Folk Art Potters of Japan

Beyond an Anthropology of Aesthetics

For Molly.

How nice to see you
again after so many years.
So this book is to commem-
orate Berkeley '84 & '86,
as well as 10 years with
Lux —

lots of love

Brian

24. iv. 98

ANTHROPOLOGY OF ASIA SERIES

Series editor
Grant Evans
University of Hong Kong

Asia today is one of the most dynamic regions of the world. The previously predominant image of 'timeless peasants' has given way to the image of fast-paced business people, mass consumerism and high-rise urban conglomerations. Yet much discourse remains entrenched in the polarities of 'East vs. West', 'Tradition vs Change'. This series hopes to provide a forum for anthropological studies which break with such polarities. It will publish titles dealing with cosmopolitanism, cultural identity, representations, arts and performance. The complexities of urban Asia, its elites, its political rituals, and its families will also be explored.

Dangerous Blood, Refined Souls
Death Rituals among the Chinese in Singapore
Tong Chee Kiong

Anthropology and Colonialism in Asia
Reflections on the Japanese, Dutch, Chinese, and Indian Experiences
Edited by Jan van Bremen and Akitoshi Shimizu

Hong Kong
The Anthropology of a Chinese Metropolis
Edited by Grant Evans and Maria Tam

Folk Art Potters of Japan

Beyond an Anthropology of Aesthetics

Brian Moeran

CURZON

First published in 1997
by Curzon Press
15 The Quadrant, Richmond, Surrey, TW9 1BP

© 1997 Brian Moeran

Typeset by LaserScript, Mitcham, Surrey

Printed in Great Britain by
Biddles Limited, Guildford and Kings Lynn

British Library Cataloguing in Publication Data
A catalogue record for this book is available from the British Library

Library of Congress in Publication Data
A catalogue record for this book has been requested

ISBN 0–7007–0605–4

Fuji no shirayuki
Asahi ni tokete
Tokete nagarete
Mishima ni ochiru.
Mishima jorōshu no
Keshō no mizu.

The white snow on Mt. Fuji
Melts in the morning sun,
Melts and flows down,
Flows down to Mishima.
And in Mishima the prostitutes.
Use it in their makeup.

Popular Ballad

For Anchan
and
In Memory of Sakamoto Fujio

CONTENTS

PREFACE

This book is about a group of potters who live in a small community called Sarayama in the south of Japan and who make what is known as Onta ware. It concerns certain problems arising from the production, marketing, and aesthetic appraisal of a kind of stoneware pottery that is generally referred to as a 'folk art' or 'folk craft' (*mingei* in Japanese).

When I first published the results of my research, in *Lost Innocence: folk craft potters of Japan*, I used the phrase 'folk craft' to translate *mingei*. During the decade and a half since it was first written, however, I have come to feel that my usage was a little too purist. After all, one of the points made then (and repeated here) is that – as in other forms of art appreciation – people have different interpretations about what constitutes *mingei* depending on their position in the art world: for the potters whom I studied, Onta pottery was little more than a 'craft'; for Yanagi Sōetsu, founder of the Japanese *Mingei* movement, and other connoisseurs, it was closer to 'folk craft'; while for dealers and the general public, it could easily shift to being a 'folk art', 'art-craft', or even 'art'. However, all of them used the term *mingei*, and all of them knew precisely what *mingei* meant for them. As I have had occasion to remark elsewhere in the context of the language of aesthetics, keywords like *mingei* (as well as *shibui*, *sabi*, *wabi* and a host of other, apparently untranslatable, terms used to set apart a specifically 'Japanese' appreciation of beauty) serve to disguise differences of opinion and so to unite aesthetically like-minded people into an 'art world'. In view of all this, I shall here use the phrases *mingei*, arts and crafts, folk craft, and folk art fairly indiscriminately, since my concern is not with definitional problems so much as with the social and ideological processes surrounding the production, marketing, appreciation, interpretation and discussion of a certain kind of pottery in Japan.

There are two further reasons to justify this terminological eclecticism. Firstly, pottery holds a position in Japan's aesthetic hierarchy which is far and away superior to its position in – say – British or American arts, and certain kinds of Japanese pottery, particularly when connected with the tea ceremony, are often regarded as 'Art' (with a capital A). During the post-war years, such appreciation has enabled one or two *mingei* potters – most notably Hamada Shōji – to produce work that has been given the highest artistic accolade, not only in Japan but also in Europe and America. It is probably Japan's own aesthetic valuation of pottery – as well as that country's emergence as a top-ranking economic power since the 1970s and 80s, the international recognition of certain Japanese potters (whose fame abroad in some cases stemmed primarily from their early involvement in the Japanese *Mingei* movement), and a handful of serious collectors – which has prompted certain European auction houses from the mid-1980s to try to raise the western category of pottery from 'craft' to 'art' (i.e. to 'ceramics') – by handling the 'works' of, among others, Hans Coper, Lucie Rie, Michael Cardew, Elizabeth Fritch, and Bernard Leach (whose pots already commanded higher prices in Japan than they did elsewhere).

Secondly, the use of a single fixed category is also made difficult by the fact that processes of production and appreciation of folk art works are two-way. The argument put forward in this book is that the development of the concept of Japanese *mingei* in Japan owed much to the ideas of William Morris and the Arts and Crafts movement in Britain in the late nineteenth century. Nowadays, though, many European and American studio potters have taken on board Yanagi Sōetsu's *mingei* philosophy – often as part of an aesthetic exoticism which has existed between Europe and Japan, at least since 1688, when John Stalker and George Parker first published *A Treatise of Japanning or Varnishing*. It is thus virtually impossible to disentangle satisfactorily all those terms connected with arts and crafts mentioned above, since *mingei* is a world-wide phenomenon not just appreciated but practised by potters in Europe and the Americas, as well as in Japan. In other words, nowadays art works by whatever name are everywhere designed, thought about, made, collected and consumed in a world system in which different values are brought to bear by different people in different contexts, depending on their aims and intentions. It is the intricacies of the functioning of this global system that have prompted me here to argue for an *anthropology of values*.

For better or for worse, and in spite of the misgivings expressed in the original Preface to *Lost Innocence*, I have decided to start again. This is partly because I have learned much more about the protagonists of my tale – William Morris, Bernard Leach and Yanagi Sōetsu – in the interim since that book was first published; and partly because I have conducted further research into pottery as an art form (described here in the Afterword) and understand much better, I think, the workings of the Japanese and other art worlds. One further important reason is that, during the four (yes, *four*) years that it took *Lost Innocence* to move from manuscript to book, three works were published that proved to be crucially important to my own deliberations here, and to the study of art and anthropology in general. These were Arnold Hauser's *The Sociology of Art*, Pierre Bourdieu's *Distinction*, and Howard Becker's *Art Worlds* (which actually came out of the same press as my own book). It is the arguments and insights of these books that I have tried to incorporate in *Folk Art Potters of Japan*.

Going back over already published material has not been quite the doddle that

I assured both my series editor, Grant Evans, and publisher, Malcolm Campbell, it would be before I set to work. First I had to scan *Lost Innocence* onto a computer and convert it into word processing format; then I had to think how to incorporate all the new material I had gathered; I soon found myself tinkering with the sparse, understated formal style of the original and, before long, having to rethink two of my most important arguments (about folk art and industrialization, and *mingei* and Orientalism). I have tried to frame my arguments within two discourses of anthropology: one concerned with art and aesthetics; the other with Orientalism. Hopefully, this will attract the attention of my colleagues and lead to some form of anthropological dialogue that recognizes that 'Japan' exists outside the narrow focus of Japanologists, and that Japanese art is as important to the anthropology of art as the arts of Africa, the Americas, aboriginal Australia, Melanesia, and anywhere else *but* that enormous landmass stretching one third of the way around the northern hemisphere and called Asia.

Anything else? Ah yes, my friends the potters. I'm sorry, I don't seem to be capable of writing anything remotely popular or fun. So what I've done is include a lot of new photos – well, old ones really – taken by an American west coast potter, Bob Sperry, back in 1963. Hopefully, they will help you skim over all those off-putting tables and help brighten what may otherwise prove to be rather a heavy day. And if you've got a coffee table at home, you'll know where to put this book!

Brian Moeran
Hong Kong

ACKNOWLEDGEMENTS

My greatest debt will always be to the people of Sarayama itself. When I first went to do fieldwork there, they permitted me to live in their community, endured my presence with remarkable equanimity, and answered my persistent questions with patience and good humour. Realizing my difficulties in grasping some of the technical aspects of production, the potters gave me special permission to throw my own rather bad pots, and to help with glazing, as well as with the loading, firing and unloading of kilns. They also invited me to play in their softball games, run in their 'marathon' races, and get drunk at their not infrequent sake parties – as I have had occasion to describe at some, informal, length in another book, *Okubo Diary: portrait of a Japanese valley* (which, at one stage, was rather infamously Stanford University Press's 'worst selling paperback'!). I am not convinced that it might still be injudicious to praise certain individuals within Sarayama itself for the help that they gave me in my research so many years ago, so I should like to thank in particular all members of the Yamamaru household for the kindness with which they treated me as a guest in their house during the first year of my fieldwork in the community. I am sure that my presence made life difficult for everyone there in one way or another. To Tsuruyo and Moriyuki I owe a special word of thanks. It is to the memory of their (grand)son, Fujio, as well as to my fieldwork 'brother', Shigeki, that I dedicate *Folk Art Potters of Japan*.

On the academic side, neither this book nor the doctoral thesis upon which it was once based could have been written without the help of a number of scholars and institutions. First and foremost among these is the School of Oriental and African Studies, London, where I started out my academic life as a very 'mature' undergraduate in Japanese, carried on to complete my Ph.D. in its Department of Anthropology and Sociology, and then, miraculously, found employment there during the heady Thatcher years when all was certainly not right with Britain, but when I was privileged to belong to a very special academic department. My thanks are due in particular to Dave Parkin, Adrian Mayer, Mark Hobart, Lisa Croll and – certainly not least – Richard Fardon who, during a period when I was homeless, lent me a *futon* and floor to sleep on and instructed me in the pleasures of island single malts.

In Tokyo meanwhile, Chie Nakane, then of the Institute of Oriental Culture at the University of Tokyo, first undertook to act as my supervisor during fieldwork and then became a helpful and engaging colleague. Despite an extremely busy schedule, she invariably managed to find the time to see me during my infrequent visits to the capital back in the late 70s, and thereafter since then. The clarity with which she has been able to discuss the various socio-cultural and theoretical problems worrying me from time to time and the interest that she has taken – both in the progress of my fieldwork and, later, career – have been both sociologically and psychologically invaluable to me. It's a pity *she* never became prime minister of Britain.

Others who have read this manuscript in one or another of its various forms and who have given me criticism and instruction include Rodney Clark, Ronald Dore, Nelson Graburn, Robert Smith, Lionel Caplan and, more recently, Grant Evans. I thank them all for their time, trouble and, in many cases, continuing friendship – as well as their interest in my wayward brand of anthropology – but particularly Nelson and Kathy Graburn's continuing, warm hospitality and even warmer greenhouse bath with its magnificent view of San Francisco's 'city lights'. (And I feel a sense of regret that this book will probably never be sold in that bookshop – regret because my interest in Japan began back in 1960 or so when I discovered the writings of Kenneth Rexroth, Jack Kerouac, and other members of the West Coast's 'beat' generation.)

My gratitude, too, goes to Bob Sperry for allowing me to use almost all the black-and-white photographs produced here. Many monographs are disappointing for the quality of the plates that they include, so I feel myself exceptionally fortunate to be able to reproduce here such excellent and historically important photos, taken by Bob on a visit to Sarayama in 1963, and so spontaneously given to me when I met him – thanks to the intervention of Joseph Newland (where are you now, Jo?) – on a fleeting, and pretty wild, visit to Seattle back in 1986. I am very grateful, too, to Lee Chi Keung for his invaluable assistance in preparing all the art work in this book.

I should also formally recognize the assistance of the Social Science Research Council of Great Britain in funding my doctoral research for three years; the Japan Foundation in granting me a fellowship that enabled me to do an invaluable second year's fieldwork in Sarayama back in 1979; and the School of Oriental and African Studies, London, for providing me with an air fare to enable me to go and talk to Bob Sperry when I was a visiting research fellow at the University of California, Berkeley.

Others who have comforted and regaled me with their pots and conversation, who have been most helpful over the past decade, and for whom I hope this book will be of some compensation in return, include Takeshi Yasuda – who, one autumn evening in a country farmhouse in north Devon, first told me of the existence of Sarayama Onta – David Attenborough, Mihoko Bekku (Okamura), Sandy Brown, Janet Leach, Kim Schuefftan, Toshio Sekiji, Don Shively, and Yōko Tanaka. They may not care for some of the opinions that I have expressed here, but they have told me great stories, listened to my moans and groans, and never failed to give me their support and assistance when I needed it. My debt to them will be repaid, at least in part, if this work succeeds in clarifying a few of the many problems that now beset the Japanese *Mingei* movement.

One thing I shall always regret is that I was never able to talk to Bernard Leach about what I had learned during my two years of fieldwork in Sarayama. We had exchanged letters, of course, and had arranged to meet again upon my return from Japan in May 1979, but – alas! – Bernard died at more or less the exact moment that the plane bringing me back from Sarayama touched down at Heathrow. Of such ironies are our lives, and deaths, made.

Which brings me to the end of what, in a north Devon registry office, I once heard Takeshi inadvertently (but solemnly all the same) refer to as a 'sudden declaration'.

INTRODUCTION

This book is about a community of potters living in rural Japan, the critics and connoisseurs who appreciate and talk about their work, and the dealers and general public who buy and sell their works. Together they form what might be called an 'art world' of *mingei* folk arts and crafts. This art world is recognizable by its institutional and other social practices, on the one hand, and by the different values that it brings to bear on its art works, in this case stoneware pottery, on the other. The following chapters trace the development and practice of Japanese *mingei* ideals, as well as the two broader aesthetic and philosophical discourses of *Japonisme* and Orientalism, and describe the intricate relations that are thereby formed between people, objects and values. In so doing I seek to go beyond an anthropology of mere aesthetics.

People have been making pottery in Sarayama for well over 250 years. Until comparatively recently, however, hardly anybody had ever heard either of the community or of the wares that it produced. The pottery was sometimes called 'Hita thing' (*hitamono*), Hita being the name of the nearest town to Sarayama, and it was bought mostly by local farmers, who used it as domestic ware because it was considerably cheaper than, what was for them 'superior', light porcelain china.

In 1927 a black teapot made in Sarayama was picked up by Yanagi Sōetsu (1889–1961) off a dusty shelf in a wholesaler's shop in Kurume, some 50 kilometres away from the pottery community (*Plate 1*). From that day on, *hitamono* became a candidate – to adapt a well-turned phrase of Arthur Danto's (1992:34) – for interpetations at times comically inappropriate for mere pots and vessels. Yanagi was philosopher, critic, and founder of what has come to be known as the Japanese *Mingei* movement. He admired the teapot from Sarayama because it accorded with his aesthetic ideals of what constituted beauty and resolved to visit the community to see for himself where and how such beautiful pottery was being made. This was the first time that anyone from the 'outside world' had taken the trouble to find out about Sarayama's wares, and the very oldest men in the community remember Yanagi's first visit very well. It was the beginning of a complicated relationship between potters and *mingei* connoisseurs which has continued to this day and which is the focus of much of this book.

1

Plate 1 Black teapot like the one seen by Yanagi Sōetsu in Kurume, 1927

Over the years, Yanagi and others involved in the Japanese *Mingei* movement have written about Sarayama's pottery, praising it for its 'natural', 'traditional', and 'cooperative' beauty. Consequently, hundreds of thousands of people have visited Sarayama's fourteen households, situated in the mountains to the north of Hita. Many of these visitors have passed through the neighbouring hamlet of Onta (of which Sarayama was once an administrative part), and it is this name – written somewhat poetically with Chinese characters meaning Small Deer Field – which is now used for the community's pottery. Most people go there as tourists; but for a significant few the trip to Sarayama is a kind of pilgrimage because the community and its pottery represent in their minds Yanagi's ideal of what true '*mingei*' or folk arts and crafts should be.

The story recounted here of the rise to public fame of Onta pottery is characteristic of what has gone on in many other rural communities in Japan where potters – and, indeed, other rural craftsmen and women – have made *mingei*. Some of the techniques of production (like the use of water-powered clay crushers) are no longer, or for one reason or another never have been, used in these communities; but all of them have made use of modern technological developments to increase production; all of them have had to learn to cater to a predominantly urban market; all of them, to a greater or lesser extent, have become tourist destinations. All of them have also experienced that shift in public taste which has transformed their craft pottery into an art form. The story of Onta pottery is thus the story of *mingei* folk art pottery all over Japan.

2

Anthropology, Ecology and Japan

In many ways, *Folk Art Potters of Japan* would seem to be just one more in a long line of rural community studies that have characterized the anthropology of Japan – from its beginning just before the Pacific War with John Embree's *Suye Mura* (1939) to the belated publication of *Women of Suye Mura* by Robert Smith and Ella Wiswell (1982), Gail Lee Bernstein's *Haruko's World* (1985) and my own *Okubo Diary* (Moeran 1985). The reader will already have noted that the Table of Contents contains many of the words and phrases that haunt other anthropological works on Japan – including Edward Norbeck's *Takashima* (1954), John Cornell's *Matsunagi* (1956), Robert Smith's *Kurusu* (1978), Ronald Dore's *Shinohata* (1978), and other villages that characterize what might conveniently be classified as *Village Japan* (Beardsley *et al.* 1959). The household system, the hamlet, community solidarity, environmental change, tradition, even the dreaded *dōzoku* extended household or lineage group – all of these have had enough scholarly print devoted to them, it might be thought, to deserve no further attention. There are two points that I should like to make here in justification of their further discussion.

The first of these concerns *ecological anthropology*. Japanese rural society is what may be called an 'irrigation culture' (Wittfogel 1955:46), in that a large majority of people in the countryside have grown rice in irrigated paddy. Almost all studies hitherto undertaken of Japanese rural society, and most of the data upon which analysis of its social institutions have been made, have been of such agricultural communities, although more recently studies have been published of coastal villages whose inhabitants have traditionally engaged in fishing (Kalland 1981; 1995), whaling (Kalland and Moeran 1992), and other sea products. Still, it needs to be recognized that during much of the post-war period a considerable number of people in rural Japan have been either only 'half' farmers, or not farmers at all, but craftsmen, shop owners, teachers, commuters, and so on (cf. Plath 1967:519–20), so that the fact that a large number of households in any one community may not practise farming as a full-time occupation can influence the social organization of that community in a manner hitherto undocumented by scholars of Japan. This book – concerned as it is with a pottery community – makes a detailed contribution to an ecological anthropology of Japanese society, as initiated by such scholars as Yoneyama (1967a; 1967b) and Shimpo (1976), and shows precisely the relationship between a community of people, their economic practices and the environment in which they live. The book argues that the social structure of Sarayama (Onta) and the organization of its households depend mainly on the way in which water is used to prepare locally-dug clay for use at the potter's wheel. As a result, it should stand as a model study, not only for the sub-discipline of ecological anthropology, but for all those interested in ecology and in what happens to people when their environment is, for one reason or another, radically changed.

My second point concerns the *anthropology of Japan*. When I first wrote the doctoral thesis that gave rise to this book, I was concerned that those studying

Japanese rural society had rarely managed to make comparisons or deductions of theoretical interest to anthropologists in general. Rather, they had at times formed (and in my opinion still form) as close-knit and introverted a clique as did the very communities they – and I myself – had studied. I thought then that the closed-in nature of Japanese society as a whole might possibly have affected the form that the studies of its social institutions had taken – a kind of cultural determinism that I would not now so easily accept. Or, I also reasoned, perhaps there was not much of general theoretical interest to be said about country farmers, apart from the ecological argument that I was putting forward, and the apparently endless pronouncements on tradition, modernization, westernization and social change that characterized the anthropology of Japan in the 1960s and 70s. In what seemed like a concerted attempt to ignore what was going on in our discipline at large, most Japanologists seemed intent on doing little more than chew on their own cultural cud. No wonder, then, that other anthropologists paid so little attention to what went on in the anthropology of Japan.

In many ways, I am not convinced that things are that much better now, although there is at least a general awareness that these days we anthropologists specializing in Japan *ought* to try to be comparative and incorporate general theoretical issues into our fieldwork studies. One thing, however, that *Lost Innocence* did attempt to do was link a remote rural community to the nation as a whole, by focusing on ways in which urban-based aesthetic ideals and a market demand for *mingei* pottery affected Sarayama's social organization and caused Onta potters to reflect upon the meaning of their work. Moreover, in that Japanese folk art had come to be a world-wide phenomenon, what started out as yet another example of anthropological fieldwork in an isolated rural community ended up as a much broader discussion of relations between what, in the 1990s, it has become fashionable to term 'global' and 'local' processes (Friedman 1994), between centres and peripheries of cultural flow (Hannerz 1992:218–23).

It is this discussion which still makes *Folk Art Potters of Japan* rather special in the context of Japanese anthropology. I was fortunate enough to discover a community that has been linked to the outside world through the pottery that it produces. Moreover, this pottery has been subjected to a form of appreciation whose content was itself influenced by European aesthetic theory – specifically that of the British Arts and Crafts movement led by William Morris, but also indirectly linked to the late-nineteenth century European tastes for things Japanese and more generally 'oriental'. This meant that I have been able to describe here not only the relation between ecology and social organization in a Japanese pottery community, but the interpretation of that relationship in the context of the Japanese *Mingei* movement, and of *Japonisme* and Orientalism. Ultimately, therefore, it is the general relation between folk art and social organization that has been of interest to me and so I have found myself tackling head-on an *anthropology of art*.

4

Anthropology, Philosophy and the Art World

In theory, anthropologists should not resort to tricks that enable them to produce a work of art – or anything else for that matter – as if from a conjuror's hat (Hauser 1982:23). Instead, they should adopt what Alfred Gell (1992:42) calls 'methodological philistinism' and remain resolutely indifferent to whether 'grace', 'lyricism', 'spirit', or – in the context of the Japanese *Mingei* movement – 'functional beauty' (*yō no bi*), is or is not a quality of a particular object. Alas, when it comes to studying art, most anthropologists have tended to forego such aesthetic agnosticism and thus be deceived by their own ideological prejudices. Unable to take a consistently objective view of the art forms of other societies, they often fail to clarify whether the criteria they are using to determine the worth of an object as 'art' are in fact their (reactionary [Gell 1996:35]) own or those of the people in whose culture the artwork is found. There has thus been a very real danger in anthropology that what has been called 'art' is little more than either an expression of western cultural bias, or personal predilection, or a strategy to enhance the value of certain individuals' private collections (an old trick common to collectors all over the world). As a result, about the only thing that has become clear from the anthropological approach to art is that nobody is quite sure what art, especially 'primitive' art, is.[1] This may partly explain why, even in the 1990s, so much attention is still being paid to definitions (e.g. Morphy 1994). Surely, there is no other area of anthropology where so little is agreed.

I myself feel that we might have made more progress in our studies of non-western art forms if we had moved away from definitions – after all, art ultimately boils down to no more than what is now consumed as art (Hauser 1982:433) – and concentrated more on finding out what it is that makes it *possible* for that splendid item of industrial *porcelainerie*, a urinal, on the one hand, or an ethnographic or archaeological artifact – say, a Kuba clay cup, Tanagra figurine, or Zande hunting net (Gell 1996) – on the other, to be seen as art. It is thus in the expressed experiences of art and in the relation of art objects to an existing art world – that is, to the social processes in which they are produced, distributed, marketed, appreciated, interpreted and discussed – rather than in art objects *per se*, that I am interested here. As we shall see, whether Japanese *mingei* is an art or not is a moot point. Ideally, Yanagi Sōetsu stressed that his concept of *mingei* (which literally means 'popular art') was not an art form. However, this book shows clearly that nowadays many people do regard *mingei* objects as a kind of art covering a broad spectrum between Art (with a capital A), on the one hand, and what Graburn (1976:6) has termed 'ethnokitsch', on the other. In other words, it has become what first André Malraux (1967) and then Jacques Maquet (1979; 1986) have called 'art by metamorphosis' rather than 'art by destination'. Onta pottery lies approximately midway between these two extremes. It is subject to more or less the same social processes as those that surround the appreciation of a Rubens oil painting, a Chippendale chair, or that pile of bricks in the Tate Gallery in London.

To talk of an anthropology of *art* as such, however, is to prejudge the issue of whether a particular object is or is not 'art', 'folk craft', 'material culture', or whatever. At this point, therefore, I need to define the particular theoretical approach to which I adhere (and so make clear my own biases). In *Folk Art Potters of Japan*, I describe and analyse what I would now call an 'art world' – a concept originally proposed by the philosopher Arthur Danto, developed into a full-blown philosophical theory by (among others) George Dickie, and given sociological credibility by Howard Becker, who has shown how, as both theory and practice, the idea of an art world might usefully contribute to a sociological or anthropological analysis of artworks.

What is now, at times disparagingly (though usually with capital letters), called the institutional theory of art emerged as a result of a *philosophical* problem about how to explain those artworks which, like Marcel Duchamp's *Fountain* or Andy Warhol's *Brillo Box*, showed 'no trace of the artist at all, either in skill or intention' (Becker 1982:140). In this respect, they share something in common with those artefacts from remote parts of the world that were 'discovered' by European artists in ethnographic museums (Melanesian and African forms by Kirschner in Dresden) and junk shops (African masks and statues by Derain and Vlaminck in Paris), and finally metamorphosed and displayed as examples of 'primitive', 'ethnographic', or 'folk' art. Unlike what happened in European and American appreciation of primitive art, however, philosophers developed the institutional theory as a means of shifting attention from the physical properties of the artwork itself to the *relation* between an artwork and the so-called 'art world' (or 'artworld') in which it was interpreted.[2] Arthur Danto, who is usually credited with having initiated discussion of the artworld, did not himself define very clearly what he meant by the phrase, other than that it embraced 'an atmosphere of artistic theory, a knowledge of the history of art' (Danto 1964:580). George Dickie (1974:29) then extended Danto's concept 'to refer to the broad social institution in which works of art have their place'. Such an institution he clarified as being 'an established practice' which conferred on artworks 'the status of candidate for appreciation by some person or persons acting on behalf of a certain social institution (the artworld)' (Dickie 1974:31, 34).

There are two immediate problems with the institutional approach as outlined here (and discussed in much greater detail by Becker [1982:145–64], as well as by Alfred Gell [1996]). Firstly, it has transpired that Dickie developed his ideas on the basis of a 'creative misunderstanding' of Danto's work (Danto 1992:38), and that he overlooked the intentional construction of the 'discourse of reasons' that could 'confer the status of art on what would otherwise be mere things' (Danto 1992:40). In other words, Danto and Dickie – and no doubt various others involved in the philosophical discussion generated by Danto's use of artworld (e.g. Sclafani 1973; Blizet 1974) – have been involved in what Dickie (1993) has since called 'a tale of two artworlds'.[3] Secondly, most of those concerned are philosophers who have tended to frame their arguments in the context of

6

hypothetical examples and so failed to say in what exactly an art world might consist. Thus, when criticisms are made, they tend to focus on logical inconsistencies in the theoretical constructs of a philosophy of art, rather than on the existence and operations of an actual art world (Becker 1982:149–50).

It is here that Howard Becker's contribution is so important.[4] As both sociologist and practising jazz pianist, he has been able to show precisely the various ways in which an art world functions. By looking at who is able to ratify an object as work of art, what characteristics that object must have to be an artwork, and how well organized an art world must be to have its opinions taken seriously, Becker not only brings to bear a critical eye on all those participating in the production, appreciation, distribution and discussion of art, but is able to make a succinct argument both for the existence of plural art worlds, rather than the singular artworld so unsatisfactorily delineated by Danto and Dickie, and for there being no clear boundaries either between different art worlds or between art worlds and other worlds of folk art, craft, commerce, advertising, academia, or whatever.

What, then, is an art world? Briefly put, it consists of networks of cooperating people; in other words,

> Of all the people whose activities are necessary to the production of the characteristic works which that world, and perhaps others as well, define as art. Members of art worlds coordinate the activities by which work is produced by referring to a body of conventional understandings embodied in common practice and in frequently used artifacts. The same people often cooperate repeatedly, even routinely, in similar ways to produce similar works, so that we can even think of an art world as an established network of cooperative links among participants.
>
> Becker (1982:34–5)

We should note that, in this definition, Becker includes as 'producers' both art practitioners and those who make up an 'art establishment' (Rosenberg 1970) of all sorts of different theorists, museum curators and gallery dealers, media commentators, government and foundation executives, collectors and buyers (cf. Maquet 1986:145) – all involved in the production, experience, consumption, mediation and trade of art.[5]

At one very basic level, anthropologists have been faced with the same sort of problems faced by philosophers: why are some objects labelled art and others not? What are the criteria brought to bear on such labelling? The main difference between anthropologists and philosophers has been that the objects with which they deal are often not part of conventional western art history and are physically different from artworks to which we are accustomed in Europe[6] – New Guinea Highland societies' body decoration, Inuit soapstone carvings, Australian Aboriginal bark paintings, and Benin ivory masks, for example – but the question of whether they should or should not be classified as 'art' (and, if so, which of the objects collected, and what kind of art precisely) is identical to that posed by such 'found' objects as Duchamp's urinal, signed *R. Mutt*, or Warhol's reconstruction of a brillo box, titled *Brillo Box*, and discussed by philosophers in the manner alluded to above.[7]

As anthropologists, we should have little difficulty in accepting that art 'is always talking for someone to someone, and reflects reality seen from a social station and in order that it can be seen from such a social station' (Hauser 1982:219). It is the institutional arrangements mentioned above and mediating between the production of artworks and their consumption which are crucial, therefore, for the anthropology (or sociology) of art. 'They form the tracks upon which artistic development moves and determine the direction a change of taste will take. They make it most clear that the artistic act of creation, like the receptive experience of art, is a social process' (Hauser 1982:489)[8] – a point emphasized in this book as it follows the various intricacies surrounding the production, marketing and appreciation of Onta pottery. Furthermore, as will become apparent from my socio-historical account of the mutual influences on the idea of arts and crafts between Europe (especially Britain) and Japan, these institutions are always themselves developing and in a process of change, so that they condition one another reciprocally and find their real meaning only in relationship to one another (Hauser 1982:489–90). Ultimately, then, it is the social organization of an art world and the ideals that its members continually negotiate both among themselves and with the world at large that distinguishes 'art' from other, similar worlds of fashion, wine, antiques, postage stamps, and other objects of material culture. Hopefully, this meets Howard Morphy's (1994:655) stipulation that 'if the anthropology of art is to make a useful contribution, then it must be by virtue of a concept of art that is sufficiently open to allow the analysis of objects from other cultures on their own terms'. It is thus a sociologically-defined 'institutional' approach (that still allows for interpetation [Gell 1996:36]) to which I myself adhere and which I have tried to put into practice in my discussions of Japanese pottery, both in this book and elsewhere (see Moeran 1987; 1990).

There is, though, a second problem faced by both anthropologists and philosophers and stemming precisely from the part that they themselves play in the classification of artworks. As Danto (1973:17) has recognized, 'the distinction between philosophy of art and art itself is no longer tenable, and by a curious, astounding magic we have been made over into contributors to a field we had always believed it our task merely to analyze from without'. So, too, with anthropology. Whatever our claims to the contrary, like philosophers, we anthropologists can never be disinterested or objective observers (cf. Wolff 1983:58). However 'detached' or 'agnostic' our academic views, however 'philistine' our methodology, the very fact that we write about artworks means that we actively contribute to, and ourselves participate in, the construction and maintenance of the art world in which the objects of our observations are themselves made, discussed, interpreted, traded and so on. In this respect, what I have to say in *Folk Art Potters of Japan* necessarily contributes to, and can become incorporated in, understandings of what *mingei* means to craftsmen and women, critics, art historians, museum curators, gallery owners, wholesale buyers, department stores, collectors and others forming the 'core personnel' (Dickie 1974:35–6) in various – sometimes separate, sometimes overlapping – art worlds in Japan, Europe and the United States. It should also have a similar effect on our understandings, interpretations, discussions and negotiations of 'art' in the context of (a separate) anthropology of art world.[9]

An Anthropology of Aesthetics, and Beyond

A second concern of both the philosophy and anthropology of art is that of aesthetics. As Jeremy Coote (1992:246) has said, 'aesthetic notions are most perfectly manifested in works of art, and are given their most refined expression in that type of discourse known as the philosophy of art'. Here again, though, there is a difference in emphases – not just between members of the art world and the general population, as Coote notes, but between philosophers and anthropologists for, while the former are concerned with the aesthetic properties that distinguish an *artwork* from a mere, though possibly identical, object[10] – and so, on occasion, with the extremely laudable delineation of a *system* of artworks (Danto 1981:112) – anthropologists tend to be more concerned with 'the aesthetics of the object in the context of the producing *culture*' (Morphy 1994:672, my italics; see also Coote and Shelton 1992:4). I would contend that we need to be more specific than this. 'Culture' should not be seen as encompassing the social practices, beliefs, institutions and objects of *whole* nations, tribes, clans or whatever, but – in the first instance, at least – of more narrowly defined art (as well as, for example, medical, finance, sporting, academic and other) worlds. In its delineation of the historical development and current practice of pottery and other arts and crafts, this book shows how the appreciation of *mingei* differs both *between* cultures (those of Britain and Japan) and *within* a single culture (that of Japan).

What, then, is meant by aesthetics? This is, to put it mildly, a tricky question to answer, since historically it has exercised the minds, extremely sharp and analytical minds, of some of the world's most intelligent men (yes, them again), and I am not able either to summarize their arguments or improve upon them here. To keep matters simple, therefore, I will follow Howard Morphy (1994:673) and understand aesthetics to refer: firstly, to the effects that physical properties of objects have on the senses (the form, the feel and weight of pots, for example, together with the textures and colours of the clays and glazes used in folk craft pottery); and secondly, to other non-material attributes perceived in objects and which become 'aesthetic' when incorporated into a socio-cultural system of values and meanings (in the context of the Japanese *Mingei* movement, for instance, such attributes as 'cooperative beauty' and 'natural' methods of production).

This is not to suggest, however, that the 'aesthetic object' is 'some eternally fixed Platonic entity, a joy forever beyond time, space, and history, eternally there for the rapt appreciation of connoisseurs' (Danto 1981:111); nor, as has often been pointed out by both philosophers and anthropologists alike, that aesthetic appreciation has to be positive in its evaluation of an object. Rather, aesthetics is historical, ideological and contingent (Wolff 1983:20), subject to the 'symbolic gymnastics' (Bourdieu 1984:80) that characterize art and art worlds everywhere. Examples of such gymnastic exercises by those participating in the *mingei* art world are discussed in the latter half of this book where I look at the way in which the practice of *mingei* differs radically from the ideals on which the movement was founded.

Although all kinds of different philosophies have been propounded with regard to aesthetics and art (subjectivism, ontological objectivism, relationism, sociological relativism, sociological objectivism, plus all their variants [Morawski 1974:9–46]), what we need to recognize is that *none* of them can be a neutral way of seeing (Danto 1981:119) and that *all* of them in their own way necessarily participate in and contribute to our understanding of artworks (to reenforce a point made earlier). In other words, in the anthropology of art and aesthetics, as well as in art itself, we are necessarily taking part in the *interpretation* of things, so that an art world is in one sense no more than a world of interpreted things (Danto 1981:135).

Even though many anthropologists and sociologists have in the past set, and still set, themselves the task of making aesthetic judgements of the artworks that they discuss, I should say here that, throughout this book, I do my utmost to remain agnostic and avoid subjective evaluations of *mingei* pottery. In this respect, therefore, as an anthropologist, I do not accept Janet Wolff's idea (1983:85–95) that there is an 'aesthetic specificity' which somehow makes art relatively 'autonomous' from other spheres of cultural practices, nor that there is some kind of apparently autonomous 'aesthetic pleasure' which acts as a critical factor in art appreciation (Wolff 1983:106), since both these arguments are themselves interpretive and hence form part of the aesthetic practices they ostensibly set out to observe.[11] Furthermore, as an anthropologist again, I would take issue with Jacques Maquet's hypothesis (1986:52–3) that absorption in an object allows for aesthetic neutrality, even though, this time as a practising potter, I may from my own experience follow Yanagi Sōetsu in believing that (a certain kind of) 'beauty' is born out of 'unconscious creation'. Nevertheless, even here it must be recognized that an artwork and its surrounding aesthetic are imbued with certain qualities and meanings because of my learned 'cultural competence' (Bourdieu 1984:2).

Similarly, given that Janet Wolff has further argued (1983:79) that 'the institutional definition of art would, of course, have nothing to say about the nature of *the* aesthetic experience' (my italics), I should comment – as an anthropologist once more – that the notion of 'aesthetic experience' is just one more process contributing to an artwork's 'immaculate conception' (Hauser 1982:18), even though such an experience has been strongly espoused by another anthropologist, Jacques Maquet (1986), as well as by Yanagi Sōetsu, founder of the Japanese *Mingei* movement, whose aesthetic ideals form the foundation of this study. Rather, as *Folk Art Potters of Japan* makes clear, there are multiple and differing experiences in the appreciation of artworks – experiences which depend on people's roles in an art world (as potters, critics, connoisseurs, collectors, buyers and so on).

It is precisely because, *contra* Danto (1981:155), different people within a single (*mingei*) art world fail to see objects in the same way; because different peoples (belonging to separate art worlds) see objects in different ways (Coote 1989); and because aesthetic phenomena are *not* specific to artworks but are part of a broader system of cultural values as a whole, that one crucial element in the anthropological study of art and aesthetics must be the existence of a set of conscious and publicized appreciative premises which are subject to interpretation and negotiation. This means that, for an object to be attributed recognition as 'art', the aesthetic appraisal of that object can*not* (*contra* Dickie [1974:38]) be made by a single individual, whether artist (cf. Haselberger 1961:342) or critic (cf. Bohannan 1961:86), but must include the opinions of artist and critic alike, and very often a host of others involved – patrons, traders, gallery owners, literary editors, and other kinds of art promoters (Mendieta y Nunez 1957), plus art reviewers, publics and audiences (Albrecht 1970:7–8). In other words, to arrive at an understanding of aesthetics, we need to recognize that 'the artist, the work of art and the art public are interacting elements' (Barnett 1970:629) for all of whom aesthetics is 'an activity rather than a body of doctrine' (Becker 1982:131).

Because of the slipperiness of all these sorts of concepts used to help define aesthetics and art (and, as we shall see, *mingei* itself), and because I spend a lot of time in this book trying to disentangle the intricate relationships which connect aesthetics to other cultural phenomena (Maquet 1979:52), and so to show how 'different values are created and associated with particular qualities' (Morphy 1994:674) historically, institutionally and linguistically, I believe that it is necessary to go *beyond* an anthropology of aesthetics. In other words, because *extra*-aesthetic values are brought into the description, discussion, appreciation, evaluation and interpretation of artworks (cf. Wolff 1983:81), we need to situate artworks not just in their art worlds, but in a broader anthropological analysis of values.

To mention the word 'value' entangles me once more in a philosophical and sociological discourse that is too complex to be dealt with adequately in an introduction to a book on Japanese folk art. Suffice it to say, most scholars would agree that the valuation and evaluation (Morawski 1974) of artworks involves a number of strictly speaking non-aesthetic (moral, magical, social, barter, and so on), as well as artistic, technological and one or two other more 'aesthetic', values (see, for example Morawski 1974; Hauser 1982; Gell 1992 and other contributors to Coote and Shelton 1992). So far as I can judge, however, nobody has attempted to work out a systematic account of these different values as used by art worlds in their dealings with artworks.

It is the intermingling of the artistic and non-artistic sectors of the art world which reveals most clearly how aesthetic (or, in less value-laden terminology, *appreciative*) values are buttressed, and at times replaced, by extra-aesthetic values. The latter I divide into five different categories: *use, technical, social, commodity exchange* and *symbolic exchange* values. It is the interaction among them and the ways in which they impinge on appreciative values, thereby leading to what is generally accepted as 'good' or 'beautiful' *mingei*, that this study of folk art potters in their dealings with critics, connoisseurs, dealers and the general public makes abundantly clear.

All of these values come into play in various ways at all times, and so – as we shall see – affect the theory and practice of Japanese *mingei*. For example, a pot can be made to be used as a pickle jar, but find itself decorating a room or museum gallery, so that the concept of use adhered to by potter and buyer is different. Or, a dealer can, on the basis of known demand, request all kinds of glazes and decorative forms which technical constraints in use of the kiln, or in the very nature of the clay used, make it impossible for the potter to satisfy. Or, a critic may make suggestions regarding what constitutes 'good' form or 'beauty' in appreciation, only to find that such forms go against the practical function for which a particular pot is made. Or, a potter may find himself elevated to national fame, not (oh, heresy!) because of the actual work that he produces so much as because of close social connections with particular museum curators and art critics, who publicly praise his pots and award him prizes of one sort or another (often, as hinted at earlier, to raise the value of their private or institutional collections). Or, a dealer may set a price for a particular bowl or vase on the basis of a potter's reputation and previous similar bowls or vases, only to find that a collector will not buy the work in question because it is either too expensive or too cheap; in other words, because it does not meet *his* (or her) overall assessment of the use, technical, appreciative, and social values therein. So, a proposed exchange of money for a commodity is usually accompanied by some kind of symbolic exchange in which all other values come to play their part. In my opinion, it is only by taking into account all these different values surrounding the production, distribution, appreciation and discussion of material objects – each of which takes on a different amalgam of constantly shifting and inconstantly weighted values – that we can arrive at a cultural determination of what does and what does not constitute 'art' in different societies.[12]

Pottery as an Art Form

And how does pottery fit into the category of 'art' in Japan? Although this book is primarily about *mingei* folk craft pottery and its close connection with a set of aesthetic ideals that emerged with the Arts and Crafts movement in England in the latter half of the nineteenth century, and although, as a result, it focuses rather more on European than on Japanese art history, we need to look at the socio-historical context in which Yanagi Sōetsu developed his *mingei* ideals. So, let us take a brief look at the early development of modern Japanese pottery, before turning to folk art itself.

Although certain forms of Japanese pottery, in particular those connected with the tea ceremony, have been seen as 'artistic' since feudal times, what is now referred to in Japan as 'creative ceramic art' (*sōsaku tōgei*) is a fairly recent phenomenon.[13] During the early part of the Meiji period (1868–1912), not only was the distinction between 'art' and 'craft' as blurred in Japan as it was in Europe at the beginning of the nineteenth century (R. Williams 1976:32–5); the Japanese also failed to distinguish between 'craft' (*kōgei*) and 'industry' (*kōgyō*). It was only the development of modern industry in Japan that gave rise to the gradual autonomy of the two latter concepts, while the distinction between 'art' (*bijutsu*) and 'craft' (*kōgei*) for the most part followed western precedent. More specifically, emergent linguistic distinctions between such words as 'pottery' (*yakimono* or *setomono*), 'china' (*tōki*), and 'ceramics' (*tōgei*) have in fact been closely tied up with the development of the social institutions that have surrounded their production, marketing and aesthetic appraisal.

One series of events which not only indirectly helped the formation of the contemporary art world, but which also appears to have had great influence on Japanese perceptions of what should, or should not, be included in the category of 'art', was the holding of Great Exhibitions, or 'World Fairs' (Benedict *et al.* 1983), in various major cities in Europe and the United States during the latter half of the nineteenth century. The word 'art' (*bijutsu*), for example, was first used in its modern sense (as a translation from the German) during the Viennese World Exposition in 1873, and it was from this time that the Japanese began to follow the demarcation made by western aesthetics between 'fine' (painting, sculpture, architecture) and 'applied' (pottery, metalwork, lacquerware) arts.

The Japanese participated in three of the seven dozen exhibitions held between 1862 and 1910 (Conant 1991:79) and pottery was one of the crafts that they contributed most frequently, primarily because it was seen by the Meiji government to be of vital importance to the country's export market. Potters' frequent successes at these international exhibitions had two long-term effects on the organization of art, and on the development of pottery as an art form (discussed in more detail in the Afterword to this book). Firstly, the government was encouraged to establish a number of *formal art institutions*, including museums. One person who not only recognized the aesthetic merits of Japanese craftwork in general, but who actively supported the development of formal methods of art training, was Ernest Fenellosa, then employed at the University of Tokyo. Almost single-handedly, he organized a movement that included an artists' club, an art *aficionados'* group, art exhibitions, and most of the market institutions then characteristic of the western art world. As Chisholm (1963:54) has pointed out, 'to a westerner . . . these forms of artistic organization seemed natural, but in Japan they were innovations which transformed earlier patterns of hereditary guilds of painters, on the one hand, and the private cultivation of art by gentlemen, on the other'. In short, primarily as a result of western 'intervention', an 'art world' had been effectively created in Japan by the mid-1880s.

Ironically, however, although the social mechanisms now existed for the development of this art world, they did not embrace those crafts from whose international success their formation had resulted. Thus craftsmen were not allowed to send in contributions to the annual Ministry of Education (Bunten) or Imperial Art (Teiten) exhibitions,[14] but were for a long time confined to the yearly crafts exhibition run by the Ministry of Commerce and Agriculture. In view of the importance of the former during the late Meiji and Taishō (1912–26) periods, exclusion from such exhibitions was tantamount to an official denial of the 'artistic' quality of Japanese craftwork.

The second long-term result of Japan's participation in the world fairs of the latter half of the nineteenth century was that potters themselves developed an interest in their craft traditions. In other words, they first became conscious of, and then in some cases created, a sense of *history*. The fact that people in Europe and the United States highly appreciated the works contributed to the world fairs encouraged some Japanese to reexamine their own traditions and aesthetic values. Those concerned with the development of Japan's crafts realized that not everything they had borrowed from western culture was necessarily better than that which they themselves could produce. It was this attitude that facilitated the construction of museums, the formation of associations promoting Japanese arts, and the publication of the country's first art magazine, *Kokka* (in 1889).

Around the turn of the century, this concern with traditions led to a revival among many famous and old aristocratic families of the tea ceremony, which had been more or less forgotten during the first decades of Japan's modernization. Although this popularity in turn stimulated the antique market as *aficionados* sought tea ceremony utensils, and pottery in particular, it led to two rather different approaches to ceramic history. In the first place, there were some – primarily businessmen, doctors, and scholars – who objected to the aristocracy's passionate devotion to tea, and to the way in which tea utensils were 'appreciated'. They consequently began to set up a number of associations during the first decade of the twentieth century to study pottery. Some of these groups (for example, the Saikōkai) were particularly interested in its 'artistic' aspects. They also appear to have been influenced by western attitudes towards Chinese ceramics of the Sung and Ming periods, for they turned their attention to the investigation of Kakiemon, Nabeshima, and old Kutani porcelain wares. Others (such as Kawai Kanjirō in his earliest work) studied traditional ceramic techniques, examining kiln sites in China and Korea, collecting shards for further study, and even imitating classical ceramic styles. At the same time, there was a growing awareness of pottery *per se*, and this led to a theoretical debate about what precisely should constitute 'art' or 'craft'. It was in this kind of milieu that Yanagi Sōetsu's notion of *mingei* evolved.

But if one trend in early twentieth-century Japanese potters' consciousness of history rejected the tea ceremony in favour of Chinese and Korean styles and an emergent sense of 'individuality' (through such notions as 'artistic consciousness' and 'self-consciousness'), the second was firmly rooted in the discovery of Japanese traditions, so that here Yanagi might be said to have played a central part in the development of Japanese ceramics generally. In the late 1920s and 30s, a number of potters became interested in the technical side of tea ceremony wares and began to investigate some of the famous old Japanese kiln sites. Katō Tōkurō seems to have been the first potter to do this (in 1928), but it was Arakawa Toyozō who attracted public attention. While examining an extremely famous straight-sided *tsutsu* Shino tea bowl in a private collection, he noticed that around its foot rim there was a reddish clay which was very different from that found in Seto (one of Japan's main pottery centres). This suggested to him that Shino wares had not been made in Seto, as was then thought, and Arakawa set out to excavate a number of old kiln sites in an area northwest of nearby Tajimi in an attempt to find out from where precisely Shino wares did originate. In May 1930, he discovered shards made of clay with exactly the same texture as that of the tea bowl he had seen a few months earlier. He also unearthed a Shino tea bowl of the Momoyama period (1568–1603) that was later designated a national treasure.

Coincidentally with Arakawa's excavations, the chairman of the Osaka Mainichi Newspaper Corporation arranged for the excavation of a number of kiln sites in the Takeo/Kuronda/Arita area of northwest Kyushu. The potter Nakazato Muan, too, was financed by local families to investigate the origins of Karatsu wares in Saga and Nagasaki prefectures.

The result of all this activity was that several potters began to devote themselves to the imitation of the techniques they had discovered in these old pots. Arakawa, for instance, built an old-style kiln in the Mino area and devoted his time and energy to reproducing Shino wares like those that he had first discovered nearby; Nakazato Muan tried to copy the *madara* style of Karatsu wares with straw ash glaze; and Kaneshige Tōyō developed methods by which he might reproduce the quality of Momoyama-period Bizen ware. Indeed, it is probably not an exaggeration to say that it was these potters who laid the foundations for the creation of the history of Japanese ceramics as we know it today. Certainly, events during the Taishō and early Shōwa (1926–1989) periods not only encouraged the development of the art world whose institutions had been set up during the latter part of the Meiji period; with the inclusion of the category of 'art-craft' in the 1927 Teiten, or Imperial Art Exhibition, they firmly established pottery as an art form.

Folk Art

One theme pervading this book about the Japanese *Mingei* movement and Sarayama's community of potters is that of nostalgia. In certain respects it might be said that the Japanese feeling for nostalgia, or *natsukashisa*, is a peculiar cultural trait. From very early times, Japanese literature has reflected the people's

Plate 2 Black *senbe* rice cracker jar with *yuhada* trailed overglaze

concern for the passing of time – epitomized perhaps by the sense of *mono no aware*, or 'sadness of things', that pervades the tenth century novel, *The Tale of Genji*. Nowadays, too, people can frequently be heard exclaiming how wistful they feel upon encountering an old acquaintance, revisiting a haunt of the past, or simply doing something that they have not done for some time. To some extent, I would suggest, this concept of *natsukashisa* helps the Japanese strengthen tenuous personal relationships. But there is more to nostalgia than this. One thing that struck me during fieldwork was that both critics and craftsmen seemed to be looking wistfully to the past in an attempt to come to terms with the present, and were thus involved in what Eric Hobsbawm and Terence Ranger (1983) have referred to as the 'invention' of traditions. This we have just seen in the rediscovery of Japanese pottery by people like Katō Tōkurō, Arakawa Toyozō, and Nakazato Muan. Others, like Yanagi Sōetsu, looked elsewhere – seeing the medieval European guild as the perfect example of the way in which 'beauty' was created by craftsmen who cooperated in a particular social and moral order. Potters in Sarayama did not have to refer so far back in time in their search for community. For them, there had always been a social and moral order until the community was broken up by the effects of the boom in Japanese folk crafts during the 1950s and 1960s.

Nisbet (1970) has shown that this nostalgia for community is to be found in a large body of European thought, especially of European sociology, during the nineteenth century.[15] It would appear that in any society undergoing the sort of radical changes that were induced by the Industrial Revolution in northern Europe, people are likely to fall back on the concept of community as a means of restoring social order. While not adhering to the Marxist view that economic structure and stages of social technology necessarily condition certain forms of art (e.g. Bukharin 1972), I do think that a general premise can be made about the relation between folk art and social organization: not only has the Industrial Revolution affected the way in which we see art, but the rise of industrialism, and its concomitants, urbanization and mechanization, has led many of us to look with a certain nostalgia either *back in time* to those forms of art or craft which somehow evoke a pre-industrial, golden age of simplicity, or *across in space* to objects produced in other, less 'civilized' cultures. When established art forms fail to meet the criteria of simplicity, new forms are likely to be invented or borrowed by those with a special interest in the arts. At this stage what has hitherto been seen as 'rubbish' may be elevated to the more durable category of 'art' (Thompson 1979). Thus, on the one hand, William Morris could rediscover the beauty of handmade British arts and crafts made prior to the industrial revolution; and, on the other, French painters such as Van Gogh and Gauguin could discover *ukiyo-e* woodblock prints used as wrapping paper for early Japanese pottery exports and make them into art. Thus, too, with *mingei*, whose underlying philosophy was probably first brought to Japan from England by two potters-to-be, Tomimoto Kenkichi and Bernard Leach; whose artworks were then (re)discovered by Yanagi Sōetsu in the temple markets of Kyoto in Japan; and whose newly-propounded ideals were then disseminated back to England, Europe and America where they were once more 'discovered' by other practising artists and craftsmen.

The term 'folk art' was originally applied to arts and crafts made in the peasant villages of Europe (Graburn 1976:21; Harmon 1974:470), and was for some time used to refer specifically to European folk art (Gerbrands 1957:19). Arnold Hauser suggests that 'if we understand by folk art the artistic production of uneducated rural people which is created for their own use without previous prototypes (and so in this sense, naive and unsophisticated), it could be considered in certain circumstances and at certain times as the original form of art' – an attitude which is very close to that adopted by Yanagi Sōetsu with regard to *mingei*. The term 'folk' has been used interchangeably with 'popular', although the distinction is not absolute and Hauser (1982:562) would claim that there are few real points of contact between them. Still, in Japan, Yanagi Sōetsu

17

himself at one stage used the phrase 'people's art' (Yanagi 1949:7) to describe the kind of artisan work that he later preferred to call *mingei*, or 'folk craft'.

A number of characteristics of folk arts have been noted: they are *useful*, being made according to *traditional* methods, with readily available *natural* materials, and often make use of *simple* techniques in production which tend to demand *collective* work and to produce a simple style evolving naturally out of the craftsman's repetitive use of established patterns (Harmon 1974:471–474). Adolf Tomars (1940:167) has also argued that folk arts have no professional specialist who lives by practising the folk art concerned and that, in general, they are marked by a concern for 'communal growth' rather than for individual work; a comparatively slow rate of change; no aristocratic patronage; and no abstract theory regarding technique.[16]

Tomars's list of folk art characteristics expresses an ideal, perhaps, that no longer exists, for over the past few decades artists, museum curators, anthropologists, and dealers of one sort or another have patronized folk arts all over the world. As a result, craftsmen have often become professional specialists and may well be known by their individual names. 'Communal growth' is overlooked as individual craftsmen continually experiment with new shapes and designs. Although a stylistic simplicity may be retained, this is frequently only because it is an essential part of an abstract theory of folk art. Craftsmen find themselves involved in a definition of folk art which may well include an emphasis on beauty (Becker 1978:865–866), put forward by outsiders not directly involved in the craft concerned.

These are all problems faced by the potters who live in the community of Sarayama, where I conducted fieldwork for two years from April 1977, and which I have continued to visit regularly since then. From the late 1920s, Yanagi Sōetsu published a series of essays in which he argued that, ideally, 'beauty' derived from the fact that folk crafts were functional, made by craftsmen who relied on traditional methods of production and on the use of natural materials. These were not individual 'artists' but 'unknown craftsmen' who worked 'unconsciously' in a spirit of cooperation with one another, without regard for financial gain.

Onta potters found themselves involved in the Japanese *Mingei* movement because their work and the social organization of their community closely conformed to Yanagi's (so-called) aesthetic ideals. However, since the mid-1950s, a rapid expansion in domestic consumption brought on an equally rapid growth in the Japanese economy as a whole. What Ronald Dore (1967:24) once referred to as 'the landslide into westernization' affected all sections of Japanese society. The community of Sarayama was brought into more immediate contact with the outside world by an improvement in communications; potters were able to adopt one or two technological innovations in production as a result of developments in the ceramic industry. Such advances, together with a sustained increase in the market demand for *mingei* (itself a product, as I will argue, of Japan's economic development and concomitant processes of westernization), led to a number of adaptations in Sarayama's social organization. These social changes have been interpreted as aesthetic changes by the present leaders of the Japanese *Mingei* movement, who have suggested that the standard of Sarayama's pottery has thereby deteriorated. The potters, for their part, argue that they cannot now fulfill *mingei* aesthetic ideals, because they have to take into account technical aspects of production and consumer demand when making pottery. They find themselves caught between the expectations of their critics, on the one hand, and those of their buyers and general public, on the other. This book is an account of the extent to which they satisfy and fail to satisfy the two groups, of how they try to adapt to changes induced by national economic growth, and of what happens to their community as a result.

This study, therefore, concerns the total social processes surrounding the production, marketing, and appreciation of a type of stoneware pottery which is known in Japanese as *ontayaki*, or Onta pottery, and is made in the community of Sarayama, Kyushu, Japan. In Chapter 1, I shall give an outline of the historical background of the Japanese *Mingei* movement, including details of some aspects of its founder's ideology and how it was influenced by the ideas of William Morris and the British Arts and Crafts movement. I shall then discuss the organization of Japanese rural society in general and provide a more detailed study of the social structure and organization of Sarayama itself (Chapters 2–5). From Chapter 6, I shall turn to the general theme of social change and the aesthetic appraisal of Onta pottery. I hope to show how environmental changes and improved economic conditions have led to a breakdown of community solidarity and to the emergence of what might loosely be termed 'individualism', and how these changes have been seen by leaders of the *Mingei* movement to give rise to a deterioration in the quality of Onta pottery (Chapters 6–8). In Chapter 9, I examine Yanagi's folk craft ideology in more detail and show how many theoretical premises cannot be fulfilled because of problems arising in the production and marketing of Onta pottery. In the final chapter, I sum up the main points made in the book before speculating about possible links between the concept of folk art and the nature of the society in which such a concept is found, and tracing in further detail the way in which folk art ideals travelled from England to Japan in the first two decades of this century. The intricacies of this long-term aesthetic intercourse then lead me to examine, and question, the relationship between folk art, *Japonisme* and Orientalism.

And now, if you're sitting comfortably, I will begin . . .

Chapter One

THE JAPANESE *MINGEI* MOVEMENT

Two events seen to be of vital significance to the development of nineteenth-century European thought were the French Revolution and the Industrial Revolution. The development of Japanese thought in the late nineteenth and early twentieth centuries was influenced by no less dramatic a series of events. In 1868, the Meiji Restoration brought an end to the feudal system that had characterized the country's government for the previous three centuries, and laid Japan open for the first time to the influences of modern Western civilization. During the next few decades the country underwent a number of political, administrative, and economic changes that were the prelude to Japan's emergence as a leading industrialized nation in the mid-twentieth century. Such events in both Europe and Japan had a major effect on people's appreciation and understanding of art.[1]

The British Arts and Crafts Movement

In his discussion of English culture and society, spanning nearly two centuries from the Industrial Revolution to the mid-twentieth century, Raymond Williams writes:

> An essential hypothesis in the development of the idea of culture is that the art of a period is closely and necessarily related to the generally prevalent 'way of life', and further that, in consequence, aesthetic, moral, and social judgements are closely interrelated. Such a hypothesis is now so generally accepted, as a matter of intellectual habit, that it is not easy to remember that it is, essentially, a product of the intellectual history of the nineteenth century.
>
> (Williams 1958:137)

Isolating a number of key words that took on new and important meanings during this period, Williams proceeds to trace the idea of 'culture' as it was expressed in the social criticism of writers from William Cobbett to George Orwell. These key words include industry, democracy, class, art, and culture; among these, it is the concept of 'art' in particular that I wish to discuss in this book. The variety chosen has been labelled 'folk art' (*mingei* in Japanese), but – as is often the case with pre-packaged foods – it is not always easy to distinguish the taste of the contents of one label from those of other, similar labels. Thus, 'communal art', 'decorative art', 'popular art', 'arts and crafts', 'art-craft', 'folk craft', and the deceptively bland 'craft', are all blended into the pot-pourri of western and eastern aesthetics which now characterize not only *mingei* pottery in Japan, but so-called 'studio' pottery in England and the United States. *Mingei* is that variety of art which was once referred to by an American artist who visited Japan in 1886 as 'the debris of civilization' (La Farge 1986:84).

It is virtually impossible to ascertain exactly who is responsible for the formulation of the general aesthetic-*cum*-moral theory that now accompanies most discussion of 'folk art'. However, during the last decades of the eighteenth century and throughout most of the nineteenth century, a number of English writers began to discuss themes that later came to dominate the writings of Yanagi Sōetsu (1889–1961), the founder of the Japanese *Mingei* movement. This point is important, since it is often intimated that Japanese folk arts are somehow 'unique' and 'different' from what – to the uninitiated – might appear to be similar developments in other parts of the world. Here my argument is two-fold. On the one hand, I will suggest that Yanagi's *mingei* philosophy was heavily influenced by the ideas of William Morris, ideas which were brought to Japan by men who later became friends of Yanagi – the Japanese potter, Tomimoto Kenkichi, and the English potter and etcher, Bernard Leach. On the other, I will propose that the philosophy of *mingei* is the sort of moral aesthetic that tends to arise in *all* industralizing societies that experience rapid urbanization and a shift from hand to mechanized methods of mass production.

Probably the earliest example of a folk art movement is that which occurred in England during the second half of the nineteenth century, approximately 100 years after that country had industrialized. What is known as the Arts and Crafts movement flourished in Britain during the 1880s and 1890s and aimed to counter some of the social, moral, and aesthetic disintegration that was seen to have been brought about by the industrial revolution, which was itself felt to be somehow 'unnatural'. One of the first to speak out against the way in which, in his opinion, crafts were being destroyed by industry was Thomas Carlyle (who coined the word 'industrialism' [Williams 1958:85]). In 1829 he published a diatribe in *The Edinburgh Review*, in which he deplored what he saw as the mechanization of man's hand, head, and heart:

> Our old modes of exertion are all discredited, and thrown aside. On every hand the living artisan is driven from his workshop, to make room for a speedier, inanimate one. The shuttle drops from the finger of the weaver, and falls into iron fingers that ply it faster. For all earthly, and for some unearthly purpose, we have machines and mechanical furtherances . . . We remove mountains and make seas our smooth highway; nothing can resist us. We war with rude Nature; and by our restless engines, come off

21

victorious and loaded with spoils . . . Not the external and physical alone is now managed by the machinery, but the internal and spiritual also. Here, too, nothing follows its spontaneous course, nothing is left to be accomplished by old natural methods . . . The same habit regulates not our modes of action alone, but our modes of thought and feeling. Men are grown mechanical in head and in heart, as well as in hand. They have lost faith in individual endeavour, and in natural force, of any kind. Not for internal perfection, but for external combinations and arrangements, for institutions, constitutions – for Mechanism of one sort of other, do they hope and struggle. Their whole efforts, attachments, opinions, turn on mechanism, and are of a mechanical character.

(quoted in Williams 1958:86)

Another precursor of attitudes that were later adopted by the Arts and Crafts movement was the architect Pugin (1812–1852) who, in the late 1830s, published books in which he aimed to combat 'the present decay of taste'. Pugin was also responsible for two ideas that were taken up by such later critics as Ruskin and Morris, and by Yanagi in Japan: first, that of the functional approach to beauty; second, the idea that the art of a period could be used to judge the quality of the society that was producing that art. John Ruskin (1819–1900) was essentially an art critic before he became a social critic, but the two aspects of his writings should be taken together and seen as a whole. His central concern was with beauty, a word that he usually spelled with a capital B and that was virtually interchangeable with Truth. Beauty was the absolute standard of perfection, not only in works of art but in man as well.

Ruskin followed Pugin in thinking that there was a close relation between the quality of a society and the quality of its art. What started out as a quest for Truth and Beauty, therefore, ended up as a moral indictment of Victorian society and of the new wealth generated by industrial capitalism.

And observe, you are put to stern choice in this matter. You must either make a tool of the creature or a man of him. You cannot make both. Men were not intended to work with the accuracy of tools, to be precise and perfect in all their actions. If you will have that precision out of them, and make their fingers measure degrees like cog-wheels, and their arms strike curves like compasses, you must unhumanize them . . . On the other hand, if you will make a man of the working creature, you cannot make a tool. Let him but begin to imagine, to think, to try to do anything worth doing; and the engine-turned precision is lost at once.

(Ruskin 1985:84–5)

Ruskin's conception of art and society may be said to be organic in that he stressed their interrelation and interdependence. The beauty of form in art was connected with the fulfillment of its function; the fulfillment of function depended on the coherence and cooperation of all parts of the social organism.

Ruskin argued that if a society was not regulated in such a way as to permit each man to fulfill his function, then the system was to blame. It was here – in his influential essay *The Nature of Gothic* – that he took issue with the idea that production should be geared to the laws of supply and demand.

> We have much studied and much perfected, of late, the great civilized invention of the division of labour; only we give it a false name. It is not truly speaking, the labour that is divided, but the men: – Divided into mere segments of men – broken into small fragments and crumbs of life; so that all the little piece of intelligence that is left in a man is not enough to make a pin or a nail, but exhausts itself in making the point of a pin or the head of a nail.
>
> (Ruskin 1963:180)

William Morris (1834–1896) – poet, designer, critic, and socialist – took over from where Carlyle, Pugin and Ruskin left off. Born in 1834, Morris was intended by his parents to enter the Church, but decided to become an architect and artist instead. During an intensively active and full life of just over sixty years, he participated in projects that ranged from painting frescoes on the upper walls and roof of the debating hall of the Oxford Union to translating Icelandic sagas, and finally entering the political arena as a forceful spokesman for Socialism. During most of this time, he also ran the now famous Firm of 'Fine Art Workmen in Painting, Carving, Furnitures and the Metals' for which he and his friends – in particular Dante Gabriel Rossetti, Edward Burne-Jones, Ford Madox Brown and James Webb – designed quality work, in the belief that 'good decoration, involving rather the luxury of taste than the luxury of costliness, will be found to be much less expensive than is generally supposed' (Lindsay 1979:121–22).

Under such circumstances, perhaps, it is not surprising to find that Morris wrote about, as well as practised, art. Yet these writings could be deceptive for – strongly influenced by both Carlyle's *Past and Present* and Ruskin's *The Nature of Gothic* – Morris felt that the 'question of popular art was a social question, involving the happiness or misery of the greater part of the community' (Morris 1962a:139). In other words, his ideas about art were formed primarily as a means of working out his ideas about society – about problems of hand *vis-à-vis* machine work; about labour, cooperation and class; in short, about the effects of industrial capitalism in Victorian England.

Morris argued that man was being destroyed by industrialization. He saw people deprived of all joy in their work, saw them desecrating arts inherited from the time when that joy had been present in all its vitality. He called for a popular art, simple and functional, that was 'to be made by the people and for the people, as a happiness to the maker and the user' (Morris 1902:33). Art was for everyone, not simply for a 'narrow class who only care for it in a very languid way' (1947:115), and the best things were 'common wares, bought and sold in any market'.

23

Morris bitterly objected to what he called 'the wretched anarchy of commercial war', for he felt that commerce had by its supremacy entirely suppressed art. He also realized that nature was being polluted and destroyed by the competitive society in which he lived:

Is money to be gathered? Cut down the pleasant trees among the houses, pull down ancient and venerable buildings for the money that a few square yards of London dirt will fetch; blacken rivers, hide the sun and poison the air with smoke and worse, and it's nobody's business to see to it or mend it: that is all that modern commerce, the counting-house forgetful of the workshop, will do for us herein.

(Morris 1902:16)

To Morris the laws of nature were the laws of art, and wherever nature worked there would be beauty. As I shall show at the end of this chapter, this connection between nature and beauty is just one of a number of parallels in the aesthetic theories of Morris and Yanagi Sōetsu. It also plays a large part in my study of the pottery community of Sarayama (Onta) which can be seen as a microcosm of the world of folk art potters generally in contemporary Japan.

The Japanese *Mingei* Movement

One of the effects of industralization in Britain, then, was the emergence of a stream of social criticism which advocated a utopian sense of community to counteract what was regarded as the moral disintegration of capitalist society. In Japan a number of people began to propound similar moral theories, partly in response to, but increasingly more as outright reaction against, the rapid industrialization and urbanization of Japanese society following the Sino-Japanese War in 1894–1895. As in England and other parts of Europe, these theories were for the most part highly romanticized, calling for a return to the sort of rural communalism whereby high and low, young and old, rich and poor would all live together as one large organic family. The countryside came to be seen as a repository of such 'true' values as frugality, altruism, harmony, and cooperation. Such social criticism led, on the one hand, to the establishment of the Tolstoy-inspired 'new village' movement and, on the other, to the development of agrarianism (*nōhonshugi*) as an ideology for Japan's militarists in the 1930s. It may also be said to have had some influence on Yanagi Sōetsu's concept of *mingei*.

The whole idea of 'folk art' first received public recognition in Japan in the late 1920s, when Yanagi published his first book, *The Way of Crafts* (*Kōgei no Michi*). Yanagi was born in 1889. His father was of high rank in the Japanese navy, but died when Muneyoshi[2] was only two years old, and the boy was brought up by his mother. He was sent to the Peers' School (Gakushūin Kōtōka) before entering the Department of Philosophy and Letters at the Tokyo Imperial University in 1911.[3]

24

It was during his final year at the Peers' School that Yanagi joined a number of friends and acquaintances, who were all interested in literature and art, to start publication of the now famous magazine *Shirakaba* (*Silver Birch*). Several members of this group – including Shiga Naoya, Mushakoji Saneatsu, Arishima Takeo, and Satomi Ton – later became well-known writers as a result of their contributions to this magazine. Although Yanagi himself was not at the centre of the group, he wrote more than seventy articles for the magazine, including poems, translations, and critical essays. Publication of the *Shirakaba* continued monthly for fourteen years, until the great Kantō earthquake of 1923. During this time the Shirakaba group saw itself as 'children of the world' and sought to introduce to its Japanese readers a wide range of western artists and writers. These included Rodin, Cezanne, Van Gogh, Blake, Whitman, Ibsen, and Tolstoy. It was undoubtedly Tolstoy's work which inspired Mushakoji to set up the first of the 'new villages' (*atarishiki mura*) in Hyūga, Kyushu, in 1916.

In 1919, Yanagi was appointed Professor of Religious Studies at Tōyō University, and in the same year he published the first of a series of articles on Korean culture. Despite being harassed by Japanese police, Yanagi persisted in his praise of Korean things. His fondness for that country led to his planning, and eventually opening, the Korean People's Art Gallery (*Chōsen Minzoku Bijutsukan*) in one of the old palace buildings in Seoul.

Yanagi's early interest in Korea stemmed primarily from his liking for ceramics of the Yi dynasty. Indeed, the Japanese *Mingei* movement might be said to be partly a result of Yanagi's enthusiasm for Korean pottery,[4] for when he learned that Yi dynasty wares had for the most part been made by nameless craftsmen, he felt that there had to be a similar sort of art in Japan. He thus became interested in what initially he called 'people's art' – for the way in which it accorded with his ideals of beauty. Once he discovered that there was such a popular art in his own country, Yanagi started planning a folk art museum for Japan.

Although, in the end, Yanagi's *mingei* ideal was a combination of philosophical, religious, and aesthetic elements, in the early days he appears to have been primarily concerned with beauty. While he went around collecting all sorts of objects that fitted his idea of what was beautiful, he began to realize that his taste was hardly that of the average, educated person, and that his collection was not of the kind that could be seen displayed in the museums and art galleries of his time. Reflecting upon the matter, he gradually realized that all the objects that he liked had been made to be used in ordinary people's everyday lives. In other words, they had a 'common' nature which was a far cry from the 'aristocratic' *objets d'art* favoured by art critics, historians, and dealers in antiques. Moreover, these practical, everyday utensils had not been made by famous artists, but were the work of unknown craftsmen who produced things cheaply and in quantity. This was what gave them, in his opinion, a 'free' and 'healthy' beauty.

Yanagi was particularly fond of looking for this kind of craft work in the street and temple markets of Kyoto, to which city he had moved with his family in

1923 after the Kantō earthquake. The word that the women stall-operators in these markets used for such common or garden items was *getemono* (vulgar thing). Yanagi himself adopted this word for some time, before finding that it was picked up by critics and journalists and sometimes given unfortunate nuances evoked by the concept of vulgarity (*gete*). In order to overcome such misunderstanding, he had no alternative but to think of some other word to describe his 'people's art'. In 1925, after considerable discussion between Yanagi and two potter friends, Hamada Shōji (1894–1978) and Kawai Kanjirō (1890–1966), the term *mingei* was coined to describe the craftsman's work. This was an abbreviated term, derived from *minshū*, meaning 'common people', and *kōgei*, 'craft'. Yanagi initially translated it into English as 'folk craft' (not 'folk art'), since he did not wish people to conceive of *mingei* as an individually inspired 'high' art.

The term *mingei* was applied to things that were functional, used in people's everyday lives, 'unpretentious', 'pure', and 'simple'. Yanagi argued that *mingei* was characterized by tradition and not by individuality. Art should not be associated with the individual creator; it should be unassuming, the work of 'non-individuality'. Beauty could exist 'without heroes'.

Enquiries soon revealed, however, that the 'unknown craftsmen' had all but disappeared. Mass production and competitive pricing had effectively put a stop to public demand for craftwork. Yanagi deplored the way in which communities of craftsmen, such as potters or lacquerers, had been forced to give up their work

Plate 3 '*Getemono*' woven bamboo baskets, Sarayama

and take up some other occupation for a livelihood. He felt that it was precisely because such people had worked together over the centuries, patiently, with humility, using methods of trial and error in an 'abandonment of egoism and pride', that their work had great aesthetic value.

Clearly, the general public needed to be educated in the beauty of Japanese crafts, so Yanagi set about propagating his views in a series of articles, books, and lectures. His first complete work, *Kōgei no Michi* (*The Way of Crafts*), was published in 1928 and, in 1931, he started a magazine, *Kōgei* (*Crafts*), in which he and a close circle of friends who thought like him were able to air their views. The *Mingei* movement, as such, really began with publication of this magazine, and the number of Yanagi's followers increased considerably as a result of their reading its contents. The first edition of *Kōgei* ran to 500 copies; the last (Volume 120), to 2,000 copies. In 1952 *Kōgei* was absorbed by a second magazine, *Mingei* (first published in 1939). *Mingei* remains the official organ of the Japan Folk Craft Association (Nihon Mingei Kyōkai), which was founded in 1931 by Yanagi and friends – mainly potters like Kawai Kanjirō and Tomimoto Kenkichi.

Yanagi did not confine himself to literary activities, but spent some considerable time travelling round Japan, seeking out and actively encouraging craftsmen to continue or go back to their work. Indeed, it was on one of these trips, in 1931, that he visited the potters' community of Sarayama (Onta). Yanagi was himself encouraged in his evangelical work by a director of Takashimaya Department Store, Kawakatsu Ken'ichi, and received some financial support from private sources, wealthy businessmen such as Yamamoto Tamesaburō, owner of the Royal Hotel in Osaka, and Ōhara Magosaburō, president of the Kurashiki Rayon Company. It was the latter who provided the ¥100,000 needed for the purchase of land and the building and furnishing of the Japan Folk Craft Museum (Nihon Mingei-kan), opened in Tokyo in 1935.

There are three manifestations of the *Mingei* movement. The Folk Craft Museum exhibits objects that are seen to be 'truly *mingei*'; Yanagi intended the museum to establish a standard of beauty.[5] The Folk Craft Association promotes Yanagi's ideals throughout the country and publishes two monthly magazines. The folk art shop, Takumi, acts as a major retail sales outlet in Tokyo. Although Takumi was founded as long ago as 1933, it was only in the 1950s that sales began to show a noticeable increase, and the movement as a whole began to receive national, and even international, attention. By about 1960, Yanagi's ideas had become known, not just to a small group of people living in Tokyo, Kyoto, and Osaka, but – as a result of publicity in the media – to almost everyone in Japan. There was an enormous demand for handmade folk crafts, which in many people's minds extended to such diverse items as toothpicks and log cabins. This demand came to be labelled the '*mingei* boom' and continued until about 1974–75, since when it has gradually declined. Craftsmen who had been struggling to make ends meet before and just after the Pacific War, suddenly found themselves comparatively well-off; potters in particular benefitted financially from the boom. With all the publicity surrounding folk arts, new kilns were set up everywhere and old potteries such as Koishiwara, Tamba and Mashiko expanded rapidly.[6] So far as the purists were concerned, the day of the 'instant potter' had come to accompany the other 'instants' of everyday life in Japan – coffee, noodles, and *geisha*. The average craftsman was interested in *mingei*, not for its beauty, but for the money that was to be made from it.

One of the problems facing leaders of the *Mingei* movement is the way in which the meaning of folk 'art' or 'craft' has come to be interpreted by people who are not directly acquainted with Yanagi's works. It is the interpretation by the average consumer of what constitutes *mingei* that has saddened and frustrated the movement's leaders. What is perhaps worse, so far as the latter are concerned, is that it has also affected the way in which craftsmen themselves have come to view their work. It is these different attitudes towards what constitutes 'good' *mingei* which form the crux of this book and which lead to a more general discussion of the ways in which 'taste' comes to be evaluated in contemporary industrialized societies.

A second problem lies in the varied interpretations of Yanagi's ideals within the movement itself. In the beginning, potters such as Tomimoto Kenkichi and Kawai Kanjirō were closely involved with the concept of *mingei*, but in time their own work developed in such a manner that they felt it necessary to dissociate themselves from the *Mingei* movement. Tomimoto actually went so far as to set up his own organization, the Shinshōkai (New Craftsmen's Association), in 1947. It is said that Yanagi had in part expected this sort of thing to happen; Tomimoto and Kawai were, after all, artist craftsmen in search of a new means of expression in their own idiom. What really upset Yanagi and others close to him was the decision by one of his non-craftsmen followers, Miyake Chūichi, to break away and form his own group with its separate ideology. In 1949 Miyake built his own Japan Craft Museum (Nihon Kōgeikan) and then, ten years later, founded the Japan Folk Craft Society (Nihon Mingei Kyōdan). He also started publishing a monthly magazine, *Nihon no Mingei* (*Japanese Folk Crafts*), and in this he time and again took issue with Yanagi, arguing that the latter had made *mingei* into an art form by stressing beauty over function, by promoting such artist-craftsmen as Leach, Kawai, and Hamada, and by refusing to take economic issues into account when referring to the functional aspects of *mingei*. In many ways, Miyake's criticisms were well-founded, but the manner in which he made them was, perhaps, regrettable. Yanagi, to his credit, did not want to involve the whole *Mingei* movement in what he felt was often a personal vendetta against himself. He therefore remained silent in the face of criticism that during his lifetime was, and still is, often vitriolic.

Miyake died in April 1980, after running a 'one man band,' which – at the time – many people thought would fade away with its leader's death. The Folk Craft Association, for its part, has survived since Yanagi's death in 1961, but its new leaders have been faced with a variety of problems. Some of these have been financial: the Folk Craft Museum in Tokyo has been in need of repair; its magnificent collection of items (most of which have never been shown to the public) have urgently required proper storage facilities. But the Folk Craft Association has not had the financial wherewithal to carry out such major tasks. Its private backers have long since died, and a request to the national government for funds seems to be the only way to meet such financial problems.

Other problems have been ideological. The Folk Craft Association's magazine, *Mingei*, is published monthly and (in 1980) was being distributed to about 5,000 of its members all over the country. Yet the new leadership under Yanagi's son, Munemichi, was aware that people were not really reading the magazine. Rather, subscription was a form of passive membership; craftsmen, in particular, took the magazine to keep the 'people in Tokyo' happy.

By far the most active members of both the Folk Craft Association and the Folk Craft Society have been women. Young housewives regularly attend summer seminars; they travel round the country visiting craftsmen's workshops and buying much of their work. Yet many will argue (and they are *men*, of course)[7] that the housewives do not understand the meaning of 'true' *mingei* and cannot appreciate 'proper' beauty. It was perhaps not surprising, therefore, to find that – at the time of my research – *mingei* potters and other rural craftsmen dismissed the *Mingei* movement as another urban elitist fashion whose followers had failed to come to grips with their problems.[8] In their opinion, the new leadership somehow had to counteract disinterest, remain faithful to Yanagi's original ideas, yet update them to present-day realities. The intensity with which many craftsmen criticized the *Mingei* movement revealed, paradoxically, how much they had pinned their hopes on Yanagi's ideology.

The Japanese *Mingei* Ideal

Let us turn now to the nature of the ideals that Yanagi expounded. Inasmuch as he was concerned with the 'beauty' of objects that he labelled '*mingei*', and outlined the various criteria which in his opinion created such 'beauty', Yanagi may be said to have written about aesthetics. However, the Japanese *Mingei* movement was envisaged not simply as an aesthetic movement, but rather as something more fundamental to man's existence:

> This movement of ours is most active in the field of crafts, but it is not simply a craft movement. Rather what we are really aiming at is a clearly spiritual movement. Thus the *Mingei* movement cannot be said to exist without its ethical and religious aspects . . . I am not suggesting that a craftsman has to be a moralist or religious preacher; each man can keep to his own profession. What I do say is that a craftsman is first and foremost a human being, and as a human being his life has to be founded on spirituality . . . When one reviews the history of crafts, one cannot avoid the fact that every great period of craftsmanship was founded on an ethical and religious doctrine . . . The problem of beauty is not simply a problem of beauty; beauty cannot exist unless it contains elements of truth,

29

goodness and holiness. If we reflect on this, we will realize that it is impossible to come to terms with a folk art movement that is not spiritual. In this sense, the *Mingei* movement should try to be a cultural movement.

(Yanagi 1946:21–22)

What needs to be stressed here is that Yanagi's primary concern was with modern man's 'spiritual' attitude, and that he chose to express his vision of spirituality through the medium of *mingei*. He was, therefore, concerned with *how* folk art objects were made, rather than with such objects in themselves. Provided they were made according to a certain set of rules laid down by himself, they would naturally accord with his concept of beauty. This is a point not fully understood by many devotees of *mingei*, who concentrate on the aesthetic effect of craftwork and ignore the spiritual attitude of the craftsmen.

How, then, did Yanagi think that *mingei* ought to be made, and on what basis was he able to determine the difference between good and bad crafts? Yanagi himself emphasized that he did not intend to start a movement; he did not begin with a preconceived theory of art which he then tried to apply to Japanese crafts. Things were much simpler. He had no aesthetic ideas at all, but just looked at objects and experienced a certain 'mental shock'. It was from his own personal experience in 'just looking' at crafts that Yanagi developed his *mingei* theory. This experience he called 'direct perception' (*chokkan*), which he variously referred to as 'the absolute foot rule', 'the selfless foot rule', and 'the foot rule that is no foot rule' and which he used to determine beauty. Let me quote an adaptation of what Yanagi wrote about *chokkan*:

When you look at things, your eyes can be clouded by knowledge, by habit, or by the wish to assert yourself. But this is not the way to look at things. There should be nothing coming between the person who is seeing and the thing that is seen. A thing should be seen for what it is. This is 'direct perception' – just seeing things. You enter into the thing; the thing communicates with your heart. When the two become one, you have direct perception. To know about something, without seeing it directly, gives rise to pointless judgment.

In order to see things properly, you should look at them directly. But to do this, you must not prejudge them. Direct perception must come before criticism. If you allow your learning to come before direct perception, then your eye will be dulled. To know and then to look is the same as not looking at all. In order to come into contact with beauty itself, you have no need of intellectual analysis, for this only impedes your perception. Without direct perception, you will never understand beauty.

(Yanagi 1932:56–58)

Direct perception, then, defies logical explanation. Yanagi argued, moreover, that it was 'beyond the self' and that it offered a means of seeing crafts without the

Plate 4 Sakamoto Shigeki throwing *sake* cups, 1986

intrusion of subjectivity and all its possible prejudices. In his appreciation of Japanese *mingei*, therefore, Yanagi aimed at putting aside all concepts of what did and did not constitute beauty, and at allowing a thing to be seen for what it was and to speak for itself. Direct perception was a method of aesthetic appreciation that could be applied by anyone, and 'good' and 'beautiful' folk art could be recognized as such by anyone, provided that s/he made use of direct perception. Yanagi argued that if *chokkan* was subjective or arbitrary, then it was not 'direct' perception at all.

As we have seen, so far as crafts were concerned, Yanagi's main emphasis was on beauty. Beauty was, in his opinion, unchanging, created by an immutable spirit. Sung-period ceramics and medieval Gothic churches were products of the same spirit; 'true' man was unchanging, unaffected by cultural or historical background. The present and the past were linked by beauty.

Mingei has been roughly defined by Hamada Shōji – the internationally-known artist potter and close friend of Yanagi – as 'health, naturalness and beauty'.[9] Here, it may be useful to make two broad categorizations of the content of Yanagi's folk art theory: the 'moral' and 'utilitarian' aspects of *mingei*. The first is, strictly speaking, extra-aesthetic, since it concerns the way in which folk arts are made; the second centres on their social use. The moral aspect concerns the craftsman; the utilitarian aspect, the craft itself as object.

Let us start with the former. One word that occurs frequently in Yanagi's writings is 'nature' (*shizen*), for all craftwork should, in his opinion, be focused on nature. Craftsmen should ideally make use of natural materials, and these materials ought to be obtainable locally. The beauty of *mingei*, therefore, depended largely on the natural environment in which the craftsman worked.

But Yanagi's concept of nature had two meanings: one referred to the environment, the other to the inner self, or God. Yanagi did not accept the notion that nature was but a shadow or reflection of a higher reality. For him, nature *was* the higher reality; it sustained the masses, made them great, and gave them strength. He directly linked nature, beauty, and selflessness, and it is here that his thought differs most radically, perhaps, from western art theories and shows close affinity to Buddhist ideas. Beauty was, in his opinion, born of the natural, of the unconscious in man. For crafts to be beautiful, the craftsman should let nature do the creating; salvation came from outside himself, from what Yanagi called 'self-surrender' (*tarikidō*). *Tariki* was not denial of the self so much as freedom from the self. Just as an Amidha Buddhist could be saved by reciting the *nenbutsu* prayer and denying her self, so the craftsman could attain a 'pure land of beauty' by surrendering his self to nature. No craftsman had within himself the power to create beauty; the beauty that came from 'self surrender' was incomparably greater than that of any work of art produced by 'individual genius'. In other words, the doctrine of spontaneous self-surrender (*tariki*) in artistic *production*, as put forward by Yanagi, had its exact counterpart in the doctrine of the immediacy of direct perception (*chokkan*) in aesthetic *reception* – a ploy often practised in aesthetic philosophies throughout the world (cf. Hauser 1982:461).[10]

This argument led Yanagi to suggest that only in a communal society in which people cooperated with one another would beauty be born. Cooperation bound not only one person to another, but humanity as a whole to nature. There was always a communal beauty in good craftwork, and behind this beauty flowed the blood of love – the love of God, of nature, of justice, of other men, of work, and of things. Cooperation was built on mutual love, which was itself brought about by crafts. Folk crafts could only be called the 'communal arts' (*sic*).[11]

In the light of this emphasis that beauty derived from nature and from cooperation, it is not surprising to find Yanagi criticizing modern industrialized society. Three things in particular incurred his displeasure: mechanization, greed, and individualism. He felt that the more a society shifted from a cooperative to a capitalist system of relations, the more its crafts deteriorated. With industrial capitalism, mechanized means of production replaced handwork, and people became isolated from one another. Naturalness yielded to artificiality, and humanity was unable to be creative; while the joy of work could be found in handicrafts, it was absent in machine-made things.

Yanagi further argued that there was a close connection between the incentive for profit and the quality of work produced under a capitalist system of wage labour. Craftsmen had to feel love for their work, and this was impossible when they made things merely for sale. 'Love of profit robs a work of its beauty'. Beauty could not, in his opinion, be born under conditions of wage labour. In the twentieth century people were working because they had to, not because they wanted to, whereas in the past the opposite had been true. In the world of crafts, a master had loved his apprentices, and they in turn had responded by doing their utmost to please their master; consequently, their work had been good. In modern times, however, profit had become the sole motivation behind work; it was this greed for money that was destroying crafts, beauty, the world, and man's spirit.

Yanagi claimed that it was impossible for 'bad' craftwork to be created in a 'good' society, and concluded from this that 'a system which does not guarantee the existence of beauty cannot be called a right and proper system'. In short, he equated the beauty of crafts with the beauty of society. The concept of *mingei* beauty was, therefore, clearly dissociated in Yanagi's mind from the idea of individual talent. Anyone could create beautiful things, provided s/he was prepared to surrender her self and live in a 'proper' spiritual manner within the bounds of morality. 'The greatest crafts are born of the nameless masses', wrote Yanagi, who was convinced that real beauty could only be appreciated once one forgot all about names – names of who had produced an object, of what particular period or civilization or style that object belonged to. The commonly held theory that beauty could be produced by only a few highly talented people was, in his opinion, entirely wrong.

It is at this point that we come back to the non-intellectual approach to beauty which, it will be remembered, Yanagi argued was essential to his concept of direct perception. As far as he was concerned, intellectualism gave rise to art, while crafts were a result of 'unlearnedness' (*mugaku*). Craftsmen did not create beauty; beauty was 'born'. An intellectual understanding of beauty, and a conscious attempt to produce beauty, merely produced what Yanagi thought was ugliness.

He was particularly concerned that *mingei* would in fact end up as one of the arts, and he prophesied that the intrusion of the craftsman's 'self' in his work would lead to high prices, self-consciousness, elevation to the status of art, and an emphasis on decoration rather than on function. It is here that we come to my second broad categorization of Yanagi's craft theory: its utilitarian aspect. Yanagi argued that it was because *mingei* objects were used that they were beautiful. A pot, for example, was made not to be looked at but to be used; only when it was used could it be said to be beautiful. If an object was not used, it would lose its *raison d'être*. It was use which gave a thing life; it was misuse that destroyed it. The more a thing was used, the more beautiful it became. That was why, in Yanagi's opinion, the act of creation alone was not sufficient to give a thing beauty. All crafts had an afterlife, and beauty to a large extent derived from the way in which things were used in this afterlife.

Yanagi's concept of beauty deriving from function extended to the pricing of *mingei*; he felt that if things were to be used by the average man on the street, they would have to be cheap, and this was only possible if they were made in large quantities. He therefore rejected the generally held idea that there is an inverse relation between quality and quantity in the appreciation of beauty and art. In his opinion, works by individual artists were highly evaluated precisely because they were produced in limited numbers. Because there were so few of such artistic works, people became afraid to use them; they lost their function and became entirely decorative and expensive works that could be bought by only a few rich people. Consequently, these 'art' objects became divorced from the common people. *Mingei*, on the other hand, had to be made by and for ordinary people; it was born of the unlearned, of the unknown masses. As such, *mingei* was not an art but a craft.

William Morris, Yanagi Sōetsu and Popular or Folk Art

Having begun this chapter with a discussion of the emergence of a popular or folk art movement in Britain during the nineteenth century, I would like to end it by taking a closer look at a key figure in the formation of the British Arts and Crafts movement, William Morris, and by comparing more closely his ideas with those of Yanagi Sōetsu, founder of the Japanese *Mingei* movement in Japan fifty years or so later. This should enable us to judge precisely how 'different' and 'unique' the philosophy of *mingei* really is and so, much later on in this book, help us examine the way in which the notion of 'Orientalism' (Said 1978) comes into play – both in the practice of aesthetic ideals in Europe and the United States, and in anthropological interpretations of Japanese society.

Like Morris in England half a century earlier, Yanagi found himself growing up in a society in which medieval methods of production still survived, although steadily fading before expanding industrialism. Like Morris, too, he appears to have been good at picking up languages (Tsurumi 1976:68) and, like Morris, the friendships that he made early on were to be influential and long standing. At Oxford, Morris's friendship with Edward Burne-Jones led to his writing and publishing poems and essays in *The Oxford and Cambridge Magazine*, started by a group of friends in 1856 (Lindsay 1979:71). For his part – as we have seen – Yanagi helped his fellow students at the Gakushūin (Peers' School) start up the *Shirakaba* in which he published frequently. Both men were prolific writers: the collected works of William Morris are in 24 volumes, and those of Yanagi Sōetsu (*Yanagi Sōetsu Zenshū*) in twenty, volumes.[12]

There are further parallels between England in the mid-nineteenth century and Japan in the early twentieth century which reflect upon the nature of these writings. Both countries were in the throes of developing an 'industrial system'. At home, this meant the building of factories, a new system of wage labour, rapid urbanization, and a general upsetting of feudal values upon which social organization had hitherto been based. Abroad, it encouraged a search for raw materials and new markets, epitomized no doubt by Great Britain's expansion of its Empire, but beginning to be practised by Japan in Korea and leading to further military incursions deeper into the Asian continent from the 1930s. Both Morris and Yanagi lived at a time when old values were being cast aside, and a mass culture was developing (England in the 1870s, Japan in the Taishō period [1912–1926]). As a result, perhaps, each looked back to a past – to European medievalism, or to Japanese feudal times – when values seemed more certain and society less unstable.

All this is not to suggest that there are not differences, as well as similarities, between William Morris and Yanagi Sōetsu. For a start, Morris was a practising artist-craftsman who could talk about art from his own experience in *production*, whereas Yanagi was a connoisseur whose interpretations of *mingei* were based on *appreciation*. Morris actively sought, particularly through his factory in Merton, to put his ideas about 'relations of production' into practice; Yanagi, on the other hand, could merely encourage craftsmen in Japan to uphold his ideals as he collected work that seemed to conform to his notion of 'beauty'. In other words, Morris saw art as being closely connected with external *social* conditions, and therefore not directly the responsibility of those obliged to work under such conditions; Yanagi, on the other hand, perceived it more as a problem of internal *moral* behaviour on the part of the craftsmen concerned. This meant that each man adopted a radically different attitude towards the creation of popular or folk art. Change the nature of *society*, said Morris; change the nature of the *individual*, said Yanagi – if you wish to have beauty in your lives.

In spite of these differences of approach, however, there is much that Morris and Yanagi have in common. For a start, each objected to the idea that 'art' should be for an elite group of people and argued, instead, that it should be made available to the masses. This approach meant that both men objected to the distinction between what Yanagi referred to as '*jōte*' (upper) and '*gete*' (lower) (Yanagi 1955a:109–21; 1978:266–78), and what Morris variously called the 'Greater' and the 'Lesser', or 'intellectual' and 'ornamental' or 'decorative', arts of life (Morris 1882:174–232; 1964:279–90).[13] So far as both were concerned,

Our subject is that great body of art, by means of which men have at all times more or less striven to beautify the familiar matters of everyday life: a wide subject, a great industry; both a great part of the history of the world, and a most helpful instrument to the study of that history.

(Morris 1962b:85)

35

Morris went on to argue that such art covered all the crafts from house building, painting, joinery and carpentry, to pottery, glass-making and weaving. These constituted the 'Art of the People', or 'Popular art', which

Has in many places and in many times solaced and sustained the people amid their griefs and troubles. And a great gift such an art seems to me; an art made intelligently by the whole body of those who live by their labour; instinct with their thoughts and aspirations, moving whither they are moving, changing as they change, the genuine expression of their sense of the beauty and mystery of life: an art born of their joy and outliving their sorrow, though tinged by it: an art leaving to future ages living witness of the existence of deft hands and eager minds not too proud to tell us of their imperfect thoughts and their glimpses of insight into wonders and terrors, as they passed amid the hurry of their daily work, through the sunshine and shadow of their lives.

This, I say, is the Art of the People, and on this is founded an art which is worth anything. I do not believe that Art worthy of the name can long exist, unless it rests on such a foundation: or if it can, if it really be that there can be an art practised by and for a few well-to-do and rich people, and founded on the slavery of the many, I for one will have nought to do with it: to me it will be contemptible and dishonourable, a rag of luxury and folly.

(Morris 1964:280–81)

For his part, too, Yanagi attacked the idea that art should be for an elite few, and that beauty should be seen to be limited to the sphere of art alone:

Individualism must be made to collapse. For the sake of the union of society. Uncontrolled anarchy must be done away with. For the sake of world order. Self-consciousness must be surpassed. For the sake of the thorough pursuit of knowledge. A sense of 'being different' must be renounced. For the sake of the acquisition of normality. The attitude that art should be 'non-functional' must be changed. For the sake of the spiritual uplift of life. The habit of producing in small quantities must be overcome. For the sake of the happiness of the people. For art to choose a new direction, there must be courage.

(Yanagi 1954:52)

He went on to argue that, so far as beauty was concerned, the way ahead lay in crafts rather than in art *per se*:

What is the path of the future? As we feel our way towards the solution of this problem, I cannot help but feel that it is the hitherto ignored realm of craft (*kōgei*) that will take on importance. Surely it is crafts that will be obliged to shoulder that realm of beauty which cannot be fulfilled by art itself. Is not the mission of an art-based culture to be to evolve into a culture based on crafts? Only this kind of evolution will lead to a rebirth, rather than total denial, of art. By going beyond artistic work, beauty must develop into craft, for unless aesthetic values are able to penetrate craft work, there will be no conclusion. Only the growth of craft culture is to be welcomed after the culture based on art has come to an end. Surely this is where the proper progress of culture lies.

(Yanagi 1954:53)

In several ways, these passages epitomize the major difference mentioned above between Morris and Yanagi. Whereas the latter focuses his attention on beauty and hence on the cultural role of *mingei* (here referred to as 'craft'), Morris is more concerned with popular art as an expression of social problems – in particular, those of industry, mechanization, and what he called 'the curse of labour' (Morris 1962b:88). In spite of this difference of emphases in the work of the two men, however, both Yanagi and Morris dealt again and again with the same themes, as they outlined their ideas about a society in which art could be 'part of a great system invented for the expression of man's delight in beauty' (Morris 1962b:88). These themes centred on the new 'commercialism' and all the 'evils' that went with it: the division of labour and breakdown of cooperation as a result of the introduction of machinery, which separated man ever further from his real place in nature.

Morris, in his advocacy of socialism, decided that he had 'weighed the work of civilization in the balance and found it wanting' (Morris 1962c:135). He argued that 'not only the worker, but the world, will have no share of art till our present commercial society give place to real society – to Socialism' (Morris 1962d:143), and that commerce was no more than 'greed for money' (Morris 1962b:93). Yanagi, too, felt that the whole social system would have to change if 'true' crafts were to be revived. Both commercialism (*shōgyōshugi*) and mechanization (*kikaishugi*) deprived a work of 'heart' (*kokoro*) and without 'heart' there could be no beauty. In this respect, craftsmen must have 'love' (*ai*) towards their work, but this was impossible when all they were making were commodities. No craft could be imbued with warmth when made in the cold atmosphere of wage labour relations. It was desire for profit that destroyed not only beauty and crafts, but human spirit and the world as a whole (Yanagi 1955a:128–34).

At this point, both Yanagi and Morris argued that crafts disintegrated once society shifted from a system based on cooperation to one based on capitalism, or from what Morris (1893:49) termed a medieval 'Society of Status' to a modern 'Society of Contract'. This led to both men looking back to the medieval guilds as perfect examples of craftsmen working together. Morris, for example, defined Gothic architecture as 'a harmonious and co-operative work of art' (Morris 1893:2), while Yanagi, when asked what kind of social organization was necessary for crafts, answered:

37

Plate 5 Water jar with *hakeme* brush and *uchikake* brown overglaze decoration

That the capitalist system has killed the beauty of crafts means really that our whole system of social cooperation has got to change. In effect, the really great age of folk crafts existed under the guild system and one can more or less say that the two were inseparable. All beautiful handicrafts contain an element of cooperation so that, when one speaks of the age of crafts, one frequently recalls the middle ages in Europe, since these coincide with the typical guild.

(Yanagi 1955a:321)[14]

While Morris was primarily concerned with cooperation as an alternative mode of production to capitalist wage labour, however, Yanagi saw it as a step towards overcoming individualism.

A guild is a co-operative body which is organized in such a way as not to permit self-assertive individualism. Under the guild system, crafts move from individual to supra-individual beauty, from the beauty of each individual to the beauty of discipline, from independent to associative beauty. It moves from individual creations to the creations of the masses, from the expression of beauty by an individual to that by an age. In short, craft beauty goes beyond the realm of mere individually-made objects towards the realization of that 'kingdom which is properly constituted of Beauty'.

(Yanagi 1955a:321–22)

Another aspect of industrialization, the 'factory system' and division of labour to which both Yanagi and Morris objected was mechanization. Morris himself never wrote any lecture devoted solely to the problem of the use of machinery in crafts. It was subservience to machinery, rather than machinery itself, which he felt dehumanized craftsmen (Watkinson 1983:75–6):[15]

I have spoken of machinery being used freely for releasing people from the more mechanical and repulsive part of necessary labour; and I know that to some cultivated people, people of the artistic turn of mind, machinery is particularly distasteful, and they will be apt to say you will never get your surroundings pleasant as long as you are surrounded by machinery. I don't quite admit that; it is the allowing machines to be our masters and not our servants that so injures the beauty of life nowadays.

(Morris 1962e:177)

This attitude was shared by Yanagi:

The purpose of machinery must be to increase the freedom of handwork. It exists to assist handwork . . . A good machine is a utensil, a tool. Man is the master, machinery the slave. When this hierarchical master/slave relationship is maintained, then there is beauty in crafts.

(Yanagi 1955a:92)

Each man's attitude towards machinery led him also to express an attitude towards nature, to which mechanization was seen in some respects to be opposed. So far as Morris was concerned, the laws of art and nature were identical; for Yanagi, beauty arose from simplicity: the further processes of work were removed from nature, the more 'artificial' they were (Yanagi 1955a:190). Nevertheless, here again there is a difference in emphases. Morris thought that the formal properties of objects could be said to be beautiful or ugly according to the degree to which they corresponded to the forms of nature (Morris 1962b:85). Yanagi, on the other hand, felt – as we have seen – that nature was the power behind *mingei*: it sustained both crafts and craftsmen who were subject to its laws. 'Unknown craftsmen' (Yanagi 1972; Morris 1962b:87) produced good work precisely because they submerged their 'selves' in their work and allowed nature alone to appear. The beauty of nature was thus the beauty of 'selflessness' (*botsuga*) (Yanagi 1955a:149–50). There were three paths to beauty – 'safety' (*anzendō*), which meant reliance on nature; 'indivisibility' (*mibundō*), whereby Yanagi argued that craftsmen should aim beyond the dualities of 'beauty' and 'ugliness'; and 'self surrender' (*tarikidō*, literally 'other power'), in which beauty was left in the hands of a greater being than man (Yanagi 1954:312–33).[16]

Thus, we find once more that where Morris sought to relate his ideas about popular art to social conditions, Yanagi preferred to fall back on the individual *psyche*. The same themes keep reappearing (and no mention has been made here of other common interests, such as the importance of function and materials in craft work), but, whereas in England in the 1880s it was social conditions that underlay the call for a merging of arts and crafts, in Japan in the late 1920s and 30s the emphasis was more on the 'spirit' of the individual.

Conclusion

There are four main points that I should like to make in conclusion to this introductory chapter on the history and ideals of the Japanese *Mingei* movement. The first two of them concern the social circumstances surrounding Yanagi's concept of *mingei*; the other two concern his aesthetic doctrine of direct perception.

First of all, I have argued that the concept of a 'folk' art or craft generally occurs in highly urbanized societies at a certain stage following their industrialization. This point is important because Yanagi himself at one stage tended to emphasize the uniqueness of *mingei* and to suggest that the Japanese *Mingei* movement had no parallel elsewhere in the world (Yanagi 1946:3–4). My argument is that, on the contrary, there have been similar aesthetic ideals put forward in other societies, notably by William Morris and other leaders of the British Arts and Crafts movement in the late nineteenth century.

I have tried to show here that much of Yanagi's theory of *mingei* was not an independent development,[17] but owed much the work of William Morris. As we have seen, there are many parallels in the thought of the two men, both of whom advocated that simplicity and fitness for purpose gave rise to beauty; that crafts belonged to the common people rather than to an aristocratic elite; and that they were not created by individual genius, but resulted from a cooperative tradition; that the craftsman relied on natural materials, remained close to nature and took pleasure in his work; and finally, that commerce destroyed good craftwork. I will return to Yanagi's attitude toward the uniqueness of *mingei* and to the suggested connection between a folk art and urbanized industrialized societies in the Conclusion to this book.

At the same time, secondly, the content of Yanagi's thought also needs to be viewed at a more specifically national cultural level. Japanese aesthetics are in general frequently imbued with subconscious Shintō beliefs. Practicality and beauty, for example, are commonly associated in Japanese aesthetics, since they conform to the Shintō concept of creative action. In this respect, the combination of spirituality, aestheticism, and utilitarianism found in Yanagi's thought is close to the three creative characteristics of Shintō religion (cf. Mason 1938:195). But Yanagi himself was not a Shintō but a Confucian scholar. It is not surprising to find, therefore, that his concept of *mingei* reflects a number of Confucian principles which were expounded in a different context by Japan's nationalist leaders during the 1920s and 1930s. I am not convinced that Yanagi was himself aware of the parallels between his *mingei* aesthetics and the ideology upon which Japanese imperialism was founded; on the contrary, it is evident that he deplored Japanese military expansion abroad. But I think that these parallels might profitably be pointed out here as an example of my contention later on that aesthetic philosophies are never absolute, but are invariably socially relative.

The contrast running through Yanagi's thought between western 'material' culture and Asian 'spiritual' culture had been made periodically from the end of the Edo period, but its appeal appears to have been particularly strong when Japan suffered from both internal and external crises. This was true of the late 1880s when certain western countries were unwilling to revise their treaties with Japan. It was true once more in the early 1930s, when Japan was going through a period of economic depression and isolation. Confucianism came to play an increasingly important role in Japanese nationalism because it opposed western materialism and provided a useful ethical ideology with which to explain Japan's expansion abroad. At the same time, it gave those in power more opportunity to strengthen their authority by upholding the Confucian concepts of loyalty, filial piety, and service to sovereign and state.

These ideals emphasized the unity of society, in which everyone fulfilled his duties and responsibilities, thus bringing about peace and prosperity for all. They became the national goal after 1931 when cooperative effort was seen to be the means by which the nation would become strong, and the notion of a corporate society included the holding up of the family to be the foundation of the state. Relations between ruler and subject were regarded as the same as those between father and son; and those between superior and inferior, like those between elder and younger brothers. Economic relations were interpreted in a similar manner. Confucianists objected to the western labour/capital, management/worker type of relation and advocated instead, as did Yanagi, a return to the medieval guilds where master craftsmen looked after their apprentices and there was unity of interest in the work of both parties.

Because of its anti-western content, it was almost inevitable that Confucianism would become associated with Japanese nationalism and be used to stimulate the national consciousness. From the mid to late 1920s, Confucianism gradually came to be seen as an integral part of the 'national policy' (*kokutai*), in which harmony and selflessness were stressed (Smith 1973:103–145). This is not to say that it was ever accepted by the mass of Japanese people. Rather, Confucianism remained a philosophy which appealed to the ruling classes, to a cross section of the Japanese elite consisting of businessmen, politicians, high-ranking military officers, university professors, and scholars. All these men advocated a return to traditional ways, for they believed – like Yanagi – that emphasis should be placed on an inner spiritual transformation. It was only a short step from this spiritual change to a revival of the 'Japanese spirit' demanded by the nationalists.[18] The association between Confucianism and imperialism, therefore, was coincidental, unfortunate, but – from this intellectual vantage point of more than half a century's history behind us – not entirely unexpected.

At the same time, the Confucian *political* emphasis on loyalty and filial piety, and on harmonious relations between leaders and subordinates – as well as between managers and workers, parents and children – has been largely incorporated into *anthropological* writings on Japan which, ever since Ruth Benedict's *The Chrysanthemum and the Sword*, have focused on such aspects of social behaviour because they appear to set modern Japanese *apart* from other industrialized, western peoples. In this respect, the anthropology of Japan has often been guilty of a social Orientalism which Yanagi practised in the aesthetic realm – thereby initiating a kind of 'counter' orientalist discourse that has recently been taken by all sorts of other Japanese, from populist *nihonjinron* writers to advertising agencies, by way of businessmen seeking to explain their successes (Yoshino 1992). In short, the aesthetic theory of *mingei* is in many way a social prescription for the organization of contemporary Japanese society, so that the practices of art and anthropology here form a single endeavour.

My third point concerns Yanagi's emphasis on direct perception as the main guide to understanding beauty and here again I am concerned with the problem of absolute and relative values in the appreciation of art. The idea of 'perception' is not new to aesthetic criticism, for, as Pierre Bourdieu has pointed out (1968:601), 'the work of art only exists as such to the extent that it is perceived'. Theoretically, therefore, 'artistic criticism is always determined by the quality of firsthand perception; obtuseness in perception can never be made good by any amount of learning, however extensive, nor any command of abstract theory, however correct' (Dewey 1934:298). In fact, however, the notion of the 'pure' gaze can only be a historical invention (Bourdieu 1984:3).

The concept of 'perception' is very often religious or spiritual, and has also been known to affect anthropologists', as well as others', interpretations of art. For example, the identification between knower and known advocated by Yanagi is a belief that is found in other Asian philosophies such as Hindu Yoga and Theravāda Buddhism which are used by the anthropologist Jacques Maquet (1986:51–8) to promote an aesthetic vision that claims to be contemplative, non-discursive and disinterested. From this he has argued that the viewer should be *absorbed* into an object, so that s/he can have access to it 'as it is', and subject and object become one in a form of *non-duality*.

In spite of their protestations to the contrary, the problem for both Yanagi and Maquet is that, logically, 'perception' as such cannot define either art or beauty.

In Europe during the Middle Ages, Thomas Aquinas argued that the apprehension of beauty was non-conceptual knowledge, but that if it were conceptualized, it would cease to be direct intuition; the aesthetic joy would vanish and with it the awareness of beauty. In other words, in theory,

> So long as we are considering the purely perceptual act involved in becoming aware of complicated constructs of perceptual stimuli to the exclusion of emotional response, imaginal associations and reverie . . . it is to be assumed that any two ideally competent observers would actualize in awareness exactly the same work of art when looking at the same picture or listening to the same performance of a musical composition.
>
> (Osborne 1955:33)

In practice, however, as Osborne admits, one cannot make a critical judgment on the basis of direct perception because that judgment will not be a 'direct' comment but a later reflection upon the original experience. In this respect, *mingei* criticism aims to make people aware of and then formulate 'feelings, notions, and ideas which appear fleetingly in the recipient during the artistic experience and remain unarticulated' (Hauser 1982:471).[19] Because it would seem inevitable that Yanagi's concept of direct perception (*chokkan*) cannot in fact logically provide a standard of beauty, extra-aesthetic values are bound to occur in the appreciation of Japanese folk art.

I have already outlined these extra-aesthetic values in my discussion of Yanagi's emphasis on the way in which he felt that *mingei* ought to be made. In his opinion, beauty could be adversely affected if craftsmen preferred to make use of modern technology in production, rather than use only local natural materials; if they put their own individual interests before those of the community in which they worked; if they became too interested in financial reward and increased production beyond a given point of 'equilibrium'; if they allowed their work to be priced beyond a reasonably low level; and if they produced work that was decorative rather than purely functional. Throughout the rest of this book, I will come back to each of these points as I attempt to show how the methods by which pottery is made in Sarayama, and the social organization of the community, have affected *mingei* leaders' critical appraisal of Onta pottery in particular, and – by implication – of folk art pottery in general.

My fourth and final point stems from Yanagi's concern for social and moral attitudes in his discussion of *mingei*. By emphasizing such theoretical concepts as 'direct perception' and 'self-surrender', Yanagi made it clear that beauty could be understood and created by anyone in Japanese society, regardless of his or her rank or education – a belief held by such other eminent connoisseurs as Kenneth Clark (Price 1989:8), and echoed in the anthropologist Gregory Bateson's concept of 'grace' (Bateson 1973:235–6).[20] And yet, as the whole folklore of Yanagi's 'discovery' of *getemono* reveals, 'nothing is more distinctive, more distinguished, than the capacity to confer status on objects that are banal or even "common"' (Bourdieu 1984:5). In other words, in spite of all assertion to the contrary, 'we can talk of folk art only when class and cultural differences exist and only in antithesis to the art of non-popular cultural strata. Folk art is not a communal art but – like artistic production in general – a class or caste art' (Hauser 1982:568). It is also a product of a 'cultural eye' (Coote 1992:248).

In the context of anthropology, Yanagi's and others' romantic idealism towards folk arts and artists is not unlike that of European and American anthropologists towards 'primitive' people during the course of the nineteenth and twentieth centuries. Both groups have suggested that 'there is no individual interest, that individuality as we know it is solely a modern form, that in the natural condition human kind tends to the collective' (Miller 1991:65). In this respect, art and anthropology have practised what would seem to be the same ideological discourse – a discourse which, in the context of the appreciation of Japanese art forms and explanations of the functioning of Japanese society, as mentioned above, is orientalist. This is a theme to which I shall return at the end of this book.

In the context of Japan, Yanagi performed at a level of *aesthetic* explanation the kind of 'symbolic gymnastics' (Bourdieu 1984:80) executed by cultural interpreters at the level of *social* explanation. By delineating an ideal image of beauty in which people lived in a spirit of cooperation and self-denial, Yanagi – perhaps unwittingly – foreshadowed the way in which present-day Japan has come to be described by anthropologists, sociologists and others interested in portraying Japanese society and culture. According to such interpretations – generally referred to as *nihonjinron*, or 'what it means to be Japanese' (Dale 1986, Yoshino 1992) – the Japanese are not 'individualistic', but prefer to work within the confines of a 'group' where, by surrendering their selves, members can live in harmony and cooperation with one another. In this context, if the idea of artistic distinction alluded to above *is* allied to one of class, it immediately opposes the culturally-held view that there is *no* class structure in Japanese society, in spite of the fact that all Japanese live and work in a capitalist economy. Thus, both aesthetic and social explanations deny the efficacy of a Marxist approach to the understanding of the development of modern Japan.[21] What I intend to show throughout this book is the extent to which the practice of *mingei*, and the way in which a potters' community actually lives its day-to-day life, conform – or fail to conform – to these aesthetic and social ideals.

Chapter Two

A POTTERY COMMUNITY

Now that we have looked in some detail at the origins of folk art movements in England and Japan, as well as at the basic moral-*cum*-philosophical aesthetic surrounding the concept of *mingei*, let us turn to those who – for one reason or another – have found themselves involved in the *practice* of folk art in Japan. Here I will be concerned in particular with a community of potters who make what is known as *ontayaki*, or Onta pottery, which is often seen as epitomizing much of what Yanagi Sōetsu envisaged when he first developed his theory of *mingei*. Although Onta potters are in some respects rather special, as we shall see, the kind of lives that they lead, the pottery they make, and the production, aesthetic and marketing problems they face, are typical – in one way or another – of many other folk art potters in Japan.

Historical Background

Curiously, what is known as 'Onta pottery' (*ontayaki*) is not made in Onta at all, but in a mountain community called Sarayama, located two to three kilometres away from Onta over the other side of the Otomai Pass. The reason for this confusion[1] is that a number of places go by the name of Sarayama in Kyushu, the southernmost of Japan's four main islands. Almost all of these are connected with pottery. For example, there is one Sarayama in Koishiwara, another in Shiraishi, yet another in Nishijinmachi in Fukuoka City, and a fourth in the ceramic complex of Arita in Saga Prefecture (see *Map 1*). Literally meaning 'plate mountain', the name of Sarayama has been given to places where deposits of clay have been found and pottery made. Because of the number of such sites, the wares made in each need to be identified by some other name, usually that of a nearby community or of a larger administrative unit that includes the Sarayama concerned within its boundaries. Hence pottery is called after the town of Arita, the ward of Nishijin, the village of Koishiwara, and, in this case, the neighbouring community of Onta.[2]

The exact date of the founding of Sarayama, and the date from which pottery has been made there, is not known, but is put at approximately 1705 (Hōei 2). In that year a potter called Yanase Sanuemon is said to have left the hamlet of

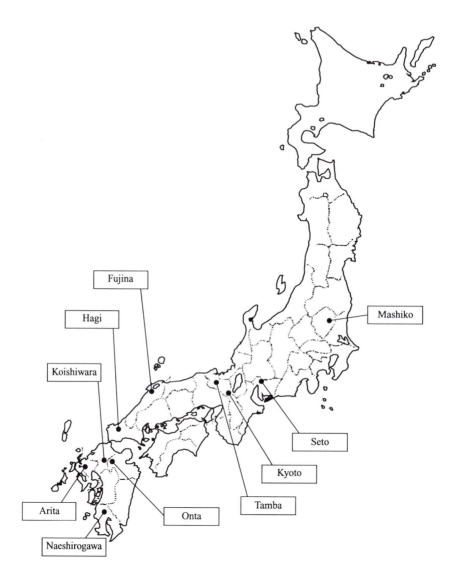

Map 1 Pottery kilns of Japan

Plate 6 View of Sarayama, Onta, 1978

Sarayama in Koishiwara, about nineteen kilometres away, and to have set up a kiln in Onta where he had discovered deposits of suitable clay.[3] Like one or two other potteries (such as Naeshirogawa near Kagoshima in southern Kyushu), Koishiwara itself was founded by a Korean potter in the mid-seventeenth century not long after Toyotomi Hideyoshi's invasions of that country between 1592 and 1596.

Three things were necessary to set up a pottery kiln: technical skill, capital, and land. It is said that the first of these was provided by Yanase Sanuemon, and the second by one Kurogi Jūbē, who came from Yanase hamlet near Ōtsuru (see *Map 2*) and was not originally a potter by trade.[4] Permission to settle was granted by the headman of the hamlet of Onta, for it was on this hamlet's land that the clay deposits had been discovered. The headman, called Sakamoto, apparently agreed to the establishment of a new community provided he be permitted to join the two men whenever he pleased. Sarayama thus began with two households, those of Yanase and Kurogi, which were later joined by a Sakamoto household that had branched from the hamlet (*buraku*) of Onta. All fourteen of the households now in the community originate from these three families.

47

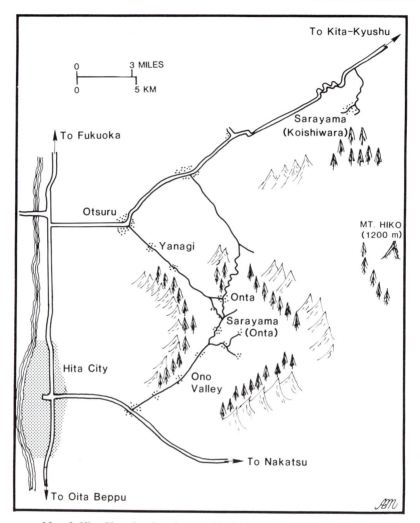

Map 2 Hita City, showing Onta and Koishiwara pottery communities

Little is known of the history of Sarayama between its founding in 1705 and its discovery by Yanagi Sōetsu in 1931. It has been suggested that in the eighteenth century the potters made their wares for a feudal lord, called Kuroda, who controlled Koishiwara (Koyama 1967:100), but there is no evidence to support this assertion. Indeed, since Sarayama was not located in Kuroda's fief, it is unlikely that the potters were called upon to fill orders for the feudal lord. They may, however, have occasionally fired pots on behalf of the sheriff (*daikan*) in charge of the imperial domain of Hita. All that is known for certain is that –

48

unlike those in Agano and other potteries directly under domain control – Onta potters did not make tea ceremony wares, but concentrated on functional pots for everyday use by local farmers: water crocks, lidded jars for pickled fruit and vegetables, ash burners, and pouring vessels with small spouts (known as *unsuke*).

During the Edo period (1603–1868), potters used to hawk their wares around the countryside, and it was only toward the end of the nineteenth century that they began selling them through wholesalers – one in Hita and another in Kurume, some 50 kilometres away in Fukuoka Prefecture. It was at the latter's shop that Yanagi Sōetsu, on one of his trips around Japan searching for 'unknown craftsmen' and their work, first learned about Onta pottery. At the pottery dealer's he saw a black teapot that immediately appealed to his sense of beauty. Asking where the pot had been made, he was told that it was a 'Hita thing' (*hitamono*) from some inaccessible pottery hamlet up in the mountains.

Yanagi's interest was aroused. He consulted various books about Japanese pottery, but failed to find any mention of *hitamono* and realized that, if he wanted to discover more about what kind of pottery was made in Sarayama and how it was made, his only alternative would be to go and see the community for himself. This he finally managed to do four years later in the spring of 1931. He had to walk most of the way up the valley from Ōtsuru, a distance of twelve kilometres. When he finally reached Sarayama, nobody there had any idea who their distinguished-looking visitor was, but all reckoned that he had to be pretty well up in the world to be able to buy all sorts of their pots (even ones that the potters were using in their kitchens) and pay for them and their postage to Tokyo in cash. They asked him to spend the night in Sarayama, but Yanagi excused himself, saying that he had an engagement elsewhere the next day, so the potters accompanied him *en masse* down the valley to the nearest bus stop. There he boarded a bus bound for Hita, promising to return as soon as he could.

Yanagi published an account of his visit to Sarayama in the Saga edition of the Mainichi Newspaper on July 13, 1931, under the title, '*Kita Kyūshū no kama o miru*' (A survey of pottery kilns of north Kyushu), and later that year the article was republished in the craft magazine *Kōgei* (Yanagi 1931). He praised Onta pottery because it had always been functional rather than decorative. Potters were ordinary craftsmen, who had no pretensions to fame, simple people whose work was clearly lacking in self-consciousness. The community of potters and their work were 'all tradition', unchanging since the first kiln had been fired back in 1705. They were also – in Yanagi's opinion – 'close to nature': clay was prepared and pounded by water-powered crushers; pots were thrown on a kick-wheel, dried in the sunshine, then glazed with local raw materials and fired in a wood-fueled climbing kiln. All this was 'natural'. Modern machinery was not used at all (Yanagi 1931:6–11).

In spite of Yanagi's praise for Sarayama and its pottery, Onta potters still struggled to sell their work. Local people in Hita for the most part disdained these dull-coloured wares with their black clay and glazes, which very often failed to prevent moisture from seeping through to the outside of the pot. Mass-produced china from Arita was, in their opinion, much better. It was light and thin; it was white and had pleasant floral designs painted on it; it didn't leak; and it was cheap. As a result, Sarayama potters found their market limited to country people living far away from towns where the Arita china was not readily available. Then came the war with its blackout restrictions; kilns were not allowed to be fired at night. As there were very few people wanting to buy their pots anyway, potters stopped production entirely until about 1947.

After three or four years, they started firing their kilns again. One advantage from the war was that a road was constructed between the Ono valley and Sarayama, and it was now possible to drive a jeep or heavy vehicle, somewhat bumpily, up from Hita to the community. It was along this road that Yanagi, true to his promise, came on a second visit to the community in 1951. This time he was not alone; the potter Hamada Shōji accompanied him and was as impressed by Sarayama's pots as Yanagi himself had been. The potters' reputation began to be firmly established among folk art connoisseurs in Tokyo and Osaka.

Sarayama's next visitor marked a turning point in the community's history. Bernard Leach (1887–1979), the English potter who had been closely connected with the *Mingei* movement throughout its early stages, expressed a desire to pay an extended visit to Sarayama. With the cooperation of both potters and prefectural authorities, Leach came in 1954 and stayed for twenty days, learning from the potters their special techniques of chattering (*tobiganna*, or 'jumping iron') and brush decoration (*hakeme*), and teaching them in return his technique of pulling handles for their pitchers.

There was wide press coverage of Leach's visit to Sarayama, and this helped make 'Onta ware' well known to those interested in *mingei*. During the next few years, visitors to the community became more frequent, and the publication of Leach's own description of Sarayama (Leach 1960) led to the arrival of foreign visitors as well. Potters expressly attribute their improved economic conditions and newly acquired fame to Leach's decision to stay for so long in Sarayama.[5]

There were, of course, other reasons for the potters' better financial position, not least of these being the improvement in the Japanese economy as a whole. It was from 1954 that the Japanese economy began to grow with great rapidity; over the next ten years, the net national product increased at an annual rate of 9.8 per cent, while the annual growth rate of the GNP averaged 14.5 per cent between 1957 and 1967. As Okada has noted (1976:170–171), 'innovations in textiles, improvements in household appliances, and rationalization of "home living" which all took place in the late 1950s were elements that helped bring about a revolution . . . in the appreciation of handcrafts on the part of the consumer'.

So, an increase in market demand brought about greater sales of Onta pottery. But to Sarayama potters, improved transportation facilities were also very important. A bus started plying between Sarayama and the town of Hita three times a day in 1956; and in this year also the railway line between Hita and Kokura, in northern Kyushu, was opened, thereby facilitating travel to Sarayama by visitors from the main island of Honshu. Communications were further improved when a communal telephone was installed in the hamlet's *sake* shop in 1957.

By the late 1950s, the media had started promoting widespread interest in Japanese folk arts and crafts, an interest that developed into what came to be called the '*mingei* boom', affecting potteries all over Japan (see, for example, Beardsley n.d.; Kleinberg 1983:219–20). Busloads of visitors began pouring into Sarayama, and potters soon found that their production was hardly sufficient to meet demand. The more they made, the more they sold. They spent less and less time in the fields, and finally from the mid-1960s began full-time specialization in pottery. The boom has brought economic stability to potter households; but it has also led to a number of problems in social relations between the community and the outside world and within the community itself. These problems will be the focus of most of the rest of this book.

Geographical Background

The community of Sarayama lies near the northeastern border of Oita Prefecture in central Kyushu. It is part of the hamlet (*buraku*) of the same name and is situated within the administrative confines of Hita City (which, in the late 1970s, had a population of 65,253 people, or 17,573 households).

Hita is a world apart from such cities as Tokyo, Osaka, and Fukuoka. Indeed, it is not really a city at all, but a town. Until the late 1980s, a rice field was still being farmed along the main shopping street. Here, in this basin of land surrounded by mountains, with its sprawling fogs in autumn and winter, with its deep haze during those sultry, humid days of summer, people live in what the city officials like to promote as Kyushu's 'Little Kyoto'. Although it cannot rival that great capital architecturally, Hita does attract the tourists, and the town is posted in the travel brochures as a place of 'water, greenery, and hot springs'. It has all the trappings of tourism: hotels and traditional Japanese-style inns, bars and nightclubs, and plenty of souvenir shops for those who wish to purchase gifts to take home to their families, fiancés, friends, and neighbours. It is in these shops that Onta pottery is sold, along with buckwheat sweet-cakes, bamboo baskets, cedarwood paper knives, and a host of other local products.

Sarayama is located about seventeen kilometres from the town centre and about 460 metres above sea level in the foothills of the Hiko-Gakumeki mountain range which effectively cuts off Oita Prefecture from the north of Kyushu with its industrial urban complexes of Hakata (Fukuoka), Tobata, Yahata, and Kokura. Sarayama is as clean, as quiet, as physically attractive as most of Japan's cities are polluted, noisy, and ugly. Situated in a narrow valley which is hardly 200 metres across at its widest point, the community consists of just fourteen households, ten of which make pottery.

Still, Sarayama looks much bigger than it actually is. Many buildings line the narrow road that winds up from Hita, and it is only at the top of the valley that the thickly wooded mountain slopes leave enough room for a dozen terraced

Plate 7 Yamani household, Sarayama, 1963

fields. These fields are no longer used to grow rice; some have been planted with cedar, others are used for stacking wood for the potters' kilns; still others have been levelled into a car park and a softball ground. Most of the buildings in the village are for purposes other than living in: garages and workshops, sheds for storing materials and pots, lean-tos for wood, and the kilns. There are six of the last in all, climbing kilns between twelve and 25 metres long, built on 30 degree inclines. The black, gaping mouths of their arched chambers are covered by asbestos corrugated roofs, and from the top of these, red-bricked chimneys now rear against the backdrop of the mountains' wooded greens.

The houses have for the most part been rebuilt since 1960, when many of Bob Sperry's photographs reproduced here were taken. There is still one old thatched farmhouse at the bottom of Sarayama, to remind potters of how they lived before the days of the *mingei* boom and their newfound prosperity. Most people now live in spacious dwellings with prestigious tiled roofs, and each household has a selection of gadgetry that has come to be thought of as essential in Japan: a colour TV, stereo set, automatic washing machine, rice cooker, self-defrosting refrigerator, and very often other luxuries such as a piano, oven, gas-heated bath, large stove in the workshop, and now the occasional *karaoke* singalong music machine which comes into its own during the community's *sake* drinking parties.

Plate 8 Yamasan (foreground), with the cooperate kiln and Kaneichi above it to the right, 1963

The workshops, too, have been rebuilt. Each forms an L-shape with its main house and faces downhill toward the south and sunlight. In front of each house is the drying yard, now concreted over, where pots are placed on their trays to lie all day in the sun. The garages are occupied by new and expensive cars, and all potters also have light vans for transporting wood or fired pots.

Yet, for all this obvious prosperity, one thing remains unchanged and is, therefore, somehow incongruous – the use of the clay crushers. Ever since Sarayama was founded, wooden crushers have been used to pound the clay with which generation after generation of potters have worked. The two streams running through the village have been stepped in a series of five-to-six-foot dams the whole length of the valley, and water is drawn from these along channels to the crushers. Each crusher is made from a large pine-tree trunk between four and five metres in length, with one end hollowed out into a scoop. Into this the river water is directed. The crusher is critically balanced on a cross-axle of wood, so that when the scoop is filled the weight of the water makes the crusher seesaw down toward the river bed. As the other end of the pine beam rises high into the air, the water flows out of the scoop and the crusher falls back with a thud onto a mound of clay piled under the far end.

Plate 9 Rebuilding Irisan's workshop in 1963, with Yamaichi behind and the cooperative kiln to the left

The noise that the crushers make cannot be expressed adequately in words. It is this sound that dominates everything that goes on in the valley, all day, all night, every day and every night, except for one respite of 24 hours from New Year's Eve. The potters can tell from the changes in the thudding rhythm of the day how much water is in the streams, whether their crushers are working, and if so, how efficiently. These pounding pine trunks are an endless source of delight to Sarayama's countless visitors, who will stop for minutes on end to gaze at these 'primitive' machines. They belong to a world of which people living in an industrialized urban Japan can only dream. The continued use of this method of preparing the potters' clay has come to be incorporated into the *mingei* ideal of what Onta pottery is and should be; it has also had considerable effect on the social structure of the community of Sarayama.

People

What sort of people live in Sarayama? Who are the buyers who purchase Onta pottery? Who are the leaders of the *Mingei* movement who give potters the supposed benefits of their advice? Although there have been some changes since

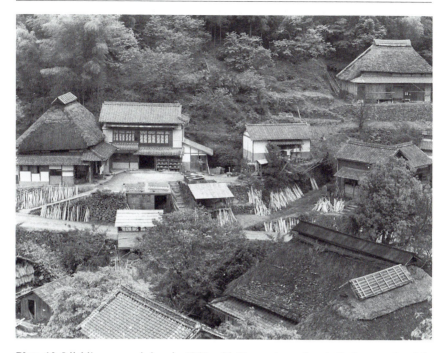

Plate 10 Iriichi's new workshop in 1963, with Yamau (now deserted) above to the right and Maruta below

the end of the 70s when I carried out my anthropological fieldwork, here are a few thumbnail sketches of some of my informants at that time.

One of the most important people in Sarayama, and a man who will often make an appearance during the course of this book, is H. Born in 1914, at the age of 20 H. was sent to study pottery in Kurume, where his father, who was not much of a potter, had eventually succeeded in getting him apprenticed. Apprenticeship in those days theoretically went on for five years, but, before two of them had passed, H. found himself called up and sent to join the army in Manchuria. Although he returned to Sarayama after his stint of 'imperial service', he soon found himself back in uniform with the outbreak of war. He managed to stay in Japan, in charge of supplies somewhere, and once he had been demobilized returned home to help run the Yamani household. He married the daughter from Kanemaru down the road and had five children. His eldest son has married and has four children of his own, and they all live together in the one house, which in 1980 included H.'s own father and mother, who were then both healthy and still able to work at the ages of 93 and 88 respectively.

H. has always taken pride in acting on behalf of others, and it was his ability to take on the role of intermediary sucessfully that led to his being looked up to as a leader. It was he who approached the Folk Craft Association and arranged for Bernard Leach to come and stay in Sarayama during his visit to Japan in 1954. As leader of the potters' cooperative, H. also managed to get Sarayama's annual pottery festival under way. As rural district councillor, he inaugurated an Ono valley softball competition. In the practical matters of everyday life, it is H. who is asked to act as go-between in marriages, land disputes, and community problems.

H.'s leadership, however, has on occasion been strongly criticized by his fellow villagers, who accuse him of being overly bossy. H. points out in defense that it is because nobody will speak his mind (except when drunk) or take the necessary decisions that he has to do the deciding for the others. Still, his ability to act at one stage aroused a certain amount of resentment among others, who could only recite, with some relish, any of H.'s misdemeanours that came to light. Some potters also objected to the unashamedly mercenary manner in which H. carried on his profession, with overlong hours, high prices, and what they saw as shoddy goods. But it was only when he started to get old and his power was on the wane that others in Sarayama began to speak out against what they saw often as having been little short of dictatorship. H. is becoming an isolated figure in the community.

One of those who has never been afraid to speak his mind is S. At 42 years of age, S. is not, in theory, old enough to be of much consequence in community affairs, but in fact he is already seen by *mingei* leaders in Tokyo as Sarayama's

Plate 11 Kurogi Toshiyasu serving beer at the community's Ebisu festival, 1977

56

next real leader. He is naturally gifted: third grade at *kendō* fencing, fifth grade at archery, second in the Hita *shigin* singing contest, the all-important position of fourth when it comes to batting at baseball. Whatever he decides to do, S. tends to do well. But, as we have already seen with H., success can lead to envy, and life in a small community like Sarayama can be very frustrating.

S.'s life has never been easy. The eighth of nine children, he was brought up by stern parents to believe that he was less than good for nothing. This was because S. was second and not eldest son of the household. His elder brother began to study pottery before S. was born, but during the war was killed in action in the Philippines, and S. suddenly found himself in favour with his father. As eldest surviving son he was now due to take over the running of the household. So he was sent, at the age of fifteen, to study pottery at H.'s and stayed there for two years. Every month he handed over a couple of pounds of rice in payment for his education and living expenses, but it seems, by most accounts, that he was not properly taught there. H. sat the lad down at the wheel head only one day a month; the rest of the time S. had to work like many apprentices in traditional Japanese crafts – being made to prepare the clay, cut wood for the kiln in the mountains, and even weed the rice paddies, rather than actually make pots.

So he was hardly able to make any pottery at all when he returned home from H.'s. Still, S. devoted himself to his work. This devotion paid off when, in the mid-1970s, he was awarded the major prize for *mingei* potters at a national ceramics exhibition. Even before this he had opposed some of H.'s schemes – such as his trying to put in machinery with which to pound the clay, or arranging for potters to report the same incomes to tax authorities each year – but S. now found that he was being called upon by outsiders concerned with the *Mingei* movement to act as spokesman for the Onta potters. He realizes the problems that this causes within the community, however, and is for the moment prepared to bide his time. He hopes that if he does emerge as Sarayama's leader, he will be able to do things more democratically than they have been done so far. He knows it takes time for things to change, though, and does not hold out much hope for the future. Another generation will grow up with its own ideas, which may oppose S.'s plans. But so long as things are done by decision of the majority, instead of on the spur of the moment by one or two individuals to further their own private interests, S. will remain content.

I. is S.'s sister-in-law, his elder brother's widow. Although, after his brother's death, she could have returned to her natal home in Kusu, halfway between Hita and Oita, she decided to stay on in Sarayama. Her father-in-law once entertained the idea of marrying I. to S., who was fifteen years her junior, but things did not turn out that way, and I. has remained a widow. Her two children by her husband were brought up in the Yamaichi household, and have now married and live in Fukuoka. They still come back three or four times a year, bringing with them their own children to visit Granny. Granny is barely five feet tall, with wrinkled, sunburnt skin and a merry laugh. She has helped look after the house, the fields, the pottery, even S.'s own children, and has thereby been a constant help and companion to his wife. She has in recent years taken charge of growing the vegetables, weeding and fumigating the rice fields, stacking the wood for drying, then tying it in bundles and taking it to the kiln before every firing. I. also works at the back of the house doing the endless task of sifting glaze materials – wood and straw ash, feldspar and iron oxide – until they are fine enough to be mixed for use in the workshop. She still sleeps with S.'s teenage children in their second-floor room behind the kitchen, and very often it is I., and not their mother – who is just as busy helping S. in the workshop – who nurses them when they are ill.

A. lives in the house opposite S.'s. The youngest of four grown-up children, she is one of two girls in Sarayama who are considered ready for marriage. Her father has already approached a relative who runs the noodle shop across the river from them, asking him to keep an eye out for a suitable young man. A. is 'open-hearted', a quality that in the opinion of the older women of the community would make her an excellent wife, but things haven't turned out well so far. A.'s mother has insisted that her daughter not marry into a farming household. The girl would be worked like a horse from morning to night, and she is too good for that. After all, she has spent several years learning how to knit in Hita and she is now qualified to teach. Her skills with the large and expensive knitting machine bought by her parents are often put to use as she mends heavy sweaters or designs and makes cardigans or woollen coats for her relatives and neighbours.

It is not as if A. is a burden on the household and her parents want her to leave. Indeed, she does many jobs that would normally be left to her elder brother's wife. Most mornings of the week A. sets off for her knitting classes in a battered and rusty Honda mini. In the town, she acts as errand girl for members of the household, buying meat and eggs from the supermarket, paper diapers from the chemist's, a pencil case or an eraser from the stationery store for one of her nieces. When one of the children falls sick it is A. who drives the girl to the doctor's. If she is around during a storm and the elementary school calls to say that little Miyuki is afraid of the thunder, A. will pick up the girl and bring her home. She does the household cooking and bathes and sleeps with the children every night. Neighbours comment wryly that her sister-in-law is going to have to work a lot harder once A. does get married and leaves home.

Those with whom the potters have to deal when selling their work live well away from Sarayama. Mr K. is in his early thirties and runs a pottery shop downtown near Hita station. He himself has been adopted into his wife's family and does not claim to know much about Onta pottery. It was his wife's father who started buying and selling pots as a sideline before the war, when he was running a coffee shop. The old man used to play around with clay himself as a hobby and is known to have made suggestions to the potters about shapes and designs. He was, however, more interested in stock than in saleable items. The Mr K. family has a large collection of old pots stacked away in its storehouse.

Now that his father-in-law is dead, Mr K. has taken over. He does not buy much, but he does not need to, since the family's main business is in real estate.

Like many other Hita buyers, Mr K. sells Onta pottery because he wants to, rather than because he has to. He admits that, as a result, he can afford to sell at fairly high prices. He realizes that this is not in accordance with *mingei* ideals, which emphasize that pots should be cheap, but he reckons that the media are much to blame for the increase in prices. As for the potters, they are not as honest as they should be in their dealings with buyers. Mr K. would like to see them sell their pots through the cooperative; that would help fix retail prices in Hita and make the potters maintain a reasonable standard in their work.

Mr T. is probably the nearest to having what might be called a patron-client relationship with the potters of Sarayama. In his mid-60s, he lives with his wife in a small house in the western part of Hita. His connection with Sarayama also started through his father, when the latter was director of the town's Industrial Crafts Institute and took a personal interest in promoting the potters' work. Mr T.'s father became involved with the *Mingei* movement when he made arrangements for Bernard Leach's stay in Sarayama in 1954. Although his father has died, Mr T. made use of his connections to start buying pots from all the potters in the community except H., whom he has always made it clear he dislikes. At the opening of every kiln, Mr T. goes up to Sarayama by taxi, and with his back very straight from his early military training, he walks from one workshop to the next and selects the pots he likes. In each pottery he is served tea and cakes, but these he tends not to touch, for he is more interested in conversation. Sometimes he will talk about the war; at other times he will enter into a monologue concerning Japan's early industrialization and contact with the west; more often he will concentrate on what he refers to as 'the great problem' besetting the *Mingei* movement. Potters will try to look attentive and adopt a fairly humble attitude in front of Mr T., but as he has a habit of saying nasty things about people behind their backs, they tend to ignore most of what he tells them. There is general agreement among the potters that they would like to stop selling their work to Mr T., but they still feel a sense of obligation toward his dead father, who really did his best to help them in the old days when pots did not sell. Mr T. is 'stuck up'; he spends his whole time corresponding with the folk craft leaders in Tokyo and telling them, and the media, that Onta is in 'dire crisis' and 'headed for destruction'. As far as potters are concerned, community affairs are none of Mr T.'s business. Nevertheless, because he is seen to be important, Mr T. usually manages to get his way with potters, who appear unable to join in concerted action against him.

One of the people Mr T. likes writing to is Dr Y., director of the Folk Craft Museum in Kurashiki, halfway between Hiroshima and Osaka. Dr Y. is in his mid-seventies and one of the last surviving members of the 'old school' of people like Yanagi, Hamada, and Leach who helped found the *Mingei* movement. He now spends a lot of his time commuting between Kurashiki and Kumamoto, where he has set up a new folk art museum, run by his daughter. He is frequently called upon to act as judge at exhibitions containing *mingei*, or to give speeches, very often at the summer seminars held by the Folk Craft

Association all over Japan. He may be seen at such events wearing what is to some a very folksy outfit, which almost invariably includes the incongruous combination of farmer's *mompe* (baggy trousers) and highly polished black leather shoes. Dr Y. is a lay priest; he speaks good English and has a nice sense of humour. The potters in Sarayama respect him highly; he has 'character' in their opinion. On one of his rare visits to the community, the potters make sure that they are all there to meet him at the entrance to Sarayama, even though they may have to wait there for more than half an hour in the rain. They obviously enjoy listening to him talk, even though Dr Y. has a habit of repeating the same anecdotes. He is, after all, the last of a generation of men who have made the community what it is.

Professor M. is very much one of the second generation of *mingei* leaders. Born in 1931, five years after the publication of Yanagi's first major work, *The Way of Crafts*, Professor M. now teaches art history at a well-known private university in Tokyo. He is also, strictly speaking, the *Mingei* movement's only professional art critic. He has written several works on Japanese art in general, but is recognized as a leading exponent of the meaning of folk art. In the 1950s he acted as secretary-cum-translator to Bernard Leach, and has now written a full biography of Yanagi. Following the death of the potter Hamada Shōji in January 1978, there was a shuffle of personnel in the Folk Craft Museum in Tokyo. Yanagi's eldest son, Munemichi, was appointed director; Professor

Plate 12 Close-up of *kushime* combing

60

M. found himself taking over the editorship of the Association's monthly magazine, *Mingei*. Followers of the *Mingei* movement are conscious that things are about to change, but none of the potters in Sarayama was optimistic about the future. In their opinion, Professor M. was too much of an ivory-tower scholar, too much the parrot of Yanagi's philosophy, to be able to understand the real problems that craftsmen such as themselves were facing. Time has shown that their apprehension was justified.

Chapter Three

SOCIAL ORGANIZATION

One of the themes running through this book concerns the inconsistencies to be found in the theory and practice of *mingei*, on the one hand, and of the organization of Japanese rural society, on the other. The way in which potters *ought* to make their wares may not be the same as they actually do make them; how they *ought* to participate in community life may well differ from how they actually do so. What is more, these discrepancies tend to interact and impinge one upon the other. Sometimes potters are unable to make their pottery according to *mingei* theory precisely because of community ideals; on other occasions they fail to fulfill community ideals because of the way in which they feel obliged to make and market their pottery.

It may be asked whether we really need to know the whole apparatus of household organization, division of labour, social cooperation and so on to understand the meaning of *mingei*, or indeed of any other art form. The anthropologist's answer is that we most certainly do. My premise, then, is quite straightforward: the production, marketing, and aesthetic appraisal of pottery are all *social* activities. Each affects, and is affected by, the other two. To understand how and why this is so, we must look at the kind of social organization that supports the production and marketing, and at the kind of people who are interested in the appreciation, of folk art pottery – in other words, at the 'art world' of *mingei*. It is here that we will encounter a dichotomy between the ideals held by people living in rural and in urban Japan (and so, in passing, I will indirectly criticize those who talk of *the* Japanese as though they form a single homogeneous entity).

Since I am concerned with the way in which the Japanese *Mingei* movement has affected social relations – and hence the pottery – in the community of Sarayama, I will begin by giving a brief account of some of the institutions that are to be found in Japanese rural society. I will then show how Sarayama itself is

---

The description of Sarayama's social organization, together with the changes that have taken place therein as described in this and the following chapters, is based on fieldwork conducted between 1977–79 and 1980–82. Subsequent visits to the community reveal that no *structural* change has taken place since the early 80s, even though elsewhere in Japan events have led to the virtual demise of the kinds of rural social institutions described in this book.

organized. I must emphasize here that the description of Sarayama's social organization outlined here and in the following two chapters is in part idealized. Later, I will show how this 'model' of rural society compares with the reality of people's everyday lives in the community.

The Household (*ie*) and Ownership of Property

Enough has been written about Japanese society for me not to go into a detailed description of its organization here. Still, I need to deal first with two general concepts – the household (*ie*) and the hamlet group (*buraku*) – which have been the focus of considerable attention by both Japanese and western scholars. I will then discuss these same concepts in the context of the pottery community of Sarayama.

In agricultural villages, the *ie* has been seen as the fundamental unit of Japanese rural society. *Ie* literally means 'house', but should perhaps be translated as 'household', for the word refers to the people living in a house as well as to its physical frame. The household is a corporate group in that it continues through time, regardless of any change in its membership; it is also a political and economic unit, whose members work together on land, making use of common property and of the household's right to irrigation water; moreover, it is widely conceptualized as such by those who do and by those who do not belong to the household concerned; it is a religious group, too, as may be seen in common ancestor worship, temple affiliation, and burial site; and it was, until the end of the Pacific War, a legal entity.

Membership of a household generally consists of an 'elementary family' – husband, wife, and children, and possibly one or both of the husband's or the wife's parents. A household may also be formed by just one man. It is also possible for non-kin, such as servants or labourers, who live in the household and form part of its work force, to be members of the *ie*. At the same time, kin who have moved out of the physical household to work permanently in a different area are not included in its membership. This means that a brother or sister can be treated as more like a stranger than a daughter-in-law or employee.

Household Head

The most important person in an *ie* is the household head, who acts as trustee of the property of the *ie* and makes use of it in a way that he thinks is most advantageous for all its members. The head used also to hold absolute authority over the affairs of all members of the household, but this is no longer legally permitted. Nevertheless, in rural society, he still has enormous influence in the running of the household and over the activities of its members.

Ideally, succession to the headship of the *ie* is based on patrilineal descent.[1] The successor should be the son[2] and not any other kind of kinsman, this son often – but not necessarily – being the eldest son of the household head. Where the household head has no male successor, adoption is frequently resorted to.

There are three possible alternatives: firstly, a man is adopted as son; secondly, a husband for a remaining daughter is imported as son-in-law and is then adopted as son; and thirdly, a woman is first adopted, then married to a man who is adopted as son. In all three cases, the man will succeed to the name of the *ie* as well as to its headship. Thus, although the Japanese say that the household is continued by rules of patrilineal descent, we must realize that in fact the *ie* is first and foremost a corporate group, and that adaptations will readily be made to ensure the continuity of this corporate group. In Japanese society generally, therefore, rules are made to help but not to hinder, and can therefore be broken for the sake of the corporate group.

Household Branching *(honke-bunke)*

A second rule of succession to the headship of the household is that the post should not be held by more than one person at the same time. The rule of residence, which is closely related to that of succession, is that there can be no more than one married couple in each generation in the house. As a result, although it is possible for two married couples of the same generation to live in a single household on a temporary basis, those who do not succeed to the post of head generally leave their home. Very often these individuals will go to live and work in urban areas, in which case they will have no more than a tenuous relationship with their natal *ie*. When these individuals live nearby in a new residential unit established by the *ie* and financed out of property belonging to it, a relationship is often set up between the two households. This is known as the *honke-bunke*, or main house/branch house, relationship.

The decision by the head of an agricultural *ie* to set up a branch household for his second son (for example) will depend largely on the amount of land owned by the main household. The personal relationship between father and son is secondary, but it may affect consideration of how much land, if any, the son will be given. If an economic tie is not established, however, the relationship between main household and branch household will soon become tenuous. Branch households may be formed not only for younger sons but for elderly parents (as in the *inkyo* system of retirement), daughters, and servants.

The Hamlet (*buraku*) and Control of Water

The Japanese word *buraku* is generally translated as hamlet. In the past, it was considered to rank in importance next to the *ie* as a social unit for group activity among farmers. The *buraku* has no legal existence now, even though in Tokugawa times (1603–1868) it conducted economic and political activities. Nowadays the village (*mura*) – or group of hamlets – is the smallest unit of government.

Whereas the household is a property-owning group, the hamlet is primarily a water-controlling unit. It is because agricultural households grow rice in their fields and because water has to be used to irrigate these fields that owners of land within a certain area have to form a group. The hamlet cannot, therefore, be viewed in isolation from the use of water (Nakamura 1977:190; Smith 1978:224–228; Sumiya 1953:47). Like the household, it is not simply a residential but an economic group (Nakane 1970:60).

The nature of the hamlet's organization has been discussed at length by Japanese scholars, who have argued that it is essentially hierarchical. Wet-rice agriculture requires the use of a lot of water over a limited period, and hamlet life is formed around the irrigation associations which control this water. As ownership of land is usually not equally distributed among households in a hamlet, the use of communal water is likewise unequal, and it is not possible to run the *buraku* along democratic principles. In other words, power is based on the right to water (Nakamura 1956:78; 1977:187–188; Sakamoto 1953:161; Shimpo 1976:1–7).

Not all hamlets throughout Japan, however, are organized in this hierarchical manner. Not every *buraku* consists predominantly of full-time farming households; there are some hamlets whose constituent households engage in forestry, fishing, or – as in Sarayama – some kind of craft. Japanese scholars have noted that there is a tendency for hierarchically structured hamlets to exist in the northeast of Japan, and democratically structured ones to be found in southwestern parts of the country. They have accordingly made a distinction between what Isoda (1951) has called 'household ranking' and 'non-household ranking' types of hamlet.[3]

A number of general features distinguish these two types. The 'household ranking' type of hamlet is usually geographically isolated. Its organization depends on the common ownership of mountain land, on the administration of irrigation water, and on the landlord-tenant system of rice cultivation. Branch households maintain close social and economic relations with their main houses. This relation is one of dependency between the two types of household and may develop into an extended household (or *dōzoku*) group,[4] in which the kinship system is based on household (rather than individual) ties. It is also the household to which prestige, status and power attach. Members of branch households and upper-ranking households usually marry out from the hamlet.

The 'non-household ranking' type of community is generally found in the southwest of Japan (where Sarayama is itself located). It is more directly affected by industrialization and improvements in communications and is consequently not nearly so isolated. Diffusion of the cash economy into rural areas has ensured that agriculture is carried out under better economic conditions; chemical fertilizers are now readily available, a fact which has enabled farmers to cultivate a greater area of land, so that they have been able to divide up hamlet common land among individual households. Branch households do not remain socially or economically dependent on their main houses, and the *inkyo*, or retirement system, of branch-house formation is commonly practised. The hamlet is often organized according to principles of age grading and governs itself by a non-kin system of seniority rather than through an extended household type of kin group. The status of individuals participating in hamlet self-government is not determined by hereditary factors so much as by present economic standing and personal qualities. There are few restrictions on marriage partners, and relations with in-laws are close. It is the individual's, rather than the household's, kindred that are often important to alliances between households in the hamlet. The 'non-household ranking' type of hamlet is particularly common in fishing communities (Dore 1959:364–366; Fukutake 1949:34–48; 1956:14–18; Gamō 1962:255–257; Isoda 1951:62–64; Johnson 1967:156–159; Seki 1962:173; Takahashi 1958:137–138).[5]

There has been some argument about the extent to which the hamlet is disintegrating in the face of administrative changes, on the one hand, and of the development of technology and the market, on the other. This argument has tended to concentrate on the concept of community solidarity, the density of which is measured by what has been seen to be nascent individualism in rural society. This is an argument of some relevance to this book since Sarayama's potters, *mingei* connoisseurs, and scholars of Japanese society all appear to value highly the notion of 'community' and take the wistful view that any change in its organization must of necessity be for the worse. The latter have always emphasized that ideally individuals are expected to subordinate their interests to those of the primary group to which they belong: in rural society, this means to the household and the hamlet. It is the household that provides 'the frame of organization in which individuals are classified' (Nakane 1967:28); it is a 'continuing entity transcending individuals' (Fukutake 1967:40), who are all but obscured by it. An individual participates in community activities only as a representative of his or her household. It is further argued that relations between individuals – such as those of an extended kin group or of a patron-client (*oya-ko*) nature – are effectively regarded as relations between households (Fukutake 1967:68; Nakane 1967:125).

The importance of the hamlet, and the loyalty and support that it ideally commands of its members, is also stressed. 'The individual is ready to set aside personal interests in favour of the community. Households within a *buraku* may feud and a man always has his enemies, but it is customary to subordinate such considerations to requirements of community interest in what are defined as important matters' (R. Smith 1961:522). Fukutake (1967:84) has argued that restraints on the individual are reinforced by the isolation and exclusive nature of the hamlet.

Because of the administrative and technological changes alluded to above, however, the ideals of both the household and the hamlet have over the years been seen to be yielding to that of individualism (Steiner 1956:197; Norbeck 1961:320; Smith 1978:202–228). Perhaps the institutions of the household and the hamlet no longer suppress individuality in the way that they used to, but it should not be inferred as a result that 'rational' or 'liberated' individualism (Fukutake 1967:216) now reigns in rural Japanese society. Individuals are still expected to subordinate their private interests to those of the household or the hamlet in which they live.

The Household in Sarayama

The *buraku* of Sarayama consists of two subhamlet groups (*koaza*) called Sarayama and Ikenzuru (Ike no tsuru). These settlements consist of fourteen and five households respectively and lie about a kilometre and a half apart. Ikenzuru, which cannot be seen from Sarayama, lies further up the mountainside, and all five of its households are inhabited by families called Kinoshita. None of them has ever intermarried with any of the four name groups living in the community of Sarayama below. Nobody in Ikenzuru has ever made pottery, although some deposits of suitable clay have been found there. One or two women from Ikenzuru are occasionally employed by Sarayama potters to help prepare clay and glaze materials, as well as do other odd jobs around the potteries. Both communities participate in recreational activities together on monthly rest days, but otherwise there is very little contact between people living in Sarayama and Ikenzuru. Their households do very different jobs, and they are situated too far apart.

Of the fourteen households in Sarayama, ten make pottery. The other four are involved in selling pottery, keeping a *sake* shop, building houses, plastering, forestry work, part-time agriculture, and running a noodle restaurant for tourists. None of the younger men from these non-potting households is around very much during the day, and building work may take the two carpenters away from Sarayama for two or three weeks on end. By contrast, men from the potter households, father and son, work in Sarayama, making pots from morning to night. Their wives prepare the clay and glazes; they turn the pots that are drying outside in the sunshine and bring them in before they are too hard if they are to be decorated. The women put handles on the coffee cups and spouts on the teapots. When the smaller pots are completely dried, they will pack them in the bisque kiln and take charge of the preliminary, low-temperature firing. They will also glaze the smaller pots, while the men, who have worked continuously at the wheel for five or six weeks at a time, glaze the larger wares. Together they load them into the multi-chambered climbing kilns, which the men then fire. After the firing, the whole household rests for two days. Then everyone turns out to unload the kiln, sort the fired pots, and pack those that have been ordered by people in places like Tokyo and Osaka. Any pots that are left over, after dealers have made their purchases, are put on the display shelves outside the potters' workshops. Then the men start throwing at the wheel again; the women return to the heavy tasks of clay and glaze preparation. Each household completes from five to eight cycles of work every year.

In Sarayama, the household is the basic unit of cooperation, and each individual is first and foremost a member of a household. The corporate nature of the household may be seen in the way all members of one household will greet, thank, or apologize to all members of another household for any one of its members' behaviour in relation to any one member of that household (Moeran 1985:128–9).[6]

Household composition in Sarayama varies from a nuclear family of parents and children (Irisai), to an extended family of parents, grandparents, children, and grandchildren (Yamani). For reasons that will be explained in due course, no household includes servants or labourers (such as pottery apprentices) among its members. Kin who have moved out of the household are not considered to be household members, unless they are schoolchildren who are being educated elsewhere.

Each household is also a religious group in the sense that it performs common ancestor veneration[7] and possesses an ancestral altar (*butsudan*), to which rice and water are offered before every morning meal. When gifts are presented to members of the household, they are customarily placed first of all before the *butsudan* as an offering to the ancestors. The importance in country life of household ancestors – and by implication the emphasis placed on the institution of the *ie* – may be seen in the way in which visitors to a household frequently pay their respects to the ancestors before greeting their host and hostess.

The value placed on the ancestors in Sarayama may further be seen in all households' strict observation of the All Souls' festival known as *o-bon* (August 13–15). Ancestors are 'met' at the households' communal graves and 'brought back' to their homes, where they are believed to reside for the three days of the festival. Household property, and in particular land, is closely associated with

Plate 13 Relatives gathered at Yamaichi for the mid-summer *obon* ancestors' festival, 1979

68

the ancestors (by whose endeavours such property was originally obtained), who are said to be enraged should a living household head for any unnecessary reason decrease household land holdings.

All households in Sarayama are affiliated to one of two temples. The Yanase, Kurogi, and Kobukuro name groups belong to the Nishi Hongan-affiliated Kyōeiji temple in Ashikari *buraku*, four kilometres down the Ono valley from Sarayama. The Sakamoto name group belongs to the Higashi Hongan-affiliated Saizenji in Kirio *buraku*, five kilometres southwest of the hamlet.

The head of the household (known locally as *sewayaku*) is the most important person in the *ie*, and he usually represents the household in community matters. Although he cannot legally hold absolute authority over the affairs of members of the household, he does exercise considerable control over them. Household finances are entirely in his hands,[8] and members of the household often have to obtain the household head's permission for any purchases other than those made on necessary food and daily household supplies. The household head also controls the activities of members, and his permission generally has to be obtained before any extra-household activity is indulged in. Finally, the household head is primarily responsible for the selection of spouses for his children, who are expected to accede to his wishes.

Succession to the headship of a household in Sarayama is based on the ideal of patrilineal descent. Theoretically, the successor should be the eldest son of the household head. As I mentioned earlier, however, these rules are flexible, and a wife or a younger son may take over the running of the household. In Yamasai, a widow for a long time controlled household affairs following the death of her husband, despite the presence of a grown-up son. In Yamako, the second son agreed to take up pottery and eventually to succeed to the headship of his household after his elder brother had made it clear that he wished to live and work in Tokyo.

Rightly or wrongly, it is generally accepted among all those living in Sarayama that only men are physically strong enough to become potters and work at the wheel full-time. A male successor is thus an absolute essential. Over the years many household heads have failed to father a son and so have resorted to adoption by one of two means: either a man is adopted as son; or a husband is brought in as son-in-law for a remaining daughter, and is then adopted as son. In both cases, the male will take the name of the household as well as succeed to its headship in due course. There is also a third method of succession to the headship of the *ie*. This involves what is known as 'secondary adoption' (*junyōshi*), whereby a younger brother will become head of the household upon the (usually premature) death of an elder sibling. In this case, the latter has often, but not always, left no surviving children. The present head of Yamaichi succeeded to the headship by this means of adoption.

When someone is adopted from outside the household as son, he is usually closely related to the present head of the adopting household – very often, as in Kaneyo, the son of the household head's or his wife's brother or sister (cf.

69

Cornell 1956:160; Smith 1956:65). When only girls are born to a household head, a son-in-law is married to one of the daughters (generally the eldest) and adopted into the household. In the past such adopted sons-in-law have tended to come from other households within the community (Yamani to Yamako, for example), but in exceptional circumstances an 'outsider' has been adopted, even though the arrangement is not usually considered to be satisfactory. The control exerted by the adopting household head over the 'son' with whom he has no blood ties tends to lead to confrontation and on occasion to the adopted son's returning to his natal home (as in the case of Irisai's father).

Household Branching in Sarayama

It will be remembered that, because of the rule that the post of household head should not be held by more than one person at a time, those who do not succeed are obliged to leave the household as they grow older. If economic circumstances permit, these individuals may be given a small amount of household land and property and establish a subsidiary, or branch, household nearby. Branch households are formed not only for younger sons of a household head, but also for daughters or servants. There is also what is known as the *inkyo* system whereby the head of a household may form a branch house for himself, his wife, and possibly a younger child upon retirement from active life. In Sarayama it has been customary for those children not succeeding to the position of household head to go to live and work in other areas, such as Hita, Fukuoka, and Kita-Kyūshū. Very often they have been adopted into agricultural and trading households in these regions.

Since Sarayama was founded in 1705, a considerable number of branch households (known locally as *shintaku*) have been formed. Although there are at present fourteen households in the community, altogether seventeen branch households have been set up by the original three main households, Yamasan, Yamasai, and the overall main household (*sō-honke*) of the Sakamoto name group (see *Figures 1* and *2*).

It can be seen that two basic types of branching have occurred. In one, second or third sons have been allowed to form branch households of their own. In this case, as described above, the main household has provided some form of accommodation and some agricultural and mountain land. I have managed to obtain information about land distribution for only one household, Yamamasu, which was formed in 1906 for a second son (Masuji) of the household head of Yamako (Kaneshichi). According to Masuji's brother, father of the present head of Yamako, the main house provided the second son with a place to live, together with some rice fields and mountain land. There was not enough paddy to feed Masuji and his family, but the latter was a carpenter by trade and thus had a cash income, which compensated for shortage of homegrown food supplies. He was able to buy more rice fields a few years later. At no time was Yamamasu economically dependent on Yamako, and there was no obligation for the former

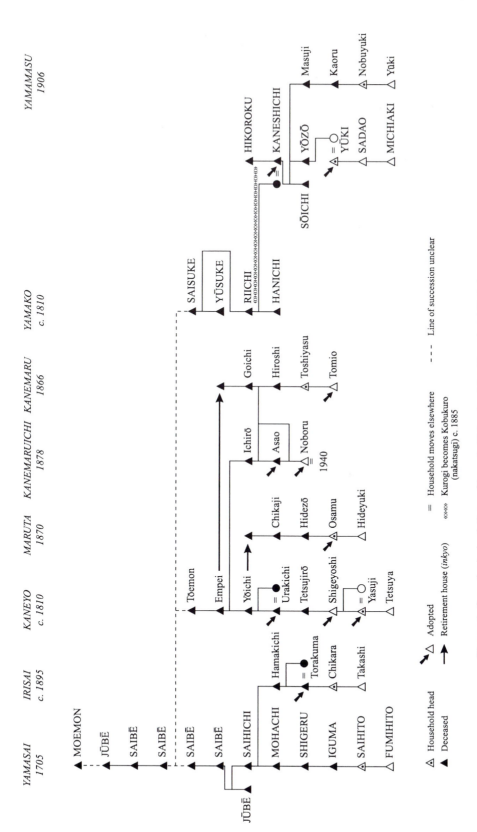

Figure 1 Genealogical relations of household heads of the Kurogi and Kobukuro name groups

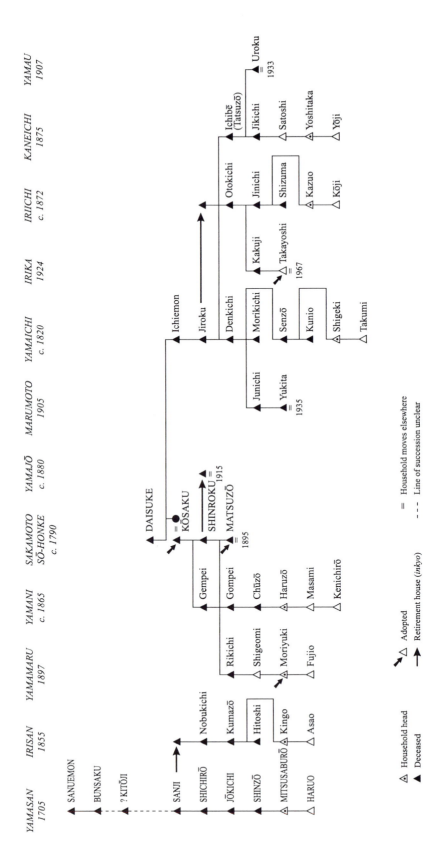

Figure 2 Genealogical relations of household heads of the Yanase and Sakamoto name groups

to give labour services to the main house. The branch house started out and remained a self-supporting unit.

Second, what is known as the 'retirement' (*inkyo*) system of forming branch households was frequently practised between 1855 and 1872. In this case, the head of the main household handed over authority to one of his sons and, taking his (second) wife and youngest remaining son (*suekko*), left the main house to set up a 'retirement' branch household (*inkyoya*).[9] The retiring head of the main household often made sure that his own branch household received a major portion of land, so that the main house was left just enough capital with which to make a living.

Of the branch households originally formed in Sarayama, five no longer exist, either because no satisfactory successor to the household head could be found or because household members moved out of the community to make a living elsewhere. Thus the Sakamoto *sō-honke* collapsed when the adopted household head went bankrupt; it is said that he emigrated to Brazil in 1895. There are now, therefore, altogether fourteen households in the community (*Figure 3*).

Extended Kinship Relations

Because branch houses are not economically dependent on their main households, there is no extended household group (*dōzoku*) in Sarayama. Kinship relations do play an important part in people's everyday lives, however, for it is through them that individuals participate in the wider activities of rural life. Such kinship ties are often framed as household relations – particularly with people related to one another through the practice of household branching. So, let us now look at the way in which personal kinship ties, in particular those formed as a result of adoption and marriage, may further serve to link one household to another.

As we have seen, adoption has frequently been resorted to in Sarayama, and on a number of occasions the adopted son (or son-in-law, *yashinai-go*) has been taken from another household within the community. In *Figure 4(a)*, two households – Yamani and Yamako – which would not normally unite because of household kinship ties or residential proximity (see next section), are brought together through adoption. In *Figure 4(b)*, Kaneyo and Maruta are main and branch households respectively, but this household relationship is reinforced by close personal-kin adoption. At the same time, Irisan becomes linked to both households owing to the previous adoption of a younger son into Kaneyo.

Marriage ties (*engumi*) have also served to link or reinforce links between households within the community (*Figure 5*). Close personal kinship ties can be seen to exist between the household heads of Yamasai (*honke*) and Irisai (*bunke*) (nephew and uncle); Kanemaru and Kaneichi (brothers-in-law); Kanemaru and Yamani (brothers-in-law); Irisai and Kaneichi (brothers-in-law); and Kaneichi and Yamani (first cousins). More distant kinship relations brought about by marriage exist between and are recognized by Yamasai and Kanemaru, Kaneichi and Kaneyo, Kaneyo and Yamasan, and Yamasan and Yamasai.[10]

As we shall see in the following chapter, personal kinship ties form an

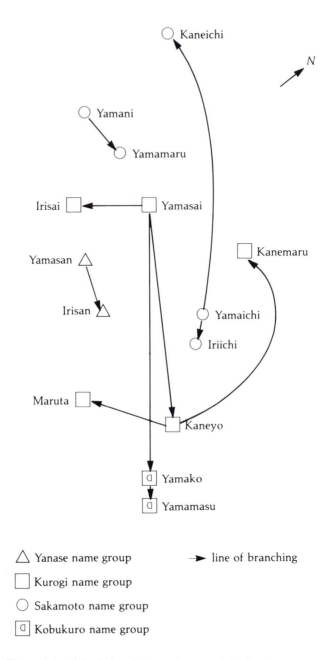

Figure 3 Spatial relations between *honke* and *bunke* in Sarayama

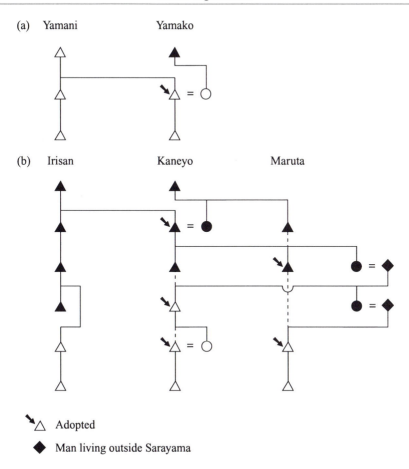

Figure 4 Households linked through personal kinship adoption ties

extremely convenient secondary means by which labour may be recruited by a household. For example, Yamani and Yamamaru are main and branch households respectively, Chūzō and Shigeomi being first cousins. At the same time, Yamani is closely tied to Kaneichi, since Satoshi's mother was Chūzō's younger sister. Finally, Kaneichi and Yamamaru are related by personal kinship ties (even though as households they are formally separate), since Satoshi's brother married the sister of Moriyuki. Moriyuki was himself adopted into Yamamaru by Shigeomi, who is Satoshi's sister-in-law's uncle (*Figure 6*).

While Yamani and Yamamaru are primarily related as main and branch households and hence cooperate for such household ceremonies as ancestor memorial rites (*hōji*), when it comes to other kinds of cooperation (such as the weeding of rice fields), personal kin ties between Yamamaru and Kaneichi, on

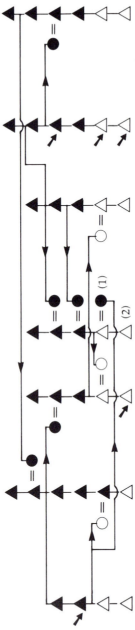

△ Adopted son

➤ Direction of virilocal marriage

(1) First wife

(2) Son by second wife

Figure 5 Households linked through personal kinship marriage ties

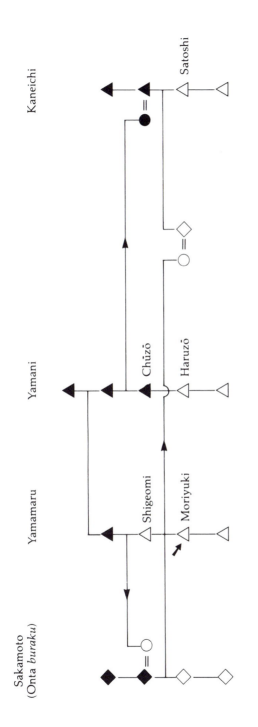

Figure 6 Personal kinship ties between Sarayama households (1)

the one hand, and between Yamani and Kaneichi, on the other, facilitate the grouping of all three households. Similarly, Yamamaru may on occasion cooperate with Iriichi or Yamamasu because of past marriage ties (*Figure 7*), even though in both cases kinship relations are becoming tenuous. Almost all households in Sarayama are thus able to form links on the basis of the past exchange of women, and of men through adoption.

Finally, we should note that personal kinship ties can be used to increase the number of households linked through household kinship ties. For example, Yamasan is linked to Kaneyo, and Kaneyo to Maruta, by marriage; household kinship ties exist between Yamasan and Irisan, Irisan and Kaneyo, and Kaneyo and Maruta; but there is no household or personal kinship tie between Yamasan and Maruta. However, these households, together with Kaneyo and Irisan, almost invariably form a quartet for cooperative work or labour exchanges.

Residence Associations

Another means by which households in the community may be linked is that of residence associations (called *kumi; tonari dōshi*). Such associations are based on principles of residential proximity and act primarily as methods of recruiting labour for community (as opposed to household) activities, such as road repairs, river weeding, recreation, and the appointment of community officials.

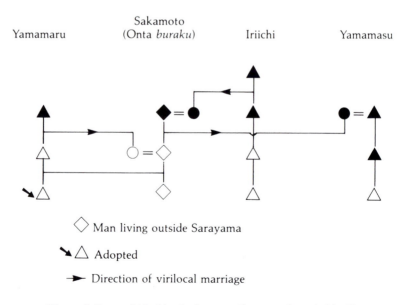

Figure 7 Personal kinship ties between Sarayama households (2)

Although residence associations tend to strengthen *honke-bunke* household ties, in that main and branch households are almost always located on adjacent plots of land, they do provide an opportunity for nonrelated households to cooperate in community tasks or sports. Yamaichi and Irisan, for example, will join together in one team to play a softball match or have an archery contest with a second team that includes Yamamaru and Yamasai. Associations are designated with reference to the top and bottom houses of the community, and households within each assocation are enumerated from top to bottom according to their location down the mountainside.

To some extent, perhaps, residence associations tend to isolate those households at the top and bottom of the community into fixed combinations (Kaneichi, Yamani and Yamamaru at one end, and Yamamasu, Yamako, Maruta and Kaneyo at the other). Those households located in the centre of Sarayama, however, have more fluid relations with other households around them. Certain households, not otherwise connected by household or personal kinship ties, are able to form links with other households through the residence associations. As a result, there are very few households that have no connection at all with other households within the hamlet. Residence associations thus prevent kin-related households from forming exclusive groups.

Age Associations

Another method of social organization – age associations – provides cross-cutting ties within the hamlet and also serves to link those living in Sarayama with people from other communities nearby. Age associations have been given some attention by Japanese scholars, who have shown that a variety of types can be found all over Japan, although most commonly in the south-western part of the country. In general, there are three factors which may affect the membership of an age group: one is topography, which may lead to the existence of two groups, not just one, in a hamlet; a second is household status, which may give rise to a distinction between original residents and more recently settled households; and the last is individual status, which may permit only first-born sons to join an age group. Any community, hamlet, or village may be divided into four age associations – child, youth, adult, and aged – of which the eldest or the youngest may be missing. The actual age limits and the internal structuring of each age association also vary from place to place (Seki 1962:131–139).

Sarayama is divided into three age associations: youth (*seinen*), adult (*sōnen*), and aged (*toshiyori*). In the past, young people, both boys and girls, regardless of whether they were eldest or youngest in their households, were required to join the youth association after leaving school. They would remain members until the time they were married at about 25 years of age. They then automatically became members of the adult association. The age at which men and women joined the old people's association was ill-defined, and members were recruited

79

Plate 14 Local primary school sports day, 1982

from their early 60s to late 70s, depending on the individual's own concept of what constituted old age.

The youth association has always been the best organized of the three associations in Sarayama. Because members used to meet regularly, friendships were formed between young people who would remain close to one another through the busier and less well organized years of adult life. In the past, members of the youth association would participate in such activities as communal reading, abacus practice, discussions, and *utai* chanting. They were also required to clean the hamlet graveyard at the *o-bon* ancestor ceremony and were generally assigned the least pleasant community tasks, such as grave digging.

During the past fifteen to twenty years, however, the youth association has come to occupy a less and less important position in young people's lives. This is partly because the youth association of Sarayama has been absorbed into a national organization of youth groups, whose membership is not compulsory; partly, too, because there has also been an improvement in communications, giving access to entertainment (such as television, films, bowling, *pachinko*, baseball, and so on) not previously readily available, so that many young people prefer not to join the youth association. As a result, there is only one fully active member of the Ono youth association from Sarayama, and young people in the community only get together for such rare events as the *bon* dance (which is not held unless there has been a death in Sarayama that year) (Moeran 1985:69–82,

124–27). The custom of cremating rather than burying the dead has also relieved young men of the unpleasant job of grave digging, so that their community activities tend now to be limited to the occasional, haphazard fire practice.

The adult association (*sōnenkai*) has never been well organized, although it makes sure to arrange an annual outing for its members (Moeran 1985:134–8). It is the only age association formed entirely of men, for many of the boys and girls who were members of the youth association leave Sarayama to get married

Plate 15 Men from the *sōnenkai* adults' age association
practising archery, 1977

or find work elsewhere. Women who are married into Sarayama join the women's association (*fujinkai*), which has acted as the female equivalent to the adult association. The women's association meets twice a month, and also goes on an overnight trip to one or another of the nearby spas once a year, but, by all accounts, it is not as active as it used to be. Members of the adult association have, for their part, usually been too busy with household affairs to participate regularly in leisure or study activities, but friendships forged during their time in the youth association have continued and have served to bring about fresh ties between households.

Traditionally, it has been the old men who have maintained authority in hamlet affairs. When household members gather for ceremonies or discussion, men are seated in order of age. The eldest men place themselves with their backs to the *tokonoma* – according to Shintō beliefs, a sacred alcove and the 'highest' point in the room. In the past, the elders customarily commanded silence when they spoke and did not expect to be questioned or argued with by members of the youth or adult associations. They controlled their household purse strings, and particularly wealthy members were known to contribute money for projects that benefited the whole hamlet. Such action naturally enhanced their status (cf. Dore 1978:205–207) and made it more difficult for younger household heads to argue with their often autocratic decisions.

In the past, the old people's association was essentially administrative, although there were occasions, of course, when the old men participated in leisure activities with their womenfolk. However, postwar education, based on ideals of democracy, has led to a weakening of the position of the old men, and some of the younger men in the hamlet have begun to speak out against the more blatantly dictatorial acts of their seniors. (The way in which the power of the elders has been gradually erased over the past two decades is the subject of a later chapter.) Membership is more or less fixed by the national pension scheme, which decrees that a man is old at 65. Nowadays, the old people's association meets periodically for a game of 'gateball' (a kind of croquet) or a 'tea' party during which plenty of alcohol is also consumed. Once a year, all the old people in Sarayama are entertained and banqueted by the rest of the hamlet's residents.

The Potters' Cooperative

The Onta Potters' Cooperative (*Ontayaki dōgyō kumiai*) is a loose association which serves basically to help individual potter households deal with extra-hamlet bodies. Only those households which fire kilns are members of the cooperative; other households in Sarayama may not participate. The cooperative is strictly limited to residents of Sarayama and is not legally recognized, nor is it affiliated with any larger, nationally organized, potters' cooperative, in the way that farming households are with the Agricultural Cooperative.

The cooperative appears to have been formed sometime between 1935 and 1937, at about the time of the China Incident, when the central government tried to stimulate the Japanese economy. All those of the same occupation (dōgyō) were required to form a cooperative association. The father of the present head of Kaneyo, was the first leader of the cooperative, since he was employed in the local village office and was also hamlet chief at the time. But his household stopped potting, and from 1945 the head of Yamani took over the job. Eight years later, however, Mr. T., director of the Hita Industrial Crafts Institute, suggested on one of his visits to Sarayama to buy pots that he was too old to do the job and that a younger man was needed. As a result, Yamani's son was appointed and remained leader of the cooperative for more than twenty years. In 1975, after some argument, two of the younger potters persuaded him to resign, and his place was taken by the next man in line of seniority, who also happened to be his brother.

Potters say that the post of leader of the cooperative is necessary, but add that it is an unrewarding task which they do not see as at all prestigious (cf. Cornell 1956:175; Norbeck 1977:98). Its occupant is required to act as spokesman for the potters, to relay information, and in general to mediate between them and the outside world. Increasing contact with the media, local government officials, and various mingei organizations has made the job of cooperative leader rather more time-consuming than it used to be, and outside bodies tend to look upon the position as one of importance. At the beginning of the 1980s, some of the younger potters felt that the selection of their cooperative leader might begin to alter in the near future, especially since the potters had by then come to be differentiated as an occupational group from the remaining non-potting households in the community.[11]

Conclusion

In this description of the social organization of the potters' community of Sarayama, I have concentrated on the household as an economic, political, and religious institution, and have traced the ways in which households in Sarayama are linked through household and personal kinship ties. I have also outlined further means of social organization, such as residence associations, age groups, and the potters' cooperative.

This discussion of household alliances in Sarayama has shown that the community is essentially of the 'non-household ranking' type. This may be seen in the facts that there is no evidence that there was ever economic dependence between a branch household and its main house; the inkyo system of branch-house formation was frequently resorted to (cf. Takahashi 1958:136); an individual-oriented type of kinship system may be found alongside a house-oriented system (Gamō 1962:255); endogamy has been practised among households in the community (Gamō 1962:256); age associations exist, and their membership is not affected by territorial or status considerations (Seki 1962:131–133; Isoda 1951:63); and finally, religious and social events in the community are the responsibility of each household in turn (Fukutake 1949:37).

Although I will go into further details of the egalitarian nature of household relationships in Sarayama in the following chapters, I should like to note here that the 'non-household ranking' system has been to some extent upheld by the age-grade system of gerontocracy. Clearly, government by older men may be seen as somewhat undemocratic, but it should be realized that the system is cyclical and that those who are young now will in due course grow old and take over the reins of community power. Thus every household should in theory take its turn at the top of the gerontocratic hierarchy, as its head gradually grows older, retires, and is replaced by his son, who in turn grows older. Ideally, this rotating system of authority prevents a household ranking system based on such criteria as wealth – a point to which I shall return when I discuss the decline of community solidarity.

Another point concerns the way in which the social organization of Sarayama might differ from that of a purely agricultural hamlet. I have already mentioned that the data for most of the sociological explanation of Japanese rural life has come from studies of farming villages. The household has been seen as a landholding, and the hamlet as a water-controlling, unit. This study, however, focuses on a community that has been only partly agricultural; people living in Sarayama have also been making pottery there since the community's founding in 1705. What interests me, therefore, is the possibility that the organization of households in the community of Sarayama may differ from that found in purely agricultural hamlets.

There are two features in particular about pottery making which contribute to egalitarian relations in the community and which may also add to our knowledge of the hamlet and the household as social institutions: the first of these is the way in which water is used by potter households to prepare clay for use at the wheel; and the second is the way in which pots have to be fired in kilns. I intend to argue that the method by which the clay is prepared for use at the wheel has in fact affected the composition of the potter's household and limited the number of potter households in Sarayama. I will also show that the ownership of kiln rights – rather than of land or water rights – has affected the economic development of potter households and their relations with other households in the community.

It is here that an anthropological account of the social organization of a group of Japanese potters can be linked to folk art aesthetics. After all,

> All artistic work, like all human activity, involves the joint activity of a number, often a large number, of people. Through their cooperation, the art work we eventually see or hear comes to be and continues to be. The work always shows signs of that cooperation. The forms of cooperation may be ephemeral, but often become more or less routine, producing patterns of collective activity we can call an art world.
>
> (Becker 1982:1)

In the opening chapter on the ideals of the *Mingei* movement, I pointed out that Yanagi Sōetsu emphasized the fact that, in his opinion, beauty derived from cooperation and self-denial, rather than from individual genius. Here I have begun to show how the lives of folk art potters also depend on social cooperation and individual self-denial, so that there is a close parallel between Yanagi's aesthetic ideal and the principles according to which Japanese rural society is organized. It is the existence of the *mingei* art world *per se*, and the various means by which that art world affects the production, appreciation, marketing and consumption of Onta and other *mingei* pottery, that underpin this anthropological approach to the study of values.

Plate 16 Small lidded jar for local Hita delicacy sold to tourists, and fired at the back of every Onta kiln chamber

Chapter Four

ECOLOGY AND SOCIAL STRUCTURE

We have seen that a major concern for Yanagi Sōetsu in the development of his theory of *mingei* was 'nature' – a word which had two inter-related meanings. On the one hand, craftsmen should ideally make use of natural materials which were obtainable nearby; for potters, this meant digging and preparing local clay and glaze materials, as well as making and firing their pots with 'natural' methods of production. On the other hand, Yanagi felt that beauty in *mingei* was born of craftsmen's 'self-surrender' to their 'nature', or unconscious. By so doing, they not only discovered a 'pure land of beauty' in their work; they were

Plate 17 Yamasai's clay crushers, with branch house Irisai's *ize* dam in the foreground, 1981

bound to their fellow craftsmen and so formed a cooperative group, or guild, which allowed everyone together to produce a 'communal art'. Nature thus came to refer, on the one hand, to the environment in which craftsmen lived and, on the other, to their spiritual and inner self.

What is relevant here, in the light of the previous chapter on the social organization of a pottery community, is that the two main institutions of Japanese rural society – the household and the hamlet – closely depend upon the environment in which they are found, since each is an economic institution depending on the use and control of land and water respectively. As a result, those living in rural pottery communities such as Onta have found that the environment has had an extremely important effect not only upon the ways in which their everyday lives are *socially* organized, but now – thanks to the *Mingei* movement – upon the way in which their work is appreciated *aesthetically*. In order to tease out this paradox further, I need now to decribe how the social structure of Sarayama and its potters depends upon the ecology of their pottery production.

Before proceeding, however, let me point out that, although from time to time I use the term 'ecology' to refer to the 'environment', I realize that strictly speaking they are not equivalent – especially given Anderson's definition (1973:182) of ecology as 'the study of entire assemblages of living organisms and their physical milieus, which together constitute integrated systems'. Mark you, such a broad view would seem to involve too many variables to be accounted for in any comprehensible study of people's social and biological relations with the environment in which they live.

Two problems arise from this. In the first place, there is little agreement as to what exactly constitutes an ecological approach in anthropology (Ellen 1979:1). A number of terms have been used to describe limited aspects of particular environmental-cultural relations: for example, 'cultural ecology' (Steward 1955), 'ethnoecology' (Frake 1962), 'cultural (or, "vulgar" [Friedman 1974]) materialism' (Harris 1968), 'anthropological ecology' (Anderson 1973), 'ecological anthropology' (Rappaport 1971), and so on. Second, anthropological research into the relationship between 'ecology' and 'society' has so far left us with 'a wealth of facts but a paucity of principles' (Freilich 1963:21). I remain unconvinced by the evidence provided hitherto that cross-cultural 'ecological' regularities do in fact exist (cf. Ellen 1978:298–299), but hope that such regularities may one day be found. It is in this spirit of optimism that I present here my 'ecological' argument about clay, water, and social structure.

The Japanese hamlet, as we have seen, is not simply a residential group, but a water-controlling unit. It is often hierarchically organized – firstly, because of landlord-tenant patterns of ownership; and secondly, because of access to water rights associated with ownership of rich paddy. These have in effect 'ecologically' structured both the organization and the size of rural hamlets. In other words, during the Edo period (1603–1868), the proliferation of households in a hamlet depended on the distribution of land and water rights, and it is the latter that may be said to have been the decisive factor in the formation of branch households (Smith 1959:24–25, 56–57; Johnson 1967:163).

Now, those living in the community of Sarayama have, until very recently, been both farmers and potters. One of the questions of theoretical interest for those studying Japanese rural society, therefore, concerns the extent to which the structure of this community and the organization of the households making up the community differ from those of purely agricultural settlements studied so far (Beardsley *et al.* 1959; Cornell 1956; Dore 1978; Embree 1939; Shimpo 1976; Smith 1956, 1978; and Yoneyama 1967a, 1967b). Although the answer is 'not much', the reasons underlying that answer are significant.

Since people living in Sarayama relied on wet-rice agriculture for their livelihood until after the end of the Pacific War, the community is like other agricultural communities in two important ways: not only is Sarayama's household system similar to that found elsewhere in Japanese rural society, but the community as a whole may be seen as a water-controlling unit. However, most households in Sarayama also make pottery. The clay used for this is extremely hard and has to be powdered before being thrown on the wheel. Clay crushers, powered by the water flowing in two streams that run through the community, are used to prepare the clay, but they can prepare only enough for two men in each household (i.e. father and one son) to work with at the wheel. My contention here, therefore, is that the nature of the clay affects, firstly, the composition of each potter household and, secondly, the expansion of potter households, since each must have access to water in order to prepare its clay. The limited amount of land available for building on, together with the angle of slope of the streams flowing down through Sarayama, has thus determined the number of households in the community able to practice agriculture and pottery.

I have already suggested that Sarayama may be classed as an egalitarian type of community such as is found elsewhere in the southwest of Japan. There are three reasons for the lack of hierarchical organization in Sarayama. In the first place, there have never been any landlords in the community, nor have households there been tenants to large landlords in neighbouring hamlets. Ownership of rice paddy and dry fields has been fairly evenly distributed among all households; their holdings are comparatively small, averaging about 2,900 square metres of paddy and 240 square metres of dry field, scattered within a three kilometre radius of Sarayama. Second, since all the paddy that has been cultivated is situated in narrow valleys in the mountains, it has not been necessary for farmers to build complicated or lengthy irrigation systems (such as are found in many of Japan's coastal plains). Many streams provide a constant source of water supply, and farmers have generally taken water directly from these streams to their fields by way of split-bamboo pipes. There was only one irrigation channel supplying as many as a dozen small fields and this was found in the valley immediately above the community. In general, however, not more than four or five narrow fields were irrigated by a single 'channel' of split-bamboo pipes laid from the mountain streams. Thus, households in Sarayama never formed exclusive groups for the control of water, and friction over the allocation of water – such as that discussed by Shimpo (1976) – has generally been avoided.

Third, unlike in agriculture, the way in which water is channelled to work the clay crushers does not affect downstream potter households. In the production of pottery, there is no critical period, such as exists in the agricultural cycle, when a household *must* have water. In Sarayama, when water is scarce, there is a shortage for everyone; when it is abundant, there is plenty for everyone, regardless of whether a household has its clay crushers upstream or downstream.

Clay Preparation and Community Expansion

Since the founding of the community in 1705, potters have had their local, hard clay powdered by water-powered clay crushers, known as *karausu* (literally 'Chinese pestle'). These clay crushers are usually in groups of twos and threes and line both streams running through Sarayama. Water is channelled so that it flows into the hollowed out scoop at the end of each crusher; the weight of the water makes the crusher seesaw down, empty the water from its scoop, and fall back with a thud onto a mound of clay placed under its far end.

Plate 18 Yamaichi's clay crushers, 1981

89

The clay crushers have always fascinated visitors to Sarayama, and those involved in the *Mingei* movement have not failed to mention the crushers in their descriptions of Onta pottery. The following passage is by no means atypical and illustrates the way in which the method of clay preparation is partly attributed responsibility for the beauty of the pottery made in Sarayama:

> As you come down from the mountain pass into the valley, you first hear the echo of the water-powered *karausu* used to pound the clay. The silence between each echoing thud is terribly long. Only a little water trickles along the channel from the river to the crusher. There is no need for things to be done in any rush, however, and it seems as though it is only our hearts that find it hard to wait. But it is because there is this gentle rhythmic sound that the village exists. If some busy-sounding machinery were to be introduced, the whole place would fall into disarray. This is something written about by Yanagi in *Hita no Sarayama*. It is probably unnecessary to reappraise Onta's pots when there is such a beautiful collection of crocks and jars in the Folk Craft Museum in Tokyo. But I still had to see these pots in Sarayama itself where they listen to the sound of the clay crushers.
>
> (Matsukata 1955:15–16)

Plate 19 Sakamoto Moriyuki and Kurogi Tomio making a new *karausu* clay crusher, 1978

Some people have considered the *karausu* to be extremely rare (Koyama 1967:101), but this is not actually so. There are two varieties of crusher to be found in Japan. One is water-powered and is generally known as *battari* or *sakontarō*; the other is foot-powered and is widely distributed over southeast Asia. Both kinds of crusher have, however, generally been used to pound rice and cereals, and the unusual thing about the crushers in Sarayama is that they have been adapted to pound clay.[1]

The question of interest to students of the structure of the Japanese hamlet is: how has the fact that clay crushers can only be used in limited numbers affected community expansion? In answering this question, I should make it clear that the description given here of community expansion is ideal in that market considerations are not taken into account. Thus, during the Meiji period (1868–1912), there were probably very few newly-established branch-household heads who wanted to take up pottery, since it was hardly an occupation that reaped much – if any – economic reward. Whether branch households actually took up pottery immediately upon being formed, or waited until later, is not known. It was suggested that Irisai, for example, the last potting branch-household to be established, may not have started pottery for some twenty years, until market conditions had improved.

In Sarayama (Onta), all pottery is made from a local clay which is rich in iron content and can be obtained from the mountain land in the immediate neighbourhood of the community.[2] As already noted, this clay is extremely hard, and it can be used for throwing at the wheel only if it is first powdered, then sifted and left to settle in tanks of water, before being dried. The rock-like substance of the clay requires something really heavy to break it up into tiny granules and give the clay the plasticity potters require. In the days before modern machinery was devised to pound the clay (and adopted now in the neighbouring village of Koishiwara), water-powered clay crushers provided the only means by which clay could be properly powdered.

Each crusher must be about fourteen feet long, and in order to seesaw properly, it must pivot at a point about one-and-a-half to two metres from the tip of the hollowed-out scoop into which the river water pours. Each crusher, therefore, must be set at about the same distance above the bed of the stream from which it takes its water. As a result, there must be a drop between each crusher or set of crushers. This effectively limits the branching of households because, firstly, access to either of Sarayama's two streams depends on land ownership; secondly, such access should be within reasonable distance (say, 200 metres) of a potter's workshop; and thirdly, the total drop of the stream between the cultivated land at the top and the bottom of the community is fixed. The last factor has limited the *total* number of farming households able to take up pottery in Sarayama; the first two factors have made *specific* limitations on which households have been able to take up pottery.

At the time of fieldwork, the total drop of the two streams did not permit the further introduction of clay crushers within the residential confines of Sarayama.

91

Land immediately above and below the community on the Sarayama stream and to the north along the Gōshiki stream was being used to grow rice.[3] Both streams flow in a series of stepped dams through the community. These dams are called *ize* and allow the *karausu* to seesaw effectively. Each household builds a dam above its clay crushers; it is ownership of land for the crushers, and the fall of the river between these crushers and the crushers of the household immediately upstream, which in the end determine whether a household will or will not take up pottery.

In the past, dams were made from large stones. They were frail constructions that were almost inevitably washed away every June by floods that occurred during the rainy season. However, during the late 1960s and 70s, almost all of

Plate 20 Irisai's clay crushers, with concreted water channel dam and main house Yamasai's crushers in background, 1978

92

the dams were concreted and their heights established once and for all. Only along the upper stretches of the Gōshiki stream, where the flow of water is never strong, have the dams continued to be made of stone.

The building of each dam originally required the permission of the household that owned land alongside the stream above, since the downstream household's dam would determine the upstream water level. The dams had to be rebuilt after the rainy season every year, and arguments sometimes broke out. An upstream household might complain that the dam downstream had been built too high and that its clay crushers had been adversely affected by the raised water level. Now that the dams have for the most part been concreted, however, such conflict between potting households rarely occurs.

The relation between dam heights, water levels, and clay crushers has to some extent affected the siting of branch households during the forming of the community. *Bunke* have generally been placed *downstream* of their main households when they were to take up pottery as well as farming. In this way, the establishment of a new dam would affect only the main house forming the *bunke* (see *Figure 8*).

There was never any particular rule about the formation of potter households in Sarayama. However, it can be seen that those households which were established early in the nineteenth century had residences and dams located at a considerable distance from their main households. As more and more branch houses were formed, access to the streams became more difficult and pottery *bunke* could only be established with their dams immediately below the clay crushers of their main households (cf. for example, Yamasai/Irisai and Yamaichi/Kaneichi). Actual residences, however, were at times placed at some distance from *honke* because of a shortage of land space (e.g. Yamaichi/Kaneichi).[4] If we look at the estimated dates of branching of households within Sarayama, we can see that almost all potting households were in fact early *bunke* (*Table 1*). There are exceptions, of course. Maruta, for example, was formed because a first son did not want to take up pottery in the main household of Kaneyo, whereas Irisai was able to take up pottery – despite late branching – because its land bordered the Sarayama stream. However, its dam has the lowest drop of all, and clay crushers do not function efficiently when the level of the water is raised by heavy rains.

Once Irisai was established as a potter household, the drop of the beds of both streams running through Sarayama was completely utilized by dams and clay crushers. Consequently, branch households formed after 1895 were unable to take up pottery. They did not have access to water, for clay crushers could by this time be placed only at the very top or very bottom of the community. If further crushers had been established along either of the two streams, they would have encroached on agricultural land. But this land, of course, provided households with vital food supplies. The fact that Sarayama was a self-sufficient closed community relying on agriculture prevented the number of pottery households from increasing. It may therefore be argued that the development of the community of Sarayama has been limited by the twin problems of access to

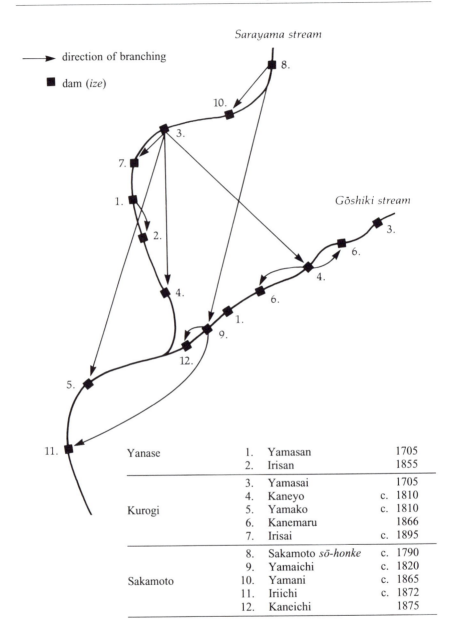

Figure 8 Locations of dams (*ize*) showing relationships between main house and branch house

Table 1 Estimated dates of household branching, together with the occupation of the branch household

Main household	Branch household	Date	Occupation
Yamasai	Kaneyo	1810	Potter/farmer
Yamasai	Yamako	1810	Potter/farmer
Sakamoto *honke*	Yamaichi	1820	Potter/farmer
Yamasan	Irisan	1855	Potter/farmer
Sakamoto *honke*	Yamani	1865	Potter/farmer
Kaneyo	Kanemaru	1866	Potter/farmer
Kaneyo	Maruta	1870	Farmer/retired
Yamaichi	Iriichi	1872	Potter/farmer
Yamaichi	Kaneichi	1875	Potter/farmer
Kanemaru	Kanemaruichi*	1878	Farmer/retired
Sakamoto *honke*	Yamajō*	1880	Retired
Yamasai	Irisai	1895	Potter/farmer
Yamani	Yamamaru	1897	Farmer/*tatami*-maker
Yamaichi	Marumoto*	1905	Farmer/*kimono*-salesman
Yamako	Yamamasu	1906	Farmer/carpenter
Kaneichi	Yamau*	1907	Farmer/plasterer
Iriichi	Irika*	1924	Farmer/stonemason

* Household now nonexistent.

water and to land. Not only has the establishment of branch houses depended on the availability of irrigated rice paddy, but the number of households engaged in the production of pottery has been limited by the necessity of their using crushers to pound the local clay.

It should be pointed out that, over the years, there have been exchanges of land adjacent to two dams and that these have affected households' 'rights' to take up potting in Sarayama. When Kaneichi gave up potting in 1910, its clay-crusher land below that belonging to Yamaichi was not returned to the latter (Kaneichi's main house), but was given or sold – for reasons unknown – to Maruta. This meant that Maruta, if it wanted to, could take up pottery, but Kaneichi could not. However, when the present head of Maruta decided to start a noodle shop in the late 1960s, he arranged to exchange the plot of land acquired from Kaneichi for one belonging to his main house, Kaneyo, since the latter was adjacent to his residence and therefore suitable for the new building which overlooks the river.

This exchange meant that, should Maruta – which was not originally a potting household – decide at some stage in the future that it wants to take up pottery, it still has the dam required for clay crushers to be activated, and these crushers would be situated on the full-flowing Sarayama stream. Kaneyo, on the other hand, which gave up pottery in 1928 owing to the illness of the present household head, would be able to set up only one or two crushers on its plot of land below Yamaichi's crushers on the Gōshiki stream. Moreover, matters are complicated by the fact that according to official maps there is no access to this land except through Yamaichi's land. Permission would have to be obtained from the latter should Kaneyo express a desire to restart potting. The fact that Kaneyo sold its other crusher land to Kanemaru some years ago now would make it extremely difficult for the former to powder enough clay to restart full-time pottery production.[5]

Clay Preparation and Household Composition

My second point about the method of clay preparation and Sarayama's social organization concerns the composition of each potter household. The work-rate of every clay crusher, or set of crushers is determined by the actual flow of water from the stream into the hollowed out scoop at one end of the *karausu*. The more water flows through the Sarayama and Gōshiki streams, the more frequently the crushers rise and fall; the more frequently they seesaw up and down the more clay is prepared.

Households have on average three or four crushers each, and these are lined along the Sarayama and Gōshiki streams in the way that I have just described. During the rainy season in June, these can be seesawing seven or eight times a minute. By early August, however, the crushers will have dropped their work-rate by half, and by the end of the autumn, when there has been little rain for some months, they will pound only once or twice a minute. Thus the clay prepared in late summer or autumn takes longer than that prepared in May and June (although the added sunshine in the later months helps compensate for the lack of river water when it comes to drying the prepared clay). The worst time of all is winter, when the flow of the streams tends to be slow (except following a thaw) and the crushers are so weighted down by icicles that they freeze in their sockets and fail to pivot at all.

There is also a considerable difference in the flow of the two streams, which means that Yamako, for example, whose crushers are powered by the combined flows of the Sarayama and Gōshiki streams, can prepare much more clay than Yamaichi, whose crushers are situated on the Gōshiki stream only. But the important point here is that *no* potter household is able to prepare more clay than can comfortably be used by two men working full time at the wheel. In other words. the nature of the clay and the method used to prepare it have a limiting effect on the composition of each potter household, in that the household head and only one son may work full time at throwing pots. The number of crushers owned by each household has been increased by one or two to meet the increased demand for pottery and enable the potters to turn to full-time production. No more crushers can be introduced, and they are now working at maximum capacity. And because the crushers are unable to prepare more clay, Sarayama households cannot employ either apprentices or throwers to boost production. Thus, the expansion of the community as a whole into a larger pottery-producing complex – of the kind found now in Koishiwara – is very difficult so long as the potters continue to throw with Onta clay and maintain the *karausu* to prepare it for the wheel.

Conclusion

I have here outlined the way in which the nature of the clay used to make Onta pottery has affected the social structure of the community of Sarayama. This point is important, given the way in which *mingei* connoisseurs have admired the clay crushers as an aesthetic phenomenon that makes Onta pottery beautiful.

The main thrust of this chapter has been on the relation between ecology and social structure. One point that has emerged from this discussion is that in neither pottery nor agriculture has the way in which water has been used given rise to a hierarchical form of relationships among households in the community. So far as agriculture is concerned, there has been neither a shortage of water nor an extensive system of irrigation. Irrigation water has generally been taken directly from a number of mountain streams that flow abundantly throughout the year. Every household has had free access to water, and there has been no need to form irrigation unions. Moreover, in pottery, the way in which water has been used to work the clay crushers is such that households can draw water independently of one another. If there is a shortage of water, it affects *every* household's clay crushers, regardless of whether they are located up or downstream. Neither in agriculture nor in pottery has the question of 'privilege' or 'rights' to the use of irrigation water arisen in Sarayama.

Land has also been important to the kind of relationship existing among households. In Sarayama there have never been any landlord-tenant relations. All households have had a small but adequate amount of agricultural land on which to make a living, and it has not been necessary for branch households to depend on their main houses for a supply of capital and land in exchange for labour services. *Honke* and *bunke* have maintained equal rather than hierarchical relations.

The egalitarian nature of such household relationships may also be seen in the manner in which branch households have been formed. In the previous chapter, I pointed out that many of the *bunke* in Sarayama have been retirement houses (*inkyoya*) for elderly household heads. Although, in theory, the main house should keep its capital intact for the most part, in fact the house formed by a retiring head, accompanied by one of his sons, very often received an unusually large share of land and property (Smith 1959:41). Nakane (1967:14–16) suggests that the *inkyo* system prevails where there is, among other things, reasonably equal economic standing among the households of a village.

This point is important to my argument for, although I have shown that land holdings are fairly evenly distributed among households in Sarayama, I have not yet discussed how the production of pottery might lead to some households becoming considerably wealthier than others. So far, I have deliberately omitted market considerations from my argument. The question arises then, are households of a reasonably equal economic standing; and if so, why? The short answer to this is yes, because the potters have shared a cooperatively fired kiln. The cooperative kiln has had an extremely important influence, not only on the economic standing of households, but on forms of labour cooperation among them – the subject of the next chapter.

Chapter Five

LABOUR COOPERATION

We have seen that Onta potters form a close-knit community in which their households are linked by kinship, residential and other formal ties. In this respect, Sarayama would appear to form the kind of communal society of which Yanagi Sōetsu dreamed as he depicted how craft objects could – or should – be beautiful. Let us now examine how these links have been reenforced and new ties created through projects involving labour cooperation. The description here is again idealized, in that it is valid for Sarayama only as it was at the time Bernard Leach visited it in 1954, before the *mingei* boom seriously affected community life. Later I will describe changes in social organization that have occurred as a result of the *Mingei* movement and will contrast the 'model' given here with life in Sarayama 25 years later. Thus I hope to offer a guideline by which community solidarity and the emergence of individuality may be measured.

I noted earlier that one trend in critical thought among those living in advanced industrialized societies has been a nostalgia for 'community'. People frequently hark back to the concept of community when they find their society going through a period of radical social change. In this chapter I will deal with what is generally termed by people living in Sarayama as *mukashi*, 'the past'. In other words, the 'model' presented here is not just my analytical construct: the kinds of social organization described are part of an ideal of the past, as presented by potters and others living in Sarayama. Although there is some evidence that individuals did not always subordinate their interests to those of the community, the ideal of the past denies this and says that the community has always been more important than the individual. In other words, the model *of* the past becomes a model *for* the present. The kinds of social organization described in this chapter form a set of rules according to which people used to behave and should still behave in Sarayama.

We have noted that the Japanese household is a ritual, political, and economic unit that continues through time. The *ie* system may be said to have evolved around the intensive cultivation of wet rice paddy. In a society where modern technology is either unavailable or not taken advantage of, a family or a household finds that its work force cannot cope with certain aspects of production on its own. It is then obliged to cooperate with other families or households. The forms that such cooperation takes in Japanese rural society have been noted by students of the social organization of farming hamlets, and I shall describe the composition of household groups for such activities as transplanting rice and growing mountain crops, since Sarayama households have been partly engaged in agriculture. However, most households have also made pottery, and it is the forms of labour cooperation resulting from this occupation that have not been documented in sociological studies. The combination of these two occupations of farming and pottery has meant that households in Sarayama have been more closely linked through forms of labour cooperation than is usual for rural communities generally.

Pottery Production

Before we consider the way in which households have cooperated in the digging of clay, in the acquisition of glaze materials, and in the firing of their kilns, we should see how pots are made in Sarayama (*Figure 9*).

The single indispensable ingredient of all pottery is, of course, clay. In general, a potter's ball clay should have three characteristics: plasticity for shaping; the ability to retain its shape during firing; and a rock-like hardness after firing at a suitable temperature. Four distinct processes are involved in turning raw clay into a finished pot: firstly, the clay is dug from a clay deposit and prepared into a plastic clay body; next, an object of clay is formed by pinching, modelling, squeezing, coil or ring building, using slabs or moulds, or by 'throwing' on the wheel; then, the finished pot must be completely dried; and lastly, it must be fired.

In Sarayama, raw clay was customarily dug out by the potters with pickaxes, but from the early 1970s a bulldozer has been contracted to do the job. In the space of a few days, the bulldozer can extract enough clay for all the potters to work with for the next three years. Although no precise measurements have ever been taken, potters estimate that they use between two and three tons of clay per household every year.

Once the clay has been dug from the deposit, it must be prepared into a plastic body, a job usually undertaken by women – a potter's wife, mother, or daughter-in-law. First of all, as we saw in the last chapter, because the clay is extremely hard, it has to be pounded by crushers. After the clay has been powdered, it is carried in baskets to mixing and settling tanks, where it is stirred, sieved, and left to settle. Water in the tanks is drained off, and the clay is then ladled out onto straw-matted frames where it is left to dry in the sunshine. After about a week, when the clay is of a soft ice-cream texture, it is scooped from the drying frames and placed in large porous planters or on a clay-drying kiln; there it is left to harden until it can be used on the potter's wheel. On average, the time taken for any one piece of clay to be powdered, sieved, and dried is about a month.

The next step is the forming of pottery. Although there are several means by

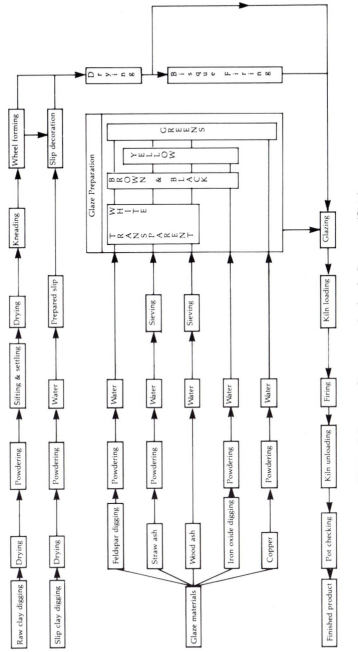

Figure 9 Process of pottery production in Sarayama (Onta)

Plate 21 Kobukuro Yōzō tending clay, 1978

Plate 22 Sakamoto Isae pouring powdered clay into a settling tank, 1979

which an object of clay may be formed, in Onta pots are almost always thrown by men on the wheel. One or two women occasionally model chopstick rests, and the wife in Yamaichi used to make about a hundred slab-moulded radish graters for every kiln firing before her son was old enough to work, but pottery forming is primarily a man's job. A potter will sit at his wheel from about eight o'clock in the morning, and throw pots continuously all day, with only an hour's break at lunch. If he is trying to meet an order deadline and fire his kiln quickly, he may well continue making pots until ten or eleven at night. During an average day's work, an experienced potter will make more than 350 teacups or their equivalent.

Once pots have been formed on the wheel, they are put out to dry – smaller dishes, cups, teapots and so on lined up on two-metre-long boards, large jars, plates and vases on single bats. Drying can take from two days to two weeks, depending on the size of the pot and the season of the year. When they are leather hard, most pots – especially plates, bowls, and smaller tea and *sake* cups – are trimmed and foot-rims formed. It is at this stage of drying, too, that parts are applied and handles and spouts are fixed to the bodies of coffee cups, teapots, pitchers, and other pouring vessels.

Potters also decorate their work with a slip clay and overglazes. Although they now purchase the slip clay from Arita, they used to dig it from a deposit close to Sarayama. When the pots are completely dry and ready to go into the kiln to be fired, they are glazed. All potters use the same ingredients to prepare their glazes: feldspar, iron oxide, copper, wood ash, and rice-straw ash. All of these have to be prepared – by clay crusher, mortar and pestle, or mixing and settling tanks. Women do these jobs and generally try to prepare enough glaze bases to last two firings at a time. As with the preparation of clay, glaze materials have to be sifted a long time before they can be mixed in the quantities required to obtain the desired colours – transparent, brown, greens, black, white, and yellow. It is usually the potters themselves who make the final decision as to how much of each ingredient should be mixed into the recipe. They will then glaze the bigger pots and leave their womenfolk to glaze the smaller ones.

Pots can be fired either before or after glazing, when they are almost completely dry. Until about 1962, glazes were always applied to unfired pots, but from the 1970s smaller items have been fired to a low temperature (about 800°C) for about twelve hours in a small (generally updraught) kiln. This process is known as bisque firing, and it has been adopted in Sarayama because bisquing helps the clay body accept thicker glazes.

Before firing, however, kilns have to be loaded. This is done by the potters while the women are glazing. Kiln loading can take as long as three days, as pots are taken from the workshop to the kiln and carefully stacked in each chamber. Some pots are piled on top of each other, and it is the women who carefully wipe off the glaze at the point of contact between the pots to prevent them from sticking together. All potters fire their pots in climbing kilns, which have from four to eight chambers each and take between 24 and 42 hours to reach a temperature of about 1250°C.[1]

Plate 23 Sakamoto Matsue sifting clay, 1963

Plate 24 Kobukuro Yoshiko sifting clay, 1979

Plate 25 Sakamoto Matsue scooping clay out of the Yamani drying frame, 1963

Plate 26 Sakamoto Satoshi scooping clay out of
the Kaneichi drying frame, 1982

The kilns are almost invariably lit early in the morning (5–6 a.m.), so that potters need spend only one night without sleep. Climbing kilns (*noborigama* in Japanese) are fired at the main mouth for about twelve hours before potters start feeding wood into the single side mouth of each chamber, working upwards. It usually takes about three hours to complete the firing of a chamber and once it has reached the maturing temperature, the next chamber up will already have reached about 850°C and the one above that 450°C from the heat overflow from the first chamber. The firing is generally done by men, but in a household where a potter is working without the help of his son, he will be aided by his wife. Once all chambers have been fired to the desired temperature, the kiln is shut down and not opened for two or more days.

Kilns are fired with wood,[2] which is brought up to Sarayama from lumber yards in and around the town of Hita. The side mouths of the kiln are fired with two-metre strips of cedar. As this wood is too thin to be of practical use in the firing of the main mouth of the kiln, potters have also arranged to have old, demolished houses brought up to the community. Thick beams are sawn up by potters (or by hired labour) into suitable lengths and used in the firing of the main mouth of the climbing kiln.

When pots have been fired, they are left in the kiln for two to three days before being unloaded and sorted. Broken pots or seconds are put on one side, while well-fired pots are placed on trays ready for sale. The potter puts aside special items that have been ordered (on average, between 40 and 60 per cent of a kiln firing). Almost all pots are sold in and around the town of Hita, although orders are filled from places as far afield as Sendai and Sapporo in the north of Japan. Buyers are generally aware of when potters are likely to be firing their kilns, and they ask them, some days before, when they may be allowed to view a kiln's contents. Potters like to have at least one day in which to unload and sort a kiln firing, but buyers tend to come to Sarayama a day early (i.e. on the day on which the kiln is being unloaded) in order to get the pick of the good pots. They wander round the workshop and outbuildings, selecting and putting aside pots that they like. The potter's bill is generally paid in cash, either on the spot (if the merchant is taking the pots with him) or on delivery. One or two dealers pay potters at the time of the following kiln opening.

Once the buyers have left – leaving the workshop looking much like the carcass of a zebra that has been eaten by vultures – potters pack up those pots that are to be sent away – to private individuals or to *mingei* shops in cities like Tokyo and Osaka. They also pack pots to be delivered to Hita shop owners, and take these down in boxes sometime during the day or two following a kiln unloading. The few pots that are left over are placed on shelves outside the workshop and are bought over the next few weeks by tourists visiting the community. Potters expect to sell almost all pots that come out of a firing unscathed.[3]

Plate 27 Putting clay to dry on the roof of a cooperative kiln chamber after firing, 1979

Plate 28 Sakamoto Matsue taking prepared clay to the Yamani workshop, 1963

Plate 29 The eight-chambered *kyōdōgama* cooperative kiln, complete with
new chimney, 1979

The Cooperative Kiln

From this outline of the way in which pottery is produced in Sarayama we can
see that it is virtually impossible for an individual potter to prepare clay and
glazes and make and fire pots by himself. He has to rely on his wife and mother
or daughter-in-law to help with the clay and glaze preparation, and his job is
made considerably easier if he has an able-bodied father or son who can help
him throw pots at the wheel, and load and fire his kiln. A large family greatly
contributes toward efficient production – one reason why the idea of the
household is so important to people living in Sarayama, and to *mingei* potters
living elsewhere in Japan.

Without doubt, the most important form of cooperation found in Sarayama is
potters' use of the cooperative kiln. Not only do many of the alliances between
potter households (described below) derive from their membership of the
cooperative kiln, but the fact that potters have fired their pots together in a kiln
whose chamber space is equally distributed has meant that the economic
standing of each household has remained similar. I am not suggesting that every
household had exactly the same income; nor that one or two households were
unable to control others for a short period because of relatively greater wealth.

However, it has not been possible for those living in Sarayama to rank households categorically according to wealth. I believe that the lack of a household ranking system has made it easier for those living in Sarayama to identify with the community as whole, rather than with selected households of similar status within the community. The cooperative kiln, therefore, has been responsible not only for cooperation among households, but for the egalitarian nature of that cooperation; ultimately, it has given those living in Sarayama a remarkable sense of community solidarity.

There are various kinds of kiln suitable for firing stoneware. Until recently, most potters in Japan have relied upon multi-chamber climbing kilns in which to fire their pots. In some communities, such as Onta, Koishiwara, and Naeshirogawa, where a number of households have lived and worked together, potters have chosen to fire their pots in the same kiln. Such communally-fired kilns are known as cooperative kilns (*kyōdōgama*), and cooperation in Onta extended in the past to all potter households, which shared the labour and expense of building, firing, and repairing the kiln.

There are three methods by which a kiln may be cooperatively fired. Either households will take it in turns to fire the whole kiln (as used to be the case in Koishiwara) or they will combine to fire an allotted number of chambers in the kiln. It is also possible, though unusual, for households to load their pots into the same chamber and share the firing of that chamber.

In Sarayama (Onta), the cooperative kiln has almost always been fired according to the second of the methods cited here. In certain circumstances, however, when potters wished to complete a firing somewhat earlier than their usual schedule allowed for, all households would combine to share kiln chambers, with one household taking the far side and another the near side of a chamber. This method of firing is known as *hazamayaki*, and used to take place just before the ancestral *o-bon* and new year festivities, since potters considered it their duty to fire before these important household events.

The first cooperative kiln is said to have consisted of four chambers. Since 1847, however, the *kyōdōgama* has always been rebuilt with eight chambers (cf. Terakawa 1975:100). These have been shared by as many as ten households.[4] From 1935 to 1948, however, the cooperative kiln was worked by eight households, and from 1949 to 1952, by seven households. These were divided into two groups of four households and of four and three households respectively, their composition being fixed by lot at the beginning of every year. When nine households were firing the cooperative kiln, those participating were divided into groups of four and five. While lots were again drawn to decide who would fire in which group, potters made sure that they rotated fairly evenly between the four- and five-household combinations.

Having fixed household firing groups, potters then had to arrange who would fire which chambers. Since chambers near the top of the kiln tended to be larger than those at the bottom, chamber combinations were fixed according to size, in order to give each household as nearly equal a distribution of kiln space as possible. Further lots were then drawn to decide which household in each group would fire which (combination of) chamber(s). Households would rotate through these combinations, taking different chambers with each successive firing throughout the year (*Figure 10*).

The fact that households sharing the cooperative kiln had to fire together meant that ultimately they were all tied to a similar work pattern – from clay digging and preparation of materials, through wheel throwing to loading and firing of the kiln. At the same time, households were engaged in wet-rice farming, so that those with more active members used to finish their work earlier than those short of labour. Thus households which had two men working at the wheel tended to finish the quota of pots that allotted kiln space allowed them some time in advance of those households in which only one potter was throwing. In such cases, it was customary for the former to give a few days' free labour in the latter's workshop.

Household number	Group	Chamber 1 2 3 4 5 6 7 8	Firing	Date
10	5x2	a b c c b d e a e a b b a c d e d e a a e b c d c d e e d a b c b c d d c e a b	1st, 6th 2nd, (7th) 3rd 4th 5th	1910–1927
9	5x1	see above 5 household gp		1927–1935
	4x1	see below 4 household gp		
8	4x2	a b c d d c a b d a b c c b d a c d a b b a c d b c d a a d b c	1st, 5th 2nd, 6th 3rd, (7th) 4th	1935–1948
7	4x1	see above 4 household gp		1949–1962
	3x1	a b b a c b c a c a a c b a b c b c c b a c a b	1st, 4th, 7th 2nd, 5th 3rd, 6th	
6	3x2	see above 3 household gp		1962–1971
5	3x1	see above 3 household gp		1971
	2x1	a b b a a b a b b a a b b a b a	1st, 3rd, 5th 2nd, 4th, 6th	

Figure 10 Allotment of chambers to households sharing cooperative kiln

Types of Labour Cooperation

Five kinds of labour cooperation may be distinguished in Sarayama: firstly, *moyai*, or cooperative labour, whereby households form cooperating groups to work on a project of common interest; secondly, *temagēshi*, or reciprocal labour, where labour given by one party is returned equally by the recipient and applied to the same task;[5] thirdly, *kō*, or group labour, in which all or selected households of the community combine to work together for a specified time for the benefit of one of their number. Each household takes it in turn to receive this labour given by other households in the association;[6] fourthly, *kasei*, or casual work, in which labour is freely given by one party, with the recipient returning the favour at some later, unspecified time and occasion; and finally, *yatoi*, or hired labour, whereby labour is given in exchange for a cash payment for services.

Moyai

All households in Sarayama used to practise wet-rice agriculture, with each family farming an average holding of between three and four *tan* (1 *tan* =.245 acre). Rice yields were low, being approximately two *koku* (360 litres) per *tan*, but harvests were sufficient to provide a household with enough rice to feed its

Plate 30 Members of Yamamaru and Yamani helping out in transplanting rice, summer 1979

members for a year. Every household also grew its own garden vegetables and various kinds of beans, sweet potatoes, and buckwheat in the mountains. It was for the latter tasks in particular that households used to form cooperative labour groups called *moyai*.

In 1954 (and until about 1965), it was customary for households in Sarayama to grow buckwheat, soy beans, red *azuki* beans, wheat, yams, and sweet potatoes on mountain land that had recently been cleared of trees. Between two and four households often formed *moyai* cooperative labour groups in which each household would provide a stipulated number of workers (generally three); and on an agreed day all households would gather together before going to work in the mountains.

First of all, the area in which trees had been felled would be cleared of roots and remaining pieces of wood. A suitably sized strip of mountainside was then burned. The ash, which served as an excellent fertilizer, was dug into the earth as the soil was prepared for sowing. Buckwheat (*soba*) was always planted first, and this crop was followed by varieties of beans (*azuki* or *daizu*), and finally by sweet potatoes (*imo*). It was possible to use the same strip of land for approximately five years, after which reforestation made cultivation impossible.

The sowing of each crop would take at least a week's work, and later on considerable time and labour were required for the harvesting of crops, when wheat had to be humped back down the mountainside to Sarayama – sometimes a distance of several kilometres. Buckwheat and beans had to be dried up in the mountains before being carried down by the men of the participating households. Women would beat, husk, and sieve the grains and the produce would then be evenly distributed among participating households. Household labour groups were not fixed, and allowed for cooperation along other than household or personal kinship ties. Thus we find that Yamaichi, for example, formed *moyai* with both Yamamaru and Yamamasu, two households with which it was not normally linked by kinship or residential ties.

Although there were some households, such as Yamaichi, that actively participated in mountain cultivation and went so far as to rent an area from outside landowners in such neighbouring communities as Ichigi or Koda, other households, like Yamasai, very often did not bother to cultivate mountain land that had been cleared of timber. There appears to have been one principle often underlying the formation of *moyai* – common ownership of mountain land. Thus Kanemaru, Yamani, Yamako, and Kaneichi formed one cooperative labour group for slash and burn cultivation, not because they were related by kinship ties so much as because they shared ownership of certain areas of land.

Moyai cooperative groups were formed not only for mountain cultivation but in order to obtain the raw materials needed for the production of pottery: clay, slip clay, feldspar, and iron oxide.

First, let us consider the preparation of clay. So far as anyone in the community can remember, there have been two kinds of cooperatives for the digging of the raw clay from deposits in and around Sarayama. The earlier period (prior to 1952) involved households in small cooperating groups which were linked primarily by kinship ties; the later period (1952–1964), which covers the date at which this 'model' of social organization of the community has been set, brought all potter households together into one group. At the same time, we should note here that the switch from several small cooperating groups to a single large one was brought about by *internal*, not *external*, causes. The fundamental principles on which such cooperative grouping of households was based did not alter until external forces, such as communications and technical knowledge, made an alternative means of clay digging possible (to be discussed more fully later).

In the early part of this century, potter households took their clay from various sources around the community. Three areas in particularly were favoured: one was above Irisai's present kiln site, another behind Yamaichi (both on privately-owned land), and the third in community-owned land above Yamako. The first area was owned by Irisai, and clay was dug by this household, together with Yamasai and Kanemaru. The second deposit belonged to Kaneyo, which was then potting, and dug by this household in cooperation with Yamasan and Irisan. The remaining households dug from community-owned land, although on occasion each took clay from its own

Plate 31 Sakamoto Shigeki throwing a large jar, 1979

113

private land. Clay in the privately-owned deposits was considered of superior quality to that in the hamlet-owned deposit.

When Kaneyo stopped potting in 1927, Yamasan and Irisan were forced to get their clay from the community-owned deposit. The Irisai-Yamasai-Kanemaru combination, however, continued to work as a separate group. In the community-owned deposit itself, households tended to work together in groups of twos and threes, since extremely cramped conditions at the work-face of the deposit did not allow more than a few men to dig at any one time.

As noted, some households also dug clay from privately-owned land, and this led to the formation of a single clay-digging group in 1952 by all potting households. The problem started when the road just above where Yamako was taking its clay crumbled away because of undermining, and became impassable. Potters decided that clay should henceforth be dug cooperatively from the point which Yamako had penetrated (which was deemed to be community-owned land!), and the work-face was widened to facilitate working conditions. Three or four times a year, each potter household would send one man and one woman to do the labourious task of clay digging. For four or five days, the men would work with picks and shovels at the clay face, while the women would carry the clay in woven bamboo panniers (*tsuchimego*) down to the path below Yamako where

Plate 32 Sakamoto Shigeki pulling a beer mug handle, as taught by Bernard Leach in 1954

eight even piles of clay were made. A ninth pile was taken directly to Yamako's clay-crusher shed. At the end of each day's work, lots were drawn by the remaining eight households to decide who would get which pile of clay, and the clay was then removed to each household's crusher shed or drying yard.

Other cooperative groups were formed for the acquisition of such other materials as slip, feldspar, and iron oxide. Deposits of slip clay existed in the Kitanamizu area, about a kilometre and a half to the north of the community, up the Gōshiki valley. Until the mid-1950s, potters used to dig from this deposit. Because of the extreme difficulty of access (the deposits are located at the top of a one-in-three incline) and the limited area in which the work was possible, two or three houses would combine to work for a couple of days on the deposit, digging when a common need arose. Two days were needed to clear away fallen topsoil and get down to the pure veins of white slip, after which four or five days were spent digging about one year's supply of slip clay. When the face of the deposit became dangerous to work in (a trench as deep as three metres would sometimes be cut out), all nine pottery households would combine to clear away earth and clay.

Groups also cooperated to get their supplies of feldspar and iron oxide as they needed it. Feldspar, which takes its name (*akadani*, red valley) from the place where it is dug, has always been obtained some fifteen kilometres away from Sarayama. This hillside has probably been used from very early on by potters of both Onta and Koishiwara, but sometime during the Meiji period (1868–1912), the landowner complained, and potters from both communities joined together to purchase the land in which the deposits are located.

Until the mid-1950s there was no form of motorized transport, and potters used to leave Sarayama before sunrise, leading their draft cows across the mountains for two or three hours before reaching Akadani. There they would hack away at the work-face, clearing away loose earth and material of poor quality, before loading their animals with good feldspar and returning home late at night. Potters tended to go together because the long day's trip made companionship desirable. Working conditions were (and still are) poor, for the feldspar seams were not broad enough to permit more than two or three men to work together with pickaxes.

Iron oxide used to be taken from a disused mine in Fukakura some twelve kilometres away. Potters would take their draft cows with them as far as Iwaya, before tethering them and walking over the mountains for another hour and a half. As the path was often difficult to follow, the potters usually took a guide (a woodcutter who knew the mountains well). The mountainside where the mine was located was privately owned, so that the potters used to dig without permission. The iron oxide was chipped with a hammer and chisel from the roof of the disused mine, a long shaft that ran several tens of metres into the mountainside. Only two or three people could work at any one time in the confined space, and this was why only a limited number of households formed any one cooperative group. Potters would take only as much iron oxide as each

115

man could carry on his back down the mountain path to where the draft cows had been left tethered.

Temagēshi

A second type of labour cooperation adopted by households in Sarayama was that of reciprocal labour (*temagēshi*), for such activities as the transplanting, harvesting, and threshing of rice and also for the weeding of paddy fields. Such groups often formed because of – and thereby reenforced – kinship ties (e.g. Yamako-Yamamasu; Kaneichi-Yamani-Yamamaru). But there was another principle that brought households together and that did not involve kinship ties: households reciprocated labour with households whose paddy fields lay close to their own. For example, Yamani, Yamamaru, Yamaichi, Iriichi, and Kaneichi joined together in various agricultural tasks because they farmed fields in the valley immediately above Sarayama, not because they were related by kinship ties (cf. Cornell 1963:113).

Potter households also used to exchange labour to prepare glaze materials, particularly straw ash. Straw ash is usually very rough in texture and must be pounded fine if it is to produce good glaze colouring. The clay crushers are much too heavy for this task, so the ash has usually been pounded by wooden mallets before being trodden down into barrels. The preparation of glaze materials is a woman's job, and in the past households worked in pairs to prepare their straw ash this way (e.g. Yamako-Iriichi).

Kō

Another form of labour cooperation, very similar to the *moyai* described above, was the *kō*, or 'mutual credit association' (Fukutake 1967:106–107). This kind of group existed primarily to facilitate rethatching of house and outbuilding roofs. On March 1 every year, two members from each household in the community assembled to cut thatch grass (*kaya*) from the community-owned mountain behind Yamako. For the following three days, the grass was cut by the men and carried down to Sarayama by the women. One face of the roof of two or three houses was rethatched every year. The decision as to whose turn it was to benefit from the *kaya-kō* each year was made on the basis of need (cf. Johnson 1967:164). However, the *kō* generally rotated in fairly strict order, unless another household's roof was seriously leaking or in otherwise poor condition and would not keep until its turn for repair came round.

Kasei

Another kind of cooperation was *kasei*, or casual work, which was by far the most frequent form of labour exchange. *Kasei* involves assistance without financial reward, and assistance received does not in theory have to be returned. However, in practice, of course, anyone who had been helped out by another household in this way was expected to repay that help at a later date when so requested.

Kasei was the most pervasive form of labour exchange in the community, overriding kinship or residential groups, even though it was those most closely related and living nearby who would be commandeered for such tasks as the construction and repair of buildings, thatching, or simply the lifting of a heavy object. In particular, such informal exchanges of labour took place among potters. The head of Yamasai, for example, recalled that after his grandfather died, leaving him at eighteen years of age as the sole surviving household breadwinner, he was not yet skilled enough to make large pots. So potters in Yamaichi, Irisan and Irisai would come and throw the required shapes and sizes for him in his workshop, while he himself went and made small pots in their workshops in exchange. Similarly, when the head of Yamaichi was taken to the hospital with acute appendicitis, potters from Yamasan, Irisan and Yamasai came to finish off half-completed pots for him. Such labour exchanges were to a large extent based on personal friendships, but when asked who they were helped by in the past, potters unanimously reply that they were helped by *everyone* in the community.

Yatoi

In 1954, so far as I could discover, there were no instances of households hiring labour within the community in exchange for a daily wage. All labour exchange was expected to be repaid in kind and not in cash. Some idea of the pervasiveness of the labour exchange groups hitherto discussed may be gathered from *Figure 11*.

Finally, it should be mentioned that on any day during which one of the forms of labour cooperation occurred, participating households invariably shared an evening meal following the day's work (cf. Dore 1978:105; Embree 1939:137), with the household that benefitted from the labour providing the feast.[7] When potters were firing the cooperative kiln together, they would also share the midday meal (provided by the household whose turn it was to fire the first chamber, *anko*). On occasions when *hazamayaki* took place, with all households sharing kiln space in the bottom chamber,[8] there tended to be fairly prolonged drinking sessions during firing. These often resulted in less inebriated potters firing the next chamber or two on behalf of their slumbering companions.[9] Without doubt, exchanges of food and drink, together with the song and dance that inevitably accompanied such festivities, strengthened community solidarity.

Conclusion

In this chapter I have described various means by which households have exchanged labour in agricultural and pottery tasks. I have suggested that cooperation in farming did not depend on kinship ties so much as on territorial factors; in pottery, households worked together to dig raw and slip clays, feldspar, and iron oxide, not just because they found it difficult to do the work successfully on their own, but because their production schedule was more or less determined by the existence of the cooperative kiln. Potters were given an equal amount of kiln space; they therefore fired more or less the same number of pots every year and consequently used approximately the same amount of clay and glaze materials.

The cooperative kiln served another important function in the community: it helped to regulate the distribution of wealth. If each potting household was allotted an equal amount of kiln space, fired the cooperative kiln the same number of times each year, all potters were likely to sell about the same number of pots. Although income from pottery was barely sufficient to buy those essentials which a household could not otherwise produce, this money was

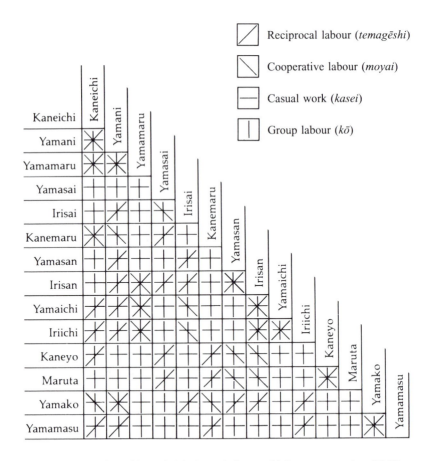

Figure 11 Linking of households through forms of labour cooperation (1960)

118

equally, distributed among all potter households. Non-potting households derived a similar, small cash income from such jobs as stone masonry or *tatami*-mat making.

As I have said, this description of community cooperation has been to some extent idealized – valid for 1954 when Bernard Leach stayed in Sarayama and before the *mingei* 'boom' had begun to affect market demand for Onta pottery. The time has come to see how Sarayama has changed since then. Some of these changes have been noted in passing: the fact that clay is now dug by a bulldozer, for example, or that the cooperative kiln is now shared by only five potter households. Now I want to concentrate on the way in which technological advances and economic improvements have led to the breakdown of community solidarity and to the rise of what might loosely be termed 'individualism'.

While the model presented in this chapter is an ideal of the past, as seen by the potters, it is also an ideal espoused by leaders of the *Mingei* movement. There are two things about the production of pottery in Sarayama that are selected for special praise by scholars and critics. One, mentioned at the beginning of the last chapter, is the fact that potters rely on natural methods of preparing clay and of making and firing pots; the other is that – like the potters of Tachikui described by Daniel Rhodes in the 1960s (Rhodes 1970:130) – they work together as a group.

Plate 33 Sakamoto Haruzō throwing pitchers, 1963

119

It will be remembered that Yanagi Sōetsu emphasized that if folk crafts were to be really beautiful, they had to be made in a spirit of cooperation and the craftsman had to surrender his self to nature. Onta potters share a cooperative kiln; they are known to help one other with all kinds of work; *therefore*, in connoisseurs' opinion, their pots are beautiful. Hamada Shōji, for example, commented on what he saw as the marvellous quality of Onta's pots at one of the annual autumn exhibitions at the Folk Craft Museum: 'the thing that is particularly striking about the way Onta potters work is the fact that the more skillful potters always help out those who are not so advanced. This makes me really happy . . . As a result, everyone's work gets better and better, and it is hard to know which pots to pick out for special praise' (in *Mingei* 276:13).

Critics realize that cooperation among potters stems primarily from the fact that they are close to nature. 'The hamlet's solidarity is really unflinching, and its heart-felt desire to preserve its tradition is stronger than any other pottery kiln's. One might almost say that this attitude has been decreed by the providence of nature' (Tanaka 1969:44). As we have seen, nature, cooperation and tradition are three crucial ingredients that make up *mingei* beauty (Yanagi 1955a:220–221). The fact that Onta pottery is made with natural materials in a traditional manner is what makes it beautiful (Noma 1955:6) – an appreciative mode that can lead to such remarkable statements as: 'whatever pottery you go to, you will find

Plate 34 Sakamoto Haruzō working with his son, Masami, 1978

120

beautiful and ugly pots mixed up together, but not in Onta. Surprisingly, every pot has good glaze colourings and there isn't a single ugly pot to be found. I suppose it must be because tradition has not been destroyed' (Yanagi 1947:253).

The traditional way of life is seen to derive entirely from nature. At the same time, as we have seen, nature affects a man's character and thereby the quality of his pots. Leach is quoted as saying of Onta: 'it is the purity of the link between man and nature that these potters have not lost. This purity gives them a warmth that is reflected in the beauty of their pots' (Noma 1965:16).

So, leaders of the *Mingei* movement have praised Sarayama because they see the potters living in a kind of ecological equilibrium, in harmony with nature and with themselves. It is this combination of spontaneity and lack of artistic intentionality which – as with westerners' appreciation of primitive art (Price 1989:89) – makes their pottery so beautiful. Yet this is where a paradox arises: because Onta pottery is seen to be beautiful and truly *mingei*, many people suddenly wanted to buy it. It was this growth in market demand that was then responsible for changes in the potters' social organization. Potters found that

Plate 35 Yanase Mitsusaburō throwing a tea bowl, 1979

121

they could sell whatever they made. The less time they spent preparing their materials, the more pots they could throw; the more they threw, the greater their income. Farming ceased to be economically viable, and cooperation broke down; considerations of status based on wealth and talent developed; community solidarity was effectively undermined. At the same time, however, precisely because potters adopted technological innovations and stopped working together, precisely because they began to make a lot of money and their individual talent came to be recognized, *mingei* leaders started to claim that the quality of Onta's pottery (and, indeed, of the pottery of other folk craft kilns throughout Japan) was rapidly deteriorating. I shall now deal with this paradox.

Chapter Six

ENVIRONMENTAL AND SOCIAL CHANGE

In the hitherto idealized description of the social structure and organization of the community of Sarayama, my argument has been, firstly, that community expansion has been limited by the way in which potter households have had to prepare clay for their wheels; secondly, that individuals worked in a multigeneration household group because environmental factors did not permit them to farm land or produce pottery on their own; and thirdly, that each household combined with other households because of these environmental factors and because it fired its pots in a cooperative kiln. In outlining the way in which households were linked by various forms of labour cooperation, I presented a 'model' of hamlet organization as it existed at the time of Bernard Leach's stay there in 1954.

This model of Sarayama's social organization is in fact the way that the community's residents now view what they call the 'good old days'. The model emphasizes that there were no permanent divisions within Sarayama's social organization. All fourteen households formed a closed community, tightly knit by kinship relations and various kinds of communal activities. While residents retained primary loyalty to their household group, they simultaneously acted as members of the community and in many cases subordinated household interests to those of the community.

There is, of course, no way of showing that the people's model reflects the true state of affairs in Sarayama more than 40 years ago now. To a certain extent it is idealized – like so many anthropological models of Japanese society generally. However, I believe that the people's model is by and large a fair reflection of community life, and that Sarayama residents did, as they say, form a community and put group before individual interests.

In fact, the ideal of loyalty to the community is still upheld, and Onta potters are quick to point out to visitors of all kinds that they do everything together and everyone is the same. Clay is dug together, they say; glaze compositions and materials are the same from one household to the next; prices are fixed; tax payments were, until 1975 (just before I conducted my fieldwork in Sarayama), paid by the potters' cooperative as a whole rather than by individual households therein; even the pottery is uniform, hardly differing in shape, colour, or design from one workshop to another. 'All together' is the motto with which the community faces the outside world. But do potters still do everything together? Is everyone the same? Nowadays, the community's social philosophy is, I think, only an ideal which is not practised, mainly because of changes brought about by improvements in communications, technology, and the market.

Fundamentally, of course, it is the general improvement in Japan's economy and the large demand for folk crafts in particular that have led to the breakdown of Sarayama's sense of community solidarity. But market demand as such is difficult to describe. Its impact can be guessed, perhaps, from the way in which local tourism more than doubled during a ten-year period between the mid-1960s and 70s and has continued to increase since then, and I shall discuss the financial implications of the – mainly tourist – demand for Onta pottery, in the following chapter. Here we will look at some of the more obvious ways in which market demand has affected potters' lives. How do the decline of social cooperation and the economic independence of each potting household affect folk craft leaders' appraisal of Onta pottery? How do potters adapt to such change, in the institutional framework of the community? Can the community as such survive the pressures put on it by the outside world?

Plate 36 Yamani's four-chambered private kiln, 1963

Technological Innovations

This discussion of social change begins with an account of the way in which labour cooperation has broken down in Sarayama. In the preceding chapter, I enumerated five types of such cooperation. Of these five, two have disappeared entirely, and one is now practised by non-potting households only. One other form of cooperation, which was formerly not found in the community, is now quite widespread. Superficially, the breakdown of cooperation among households may be said to have resulted from technological innovations and from an improvement in communications between Sarayama and the outside world. Both of these have affected the way in which the community hitherto adapted to its natural environment. They may in this sense, therefore, be seen as 'ecological' changes.

I will start, and finish, with the cooperative kiln. The cooperative kiln in Onta consisted of eight chambers. Each of these had a sloping sandy floor on which pots were placed to be fired. They could not stacked very high, and most of the available space in a chamber was wasted. In the 1950s, the technique of manufacturing strong, heat resistant kiln shelving was developed in the ceramic complexes Arita and Seto. In 1957–1958, in an attempt to increase the number of pots they could fire at any one time, potters in the neighbouring pottery village of

Plate 37 Sakamoto Masami as a teenage boy loading
the Yamani kiln with its new shelves, 1963

Koishiwara decided to buy shelves for their kilns. The innovation proved successful. The half-brother of the present head of Iriichi was at that time working in Koishiwara, and he soon told his father about what was going on. The following year, Iriichi fitted its allotted chambers in the cooperative kiln with shelves.

The use of shelving meant two things: first, the whole, and not just one third, of a chamber could be stacked with pots, without fear of their falling over; second, it allowed the firing of a large quantity of small pots, which in Onta had not hitherto been made. The economic advantages of Iriichi's decision to buy shelves were not lost on the other potters. The two firing their own kilns and then all the other households sharing the cooperative kiln agreed to put shelving into their rebuilt or newly built kilns. By 1962 all potters in Sarayama had switched from the old, sand-sloped chambers to chambers fitted with shelves.

The adoption of kiln shelving had an important effect on the community's social organization in that it induced potters to spend their time on pottery rather than on agriculture. Admittedly, they were already devoting more time than before to wheel work, because there was considerable demand for smaller pots and they were being asked to fill orders by stipulated dates. However, so long as they kept using the old-style sand-sloped kilns, there was a limit to the number of pots that could be made and fired at any one time. It did not make economic sense to fill each chamber with small pots only and increase the number of firings, because the old methods of kiln loading gave a very low yield for small items. The problem was solved by kiln shelving, which permitted smaller pots to be fired in very large quantities. At the same time, it meant that potters had to spend five or six times longer working at the wheel if they were to meet orders and continue to fire their kilns at the same rate as before.

The adoption of kiln shelving affected the distribution of labour within any one pottery household, in that from the early 1960s, both father and son began to devote their time fully to wheel work rather than farming. Women were left to prepare clay and glazes and attend to the rice paddies and vegetable patches; men came to their aid only during the really busy seasons of transplanting, harvesting, and so on.[1]

This is not to say that all pottery labour was devoted to wheel work. A lot of time was spent in the gathering and preparation of materials for clays, glazes, and firing. As I shall show, the content of pottery labour itself was about to change considerably. But another decision about how much time to give to what task had an even greater effect on social organization. In the 1960s, the Japanese government adopted a rice-curtailment policy (*gentan seisaku*). Because people in Sarayama were not growing rice for cash and because potters found that, thanks to the introduction of kiln shelving, they could satisfy a continually increasing market demand, they decided to give up wet-rice agriculture.[2] Those households that were short of manpower, Yamasai and Irisai, were the first to stop in 1966–1967. They were soon followed by all other potting households except for Yamaichi, whose head clung to the *mingei*-inspired philosophy of farming and pottery production combined (*hannō-hantō*) until the autumn of 1978.

Once potter households gave up farming, the kind of labour exchange known as *temagēshi* came to an end. Maruta also stopped farming in order to run a noodle shop and to retail Onta pottery, so the only households to continue exchanging their labour were Yamamaru, Yamaichi, Kaneyo, and Yamamasu. With Yamaichi's decision to stop growing rice from 1979, *temagēshi* was continued by only three of Sarayama's fourteen households.

In 1971, five potters purchased electric ball mills in order to help prepare some of their glaze materials. This decision brought an end to the informal labour exchange groups which used to be formed to pound straw ash. Those households which do not possess these ball mills either prepare the materials on their own or hire labour (*yatoi*) for help. They never ask to borrow the use of a ball mill.

Improvement in Communications

The social organization of households in Sarayama has also changed as a result of better communications. Since 1954, existing country roads have been widened and metalled, and methods of transportation have greatly improved. By the late 1950s, potters were able to go to places like Akadani and Koishiwara by car or three-wheeled vehicle. Instead of walking across the mountains with their cows, they drove and loaded up their cars with feldspar from the Akadani deposit. They acquired their supplies of white slip clay from Koishiwara, since it was simpler to drive the 40 kilometres there and back than to struggle for several days on end climbing the steep slope to the Kitanamizu deposit and humping the heavy clay back down to the hamlet. Potters also claimed that there was not enough slip clay in Kitanamizu to justify further digging there.[3]

Once it had become easier to travel by car, potters stopped going on foot to get their iron oxide from the mine shaft at Fukakura. Fukakura was still inaccessible by road, but new deposits were discovered in Sujiu, which could be reached by car, and so potters started going there from the mid-1960s. Whereas, in the old days, several potter households had always banded together to go and get their supplies of feldspar, slip clay, and iron oxide, they now tend to go singly.

Improved road conditions between Sarayama and Hita in particular, together with a rapidly expanding local lumber industry, led to three other important changes in labour cooperation. These concerned the preparation of fuel for firing the kilns, the practice of *yamasaku* slash-and-burn mountain cultivation, and the rethatching of house roofs in the community.

Preparing enough wood to fire a kiln involved a lot of work, as we have seen. Potter households used to spend at least a week collecting wood from the mountains and then splitting and drying it before each firing. After the Pacific War, local government authorities tried to alleviate unemployment by creating job opportunities in forestry. Government land was reforested, and cedar plantations were greatly increased throughout Oita Prefecture. Cedar was a fairly fast-growing tree, whose wood could be put to a variety of uses, from craftwork to house building. By the late 1950s, interest in cedar plantations had spread to the private sector of the lumber market. There was a big increase in planting between 1958 and 1962, and landowners round Sarayama tried to make the most of the potential economic value of their land by replacing deciduous trees with cedar.

Local government policy seriously affected household labour patterns,[4] since cedar was replacing the hardwoods which the potters had hitherto used for their kilns. Because the mountains around the community were being reforested with cedar, all the undergrowth died out. It was not just the wild undergrowth that was affected, but households' cultivated crops of beans and potatoes, which they had been growing on cleared strips of land. The cedar grew too fast to make it worthwhile for any household to go to the trouble of preparing land for its *yamasaku* vegetables, and so the old custom of *moyai* cooperative labour came to an end. I am not suggesting that the potters were sad about this: after all, it was mostly their own land on which they themselves had planted the cedar. By the early 1960s, considerations of the economic advantages to be gained from cedar-forested land and from fuller production of pottery (itself increasing each household's cash flow) far outweighed any possible nostalgia for a sense of 'togetherness' resulting from a lot of toil for little concrete gain.

But the potters' decision to plant their land with cedar in the first place was made easier by the fact that they had found a new means of procuring fuel for their kilns. The road up to Sarayama had been improved soon after Leach's visit to the community in 1954, so that heavy vehicles were able to come up the valley. Consequently, potters had only to order their wood from the lumber yards down in the Ono valley or in Hita, and great truckloads would be brought up to Sarayama. One phone call saved the potters a week's hard work cutting felled trees to suitable lengths for their kilns. The cost of having the wood brought up from the valley was more than covered by the additional time potters could thereby spend at the wheel. They were also able to invest in the planting of cedar on their mountain land.

At about the same time, two or three potting households replaced their thatched roofs with prestigious tiles. This meant that not only were they reluctant to participate in the roof thatching association (*kaya-kō*), but they also began to suggest that the community-owned land on which the thatch grass grew be converted to cedar plantations. In the mid-1960s, potters found that the *mingei* boom was making it financially possible for them to rebuild their homes. As more and more new tiled houses were put up, fewer and fewer people were prepared to participate in the *kaya-kō*. Moreover, once potters stopped farming, they no longer required their draft cows; fodder became unnecessary, so community-owned land was finally replanted with cedar at the beginning of the 1970s. The handful of residents who had not yet tiled their houses were thereby deprived of a last source of thatch, and the *kaya-kō* came to an end.[5]

Improved communications led to one more change which affected the way in which potter households once worked together. In 1963 the go-ahead was given for a completely new road to be built between Sarayama and the neighbouring

128

hamlet of Koda, in Tsurugimachi. This made access to Ōtsuru and Fukuoka much easier, and also saved the potters a roundabout trip down the Ōtsuru valley via the hamlet of Onta, which was the only way they had previously been able to travel westward (see *Map 2*). When the Sarayama-Koda road was first opened up, deposits of raw clay were discovered along the mountainside to the southwest of the hamlet near where Irisai, Yamasai, and Kanemaru had once dug their clay. It seemed much more sensible to the potters to take their clay from these new deposits, rather than continue working in the extremely cramped conditions of the community-owned clay pit behind Yamako. Since the newly found clay was right by the roadside, access was easy. So in 1964, potters arranged with two of their number, who owned the land on which the clay had been found (Yamako and Irisai), to allow them to dig there. A sum of ¥10,000 per annum was agreed upon, to be paid by each potter household in exchange for the right to take clay from the new deposits.

For the first few years after the road had been opened up, households continued to cooperate in the way that was described earlier in the model of social organization. Each household provided two of its members, one male and one female, when they were needed; a three-wheeled vehicle took the clay from the deposits to each household's drying yard or crusher shed. In due course, however, the potters began to look for new, less time-consuming methods of getting the clay out of the deposits. First, they tried to dynamite the clay from the mountainside, but this was not successful, and they gave it up after a couple of years. Then, in 1972, they found that a bulldozer could be brought up to Sarayama by heavy truck, and they hired one to shovel out the clay. One day's bulldozing supplied all the potters with enough clay to last them the next three years! It cost them ¥50,000 to hire, but it saved them the effort of two or three weeks' annual work together in the clay pits.

All of this means that not only have various forms of labour cooperation come to an end, but the amount of time devoted to the acquisition and preparation of pottery materials has been drastically reduced (*Table 2*). The time saved is now spent working at the wheel.

Market Demand

Leach came to Sarayama in 1954; the *mingei* boom started three or four years later. Many of the changes in social cooperation in Sarayama came about as a result of potters' readaptation to the environment, in response to technological innovations and an improvement in communications, as outlined above. But it was the demand for folk craft pottery that was the underlying force behind these changes. Potters adopted kiln shelving and purchased ball mills; they hired a bulldozer to dig their clay; they bought their slip and telephoned orders for wood for their kilns. All of these changes suggest that potters thought it worthwhile to alter their methods of production. It was no longer necessary to continue farming, because there was market demand for their pottery.

129

Table 2 Annual number of labour days devoted to the acquisition and preparation of pottery materials by one household (Yamaichi) in 1960 and 1977

Activity	1960			1977		
	F	M	Total	F	M	Total
Clay digging	18	18	36	0	1	1
Slip digging	10	7	17	0	0	0
Wood cutting and drying	45	40	85	30	0	30
Feldspar digging	0	2	2	1	1	2
Iron-oxide digging	0	2	2	1	1	2
Straw-ash preparation	4	0	4	4	0	4
Wood-ash preparation	5	0	5	5	0	5
Totals	82	69	151	41	3	44

Two things happened as a result of the demand for *mingei* pottery. First, potters became comparatively wealthy. Within the space of a few years, they found that they had more money than they needed for their everyday living costs. For the first time, perhaps, they were able to make use of the principle of investment: that a little money, wisely used now, could in due course generate more wealth. So they used their extra money to pay for the kiln shelves, for example, that increased the number of pots that could be fired, and hence the total income yielded by each firing. At the same time, they learned that cash could be converted into other forms of wealth – into new land, for example, into the saplings that would eventually grow into giant cedar trees, into stocks and shares, even into bars of gold.

Second, potters began to rely on the use of money to conduct their everyday affairs. In the old days, labour was the community's – and land, the household's – wealth. People had to work together, and they had to own agricultural land (or be able to work it) if they were to survive. Land provided people with rice and vegetables on which they could subsist; it gave them wood with which to build their homes, grass with which to thatch their roofs; it gave the potters clay for their pots, materials for their glazes, and fuel for their kilns. If potters sold their wares, they would use the money to buy things they could not produce on their land – a piece of fish, or cloth, or even salt. But they rarely had enough money to buy more than this. Household land, and the people who helped work the land, were more important to a man than money.

However, once potters started earning much more as a result of the *mingei* boom, they began to place more emphasis on the use of money than on working the land together. In other words, the use of cash gave rise to impersonal relations. By deciding to buy the wood for their kilns, potters were able to give more time to work at the wheel and get more money for their pots. But by using the extra cash to plant their land with cedar, potters stopped working together to

Plate 38 Sakamoto Matsue putting spouts on soya sauce containers, 1963

cultivate mountain crops. After all, more than a supply of vegetables could be bought with the results of the time that had been saved and spent making pots instead. Thus the acquisition of money as an end in itself became more important than working on the land; people ceased to matter so much.

It is hardly surprising to find that by the mid-1960s some potters had decided to stop farming. It made economic sense to use one's energies in the workshop rather than in the rice fields. It was cheaper to buy rice than to grow it – the government's requisition policy had seen to that. And since people were being paid not to plant rice in their fields, *moyai* labour cooperation came to an end and *temagēshi* labour exchange was confined to Sarayama's three farming households. This left only two forms of labour cooperation available to households, *kasei* and *yatoi*. People still give labour to their neighbours or relatives when it comes to building a new house; but building is a rare occasion, and *kasei* is now limited to minor tasks. The main method by which labour is recruited is by hiring people to help. One or two potters now employ women from Ikenzuru or non-potting households in Sarayama to help sift and settle clay, stack wood, or load and unload kilns; men are hired to saw up wood and to build or repair kilns and clay crushers, and so on. The free exchange of labour, so frequently and wistfully referred to by people talking of the past, has now almost come to an end.

Another way in which market demand affected cooperation among potter households was in the running of the cooperative kiln. In 1954 the kiln was shared by seven households, while Irisai and Yamako fired independently. By 1978 – and continuing until the present day – only five households remained members of the cooperative kiln; five others fired their own private kilns.[6]

The cooperative kiln has always been of great importance to Sarayama community life. This may be seen clearly in the somewhat mysterious circumstances surrounding the building of the first independent kiln by Irisai. The story goes that there was a doctor living in nearby Ōtsuru who was very fond of pottery, in particular of the pots made by the present head's grandfather, Hamakichi. The doctor apparently gave Hamakichi a sum of money with which to build 'an experimental kiln' and fire pots glazed with a certain type of reduced red glaze (*shinsha*) that he especially liked. It is said that the experimental kiln was originally intended for the whole community; certainly, all the potters helped to build it. But once they had completed it, Hamakichi claimed the kiln as his own. He was immediately ostracized by his co-potters, and there was a rift between the old man and his adopted son, the present head's father, with the latter eventually choosing to leave the hamlet (and his only son) entirely. Although, eventually, Hamakichi was permitted to participate once more in community life, the kiln has remained in the possession of the Irisai household to this day.

Once one potter had separated from the cooperative kiln, it became easier for others to do so. In 1948, Yamako, a household situated at the bottom of the hamlet,

Plate 39 *Hakeme* slip brushing

asked permission to build its own kiln; the cooperative kiln was too far, its head said, and it was impractical to carry pots 200 metres up the road from Yamako's workshop to the kiln and then back again after every firing. Permission was granted then and again twelve years later when Yamani used the same pretext to build itself a private kiln in 1962. Certainly, Yamani's workshop was some distance from the cooperative kiln (though nearer one, than two, hundred metres as claimed), but it was clear that its head hoped to – and in fact did – benefit from the increased demand for Onta pots by being able to fire as often as his work-rate permitted. With his own private kiln, he was no longer held back by potters who did not have sufficient manpower to keep up with his fast schedule.

It is significant, therefore, that when Kaneichi decided to take up potting again after a 60 year interval, its head did not apply to be taken into the cooperative kiln (which he had the right to fire), but built his own private kiln at the top of the community. Finally, in 1971, for completely different reasons, Yamaichi left the cooperative kiln. Its head was working on his own and found that he was neither prepared nor able to keep up with other households in his firing group. There were other things to do in life than just make pots. As a result, the cooperative kiln is now shared by just five households.

All in all there is now very little formal cooperation among households in Sarayama (*Figure 12*). Only Kaneyo, Yamamaru, and Yamamasu combine for reciprocal labour in agriculture; none of the potter households practises *temagēshi* in either pottery or farming. The custom of *moyai* cooperative labour has disappeared entirely, as has the *kō*, group labour or 'mutual credit association'. The only way in which households in the community cooperate, regardless of occupation, is informally in the exchange of *kasei* casual work (cf. *Figure 11*).

Yet there is a paradox in the way market demand has affected patterns of cooperation among households in the community as a whole, for potters have been made more aware of themselves as a group. Although the number of potters sharing the cooperative kiln has decreased, and although the potters do not exchange labour as frequently as they used to, the potters' cooperative (*dōgyō kumiai*) as a whole has begun to play an important part in their lives. This is precisely because of market demand and the renown of Onta pottery throughout Japan. The cooperative is frequently approached by local government officials concerning promotional exhibitions of pottery (linked with tourism in Oita Prefecture and Hita City); *mingei* leaders contact the cooperative whenever they want something from Onta; the media do the same when they want to make a television film or a radio programme or write a magazine or newspaper article about the pottery community. Potters therefore find themselves called together to discuss what are essentially administrative matters. For the most part they find these matters extremely irksome. There is no doubt, however, that the attention given the potters serves to unite them as a group. Community solidarity may have been weakened, but not necessarily the occupational solidarity of the potters, a point to which I shall return.

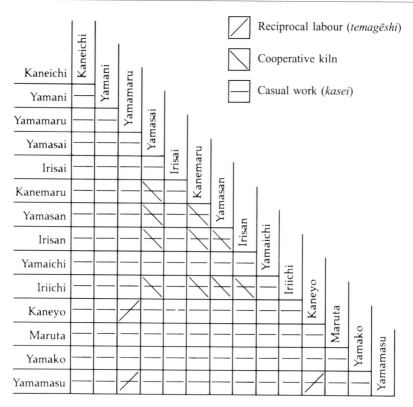

Figure 12 Linking of households through forms of labour cooperation (1979)

Conclusion

In this chapter, I have discussed environmental and social changes in Sarayama since the late 1950s, particularly the way in which various forms of labour cooperation were affected by improvements in technology and communications and by an increase in market demand. I have suggested that the adoption of kiln shelving directly influenced the potters' decision to stop wet-rice agriculture, and indirectly led to the breakdown of the cooperative kiln. Improved transportation facilities between the community and the outside world brought an end to households working together to get their raw materials; they also induced potters to buy wood for their kilns, instead of preparing it for themselves. Potters and other local landowners replanted mountain land with cedar rather than deciduous trees because of a burgeoning lumber industry in Hita. Because of the new plantations, thatching became difficult and mountain cultivation impossible. Thus the *kō* and *moyai* forms of labour cooperation also came to an end.

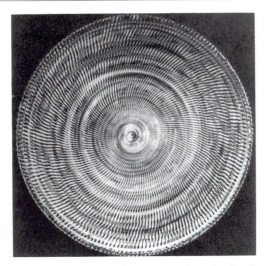

Plate 40 *Tobiganna* chattering, or 'jumping iron'
decoration, on 12" diameter plate

Such changes radically altered not only the way in which each household allocated its labour, but also how it viewed its priorities in production. As Embree (1939:306) has pointed out elsewhere, an increase in cash income has led to reliance on hired help, rather than on neighbours' cooperation, so that nowadays almost all households in Sarayama contract rather than exchange labour. There is consequently very little cooperation among households in their day-to-day living. Even informal labour exchanges have been affected. For instance, when the head of Irisai broke a bone in his wrist playing softball in 1978, nobody offered to help him out by making pots or by finishing off ones that had already been made but not turned or decorated. Instead, a small gift of money was made. Cash has become the medium by which people express their feelings for others.

I have tried to show that environmental, technological, and social variables are systematically interconnected. Thomas Smith (1959:101) has written of a previous era: 'innovations rarely if ever came simply; they hung together in clusters by a kind of inner logic; one innovation brought others in its train, and often could not be adopted independently of them'. Social changes were not *determined* by environmental changes; causality should be seen not as unilinear but rather as circular, or *reciprocal* (Friedman 1974:44; Netting 1965:95).

But the environmental changes described in this chapter are not purely 'social', for potters are involved in an aesthetic movement. Japanese folk art connoisseurs have a very clear perception of what the craftsman's relations with his environment ought to be, and any discrepancy between this 'cognized' model and the actual 'operational' model (Rappaport 1971:247) leads to severe criticism. In general, folk art beauty has been seen to disappear with the onslaught of western civilization. Almost all *mingei* pottery kilns – including, especially, that of nearby Koishiwara – have been 'ruined' by material changes that upset people's relation to 'nature': for example, the substitution of charcoal for wood in the firing of kilns, the forming of pots in plaster moulds instead of on the wheel, and the inclusion of chemical substances instead of natural materials in glaze compositions (Mizuo 1966:83).

It is not surprising, therefore, to find that, because of the social changes that occurred in Sarayama, Onta pottery was to some extent criticized by leaders of the *Mingei* movement. Tanaka Toyotarō, until 1978 director of the Folk Craft Association, has written:

> Recently people have begun to be more receptive to conventional beauty in form, colour and decoration. Whether it is because of the sudden changes that have occurred or not, I don't know, but it seems to me that the quality of the work of potters in Onta has deteriorated, as it has done in other potteries.
>
> (Tanaka 1961:8)

This remark was echoed a few years later by the potter, Hamada Shōji (1965:9): 'it is a shame how their work is gradually deteriorating', he said, before going on

Plate 41 *Kushime* slip combing

136

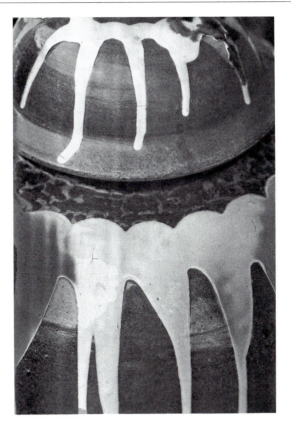

Plate 42 *Nagashi* slip trailing

to comment on a warning given by Yanagi (1961:5) on the dangers to Onta presented by local government authorities. It is they who, for a short period, prevailed upon the potters to make use of a mechanical waterwheel to step up the process of clay preparation. As a result, the quality of their pots deteriorated significantly, and it was a triumph for 'nature' – and for the beauty of folk crafts – when the potters went back to the old rhythm of life thudded out by the *karausu* clay crushers (Tonomura 1965:10). In fact, the potters rejected the waterwheel, not because of their desire to adhere to *mingei* ideals so much as because the wheel was technically inefficient and kept on breaking down.

Although potters may have discarded this innovation fairly quickly, they have not done the same with kiln shelving. Tanaka Yōko of the Folk Craft Museum pointed out (1965:24), for example, that the change in kiln-chamber loading methods had brought about poorer results with Onta slipware; she also suggested that the change in wood ash, which had come to be bought from local lumber yards, may be affecting the glazes.

Potters would probably agree in part with both these criticisms. Kiln shelving does affect the way in which flames reach the pots during firing; the new wood-ash is not as good as the old, mainly because the lumberyard people tend to burn polythene bags and plastic containers along with the wood. As noted in the previous chapter, potters are also aware of the fact that the slip clay that they now get from Arita is inferior to that which they used to dig from Kitanamizu.

They might well object, however, to the (totally extra-aesthetic) criticism that their work has deteriorated because they stopped farming. 'Onta potters were originally half potters and half farmers; if they give up farming, it will mean that they will forget the very essence of folk craft' (Miyake Chūichi, in *Nihon no Mingei* 190:7). They also have had to contend with the argument that because a bus had started plying between Hita and Sarayama, their pots were getting worse (Hamada 1965:9; Bernard Leach in conversation). In general, tourism has been seen to make the potters produce such poor work; visitors look for cheap pots; folk craft dealers only buy things that are superficially beautiful (Tanaka 1969:47). Onta pots have been seen to be 'polluted' (Mizuo 1968:110).

Arguments such as these clearly support Janet Wolff's argument (1983:81) that 'aesthetic transactions are . . . always affected by and integrated into extra-aesthetic experience and information'. In other words, the way in which *mingei* leaders apprehend folk crafts in the first place is – in spite of all 'direct perception' claims to the contrary – determined by their, and potters', everyday extra-aesthetic experiences.

This point is important because it contributes to Arnold Hauser's argument (1982:137) that a work of art always shows an ambivalence stemming from its maker's divided loyalties: between, on the one hand, the client, patron, or buyer commissioning the work, and, on the other, the artist's own class consciousness

Plate 43 *Uchikake* splashed slip decoration

and corresponding ideology. Every artist, therefore, owes allegiance to at least *two* communities. In the case of Onta potters, these communities are *social* (the community of Sarayama itself) and *aesthetic* (the folk art world in which their pots are distributed, sold, appreciated and discussed). The problem for potters is how best to balance their interests against the expectations of members of each of these communities – a problem which becomes even more acute when aesthetics collides head-on with money.

Chapter Seven

THE *MINGEI* BOOM AND ECONOMIC DEVELOPMENT

What is called the *mingei* 'boom' started in the late 1950s and continued into the early 70s. During this period, there was a sustained demand for handmade crafts of all kinds, but particularly of pottery. This demand was primarily urban; those who bought the vast majority of *mingei* objects were women. Their enthusiasm for bamboo baskets, iron kettles, woven textiles, lacquered trays and virtually every shape, size, colour and design imaginable of pottery, was kindled and fanned by the media which drew attention to *mingei* as part of an overall Japanese 'tradition' – a tradition, it was asserted, that was rapidly being lost in the face of modernization and so-called 'westernization'. This enthusiasm was satisfied in the cities themselves by department stores and other retail outlets which not only made *mingei* available to would-be buyers, but also put on major exhibitions of 'ceramic art' by such potters as Kawai Kanjirō, Tomimoto Kenkichi and Hamada Shōji – all of whom had been designated the holders of 'important intangible cultural properties' (*jūyō mukei bunkazai*) and popularly known as 'national treasures' – as well as by the English potter, Bernard Leach (Moeran 1987).

However, as has been hinted earlier, the *mingei* boom was not confined to urban areas. *Aficionados'* enthusiasm for handicrafts was also satisfied by a developing domestic tourist industry which – as with the National Railways' *Discover Japan* advertising campaign in 1970 (Ivy 1988) – encouraged (sub)urban Japanese to go off into remote parts of Japan to find traditional aspects of their culture for themselves before they were forever lost, and which, as a result, led many to make 'pilgrimages' to such out-of-the-way potteries as Tamba, Fujina, Koishiwara and Onta. It was from the twin-pronged demand through urban retail outlets and tourism that Sarayama's potters benefitted financially during the *mingei* boom; it was this same demand that allowed them to make radical changes to their former lifestyles.

In his discussion of a Japanese fishing village in the Seto Inland Sea, Edward Norbeck (1954:207) has attributed social structural change to the rise of a money economy. Once people start using cash for transactions, he says, cooperation breaks down and 'individualism' emerges. I have described a similar situation for Sarayama: the richer potters have become as a result of demand for their work, the less interested they appear to be in cooperating with others in the community. Ultimately, I shall be concerned with whether the ideal of individualism exists in Sarayama.

At the same time, increased wealth, the breakdown of community life and what is seen as emergent individualism have also been criticised by *mingei* connoisseurs and, to a lesser extent, retailers, media and general public. Because most of those living in Sarayama have been making pottery which is appreciated and marketed in the context of the *Mingei* movement, social changes resulting from the introduction of new technology, an improvement in communications generally, and increased market demand, tend to be appraised in aesthetic terms by those concerned with Onta pottery. Before exploring further this ambivalent relationship between social and aesthetic ideals, however, we need to look at the way in which Onta pottery is retailed and, by tracing the economic development of a pottery household, find out just how wealthy potters have been made by the *mingei* boom. This will then enable us to examine the way in which the trade in art works plays an ambivalent role (Hauser 1982:506) by changing their significance from an emphasis on *use* value (beauty in *mingei* pots is born of their function) to one on *commodity exchange* value (beauty is measured by how much pots cost); it will also enable us to see more clearly the various paradoxes that affect the lives of Japan's folk art potters.

Retailing

Like *mingei* generally, Onta pottery is retailed all over Japan, from Hokkaido in the north to Kyushu in the south. Some pots are ordered by post or by telephone, and are sent directly to the person or shop concerned; others pass through one or more distributors before reaching the retail market. By far the greatest number of pots is bought direct from Sarayama by dealers who visit each potter's workshop after a kiln firing. One of these dealers comes from as far away as Kamakura, near Tokyo; the majority of them have shops in and around the town of Hita, less than twenty kilometres away.

By the end of the *mingei* boom, at least fifteen buyers from Hita were regularly purchasing pottery worth between ¥700,000 and ¥8 million (averaging just over ¥2 million) from Sarayama potters every year. Two of them were distributors who forwarded pots to shops whose owners could not make the trip to Sarayama or who did not have the personal introduction necessary to start business with a potter. The other buyers from Hita used to sell varying quantities of Onta pottery, which could be found in the tourist centres of Yufuin, Beppu, and Oita, as well as in the northern Kyushu industrial complex of Tobata, Yahata, and Kokura.

Onta pottery still sells particularly well to the many people visiting Kyushu on holiday from all parts of Japan, and especially from the Kansai and Kantō regions. The number of tourists to Oita prefecture and the town of Hita doubled between 1967 and 1975, and has continued to rise since then. As a result of

141

tourist demand for souvenirs during this period, many of the buyers from Hita started dealing in Onta pottery. It is because *ontayaki* is considered by many tourists to be a medium of gift exchange, rather than simply a folk craft in the purist sense of the term, that several problems concerning 'individualism' among potters arise. This is a point to which I shall return in the following two chapters.

Income and Expenditure of a Potting Household

The *mingei* 'boom' lasted about fifteen years altogether and, although as such it may be said to be over, folk arts and crafts still sell well. Pottery in particular has been in great demand, and potters in Onta have been able to dispose of all firsts coming out of each kiln firing. In 1980, more than 90 per cent – nowadays, about 70 per cent – of these pots were sold immediately to buyers in the trade; the rest were bought by visiting tourists. Having made the long trip up to Sarayama, and not wanting to go away empty-handed, many of the latter bought misshapen and blistered seconds, although not as often or as indiscriminately, apparently, as they used to at the height of the boom.

The vital question is this: what did the boom mean to Onta potters in terms of hard cash? The answer is not simple, and has required some calculated guessing for money is not an easy topic to discuss with anyone, unless you happen to know him or her very well. In Sarayama the subject was made more difficult by the fact that potters had been under-reporting annual incomes in their tax returns by as much as 300 per cent. When I somewhat innocently began enquiring about kiln capacities and how many pots could be stacked into each firing, therefore, I received evasive answers or what I later realized were outrageously under-estimated figures. Fortunately, by the second year of my fieldwork in the community, potters had come to realize that I was neither a British spy nor an agent of the tax office. Nevertheless, questions about income and costs, capital expenditure, investments, and so on tended to be met with silence or embarrassed laughter. Fortunately, Yamaichi let me have full access to its household accounts for 1976–1978, and Kaneyo let me have its account books for 1967 and 1975. I was then favoured with the kind of luck that every anthropologist dreams of. One member of Yamaichi was clearing out her room one day and came across a diary written by her father-in-law in 1962. In this diary was written down every single item of expenditure and income for that year. These sources have enabled me to gauge the effect of the *mingei* boom on potter households in Sarayama.

In 1962 Yamaichi's total annual income came to ¥716,348,[1] and expenditure to ¥713,003. Of this income, only ¥457,344, or 63.9 per cent of the total, came from sales of pottery; the rest came from sales of land and timber, from pensions, gifts, and so on. During the course of the year Yamaichi fired its allotted chambers in the cooperative kiln six times; its average income from pottery was therefore only about ¥76,000 per firing. In May of that year the

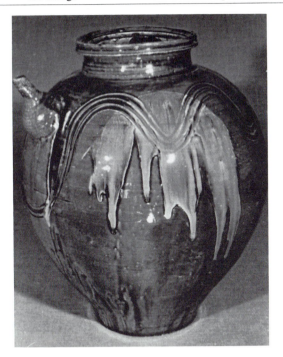

Plate 44 Large honey brown spouted vessel *(unsuke)*
with combing and green splashed overglaze

cooperative kiln was rebuilt, and shelves were put into each chamber. Yamaichi
fired twice before and four times after the kiln's rebuilding, but the deferment of
payments by buyers makes it difficult to judge exactly the differences in incomes
from the old and new methods of loading the kiln chambers. Also the present
head of Yamaichi admits that he was unable to fill his chambers completely after
the adoption of shelving, since his father made very few pots. Thus the following
figures do not support a potter's estimate quoted earlier, that kiln capacity was
increased five or six times by the introduction of shelving. In 1962 Yamaichi's
first two firings averaged ¥68,070 (pottery income from January to May
inclusive); the last four came to ¥80,301. This gives an 18 per cent increase in
income per firing.

Expenditure for the same year gives a fairly accurate picture of the way in
which pottery gave each household a source of cash income. The year 1962 was
exceptional in that capital outlay on the rebuilding of the cooperative kiln and the
purchase of shelving was extremely high (¥36,000 and ¥16,020 respectively),
coming to 43.55 per cent of total pottery expenditure for that year. Moreover, in
November, a new clay-crusher shed had to be built at a cost of ¥21,150. All these
items were to last the Yamaichi household at least ten years. The average annual

Plate 45 Rice bowl with *tobiganna* chattering

pottery expenditure for 1960–1965, therefore, was probably about ¥50,000. The cooperative kiln would also have been fired more than six times from 1963, since rebuilding interfered with the potters' schedules in 1962. More than ¥15,000 had to be spent on rice paddy repairs as well, so that Yamaichi decided to sell a lot of cedar in July to pay for the extra expenditure incurred. In a more normal year, one would have expected the household to make a modest profit of about ¥50,000, assuming that land did not yield any income apart from that gained from farming.

Income and expenditure figures belie, in my opinion, the importance of farming to potters. According to a census made in 1960, official agricultural income for all households in Sarayama was estimated at under ¥100,000 per annum. The cash return on Yamaichi's farming activities for 1962 was only ¥15,009. This sum does not show, however, the amount of money the household was saved in the purchase of foodstuffs through the consumption of home-produced rice, beans, various kinds of potatoes, and other vegetables.

By 1976 both income and expenditure had increased by seven or eight times. Yamaichi's income came to ¥5,356,518, of which more than 85 per cent derived from pottery sales. Land sales and loans feature in the accounts, mainly made to meet recreational expenses incurred in the construction of a hamlet softball ground above the community, and in the purchase of a new car. Pottery expenditure in 1976 was again unusually high because of the rebuilding of the clay-crusher shed once more and of the purchase of a new set of kiln shelves. The 1977 accounts give a somewhat more balanced picture of annual pottery expenditure. Income in 1977 came to less than that for the previous year, but the head of Yamaichi admitted to underestimation for the purpose of tax returns. The figure for pottery sales alone (from six firings in 1977, as opposed to five in

144

Plate 46 *Tokkuri sake* bottle with slip trailing

1976) should have come to ¥5,500,000, putting total income at about ¥6.5 million. He also had deposit accounts in the Agricultural Cooperative and a local bank, amounting to ¥12 million.[2]

By 1976–1977, Yamaichi had no cash income from farming, although some vegetables and rice were grown for domestic consumption. In neither case, however, were crops sufficient to feed the household for more than six months of the year.

With such high income over the previous few years, the head of Yamaichi (like almost all other potters in Sarayama) had been able to rebuild his home and workshop, pay for the construction of his household's private kiln, and later have it fitted with a chimney. Washing machines, television sets, and cars had been bought (each item three times over the years) since Leach's stay in the community. The bathroom had been renovated, and water had been taken from underground springs by pump rather than from mountain streams as of old. Expenditure of this sort may be considered to be fairly typical of potting households, for where Yamaichi laid out capital on a new kiln, other potters

Plate 47 Old style Onta pitcher with green glaze

preferred to purchase trucks, build drying kilns and woodsheds (often necessitating bulldozing away mountain land), and have their water bored from deep underground.

Although figures are not available for a non-potting household for exactly the same years (1962 and 1976–1978), household accounts for Kaneyo in 1968 and 1975 give some indication of the difference in income levels between the poorest of the potting and non-potting households in Sarayama. Kaneyo's total income in the above specified years (including withdrawals from savings) was ¥519,931 and ¥2,256,368; expenditure amounted to ¥776,836 and ¥3,216,857 respectively. Kaneyo's 1968 income did not even come up to Yamaichi's 1962 income, and by 1975 there was a difference of more than ¥2 million when Kaneyo's income is compared with Yamaichi's sales from pottery alone.

It can be seen, therefore, that a considerable difference in income levels emerged between potting and non-potting households in Sarayama. However, it must also be pointed out that potters' incomes varied immensely. Yamaichi has a four-chamber kiln, which – in the mid- to late-70s – it fired five times one year and six times the next, each firing yielding on average ¥900,000–¥1,000,000.

The capacity of its kiln, however, was – and still is – only 10.35 cubic metres, the second smallest in the community (*Table 3*). Because Yamaichi's head was often in a hurry to complete an order on time, he tended not to make as much use of available kiln space as did other potters, who very often still take the greatest advantage possible of piling pots in and on one another.

By anthropological sleuthing and by careful measurement of kiln-chamber capacities, I was able to estimate each potting household's income (*Table 4*). At the time of my fieldwork, potters with private kilns, and with sons working with them at the wheel (Yamani and Yamako), fired between seven and nine times a year. Those working on their own (Yamaichi, Irisai, and Kaneichi) fired five or six times a year. The cooperative kiln, it will be remembered, is split into two and three household groups. On average, the former fired six and the latter eight times a year. Those potters with sons working with them (Yamasan, Kanemaru, and Iriichi [father]) tended to concentrate on a greater number of smaller pots, since to some extent they had to bide their time waiting for single potters (Yamasai and Irisan) to complete their schedules. The former's incomes were probably, therefore, slightly higher than the latter's, but this difference has been ignored in my calculations.[3]

These figures would appear to be fairly accurate. In the late 70s, the total amount of traced sales of Onta pottery came to ¥74,300,000 per annum. If we subtract the wholesaler's mark-up to three retail outlets, the figure for ex-kiln sales came to ¥63,750,000. If allowances are made for Yamani's sales out of Hita, one kiln per potter household being sold at the Mintōsai pottery festival every October, and general retail sales amounting to about seven per cent of total kiln contents, the final figure is not too far from the estimated annual income given here.[4]

During the late 1960s and 70s, all potters spent a lot of money rebuilding their homes, kilns, outhouses, and so on, in much the same way as Yamaichi did. However, the latter's expenditure of just under four and a half million yen is modest in comparison with the sums spent by other potters in Sarayama, which

Table 3 Capacity (in cubic metres) of the cooperative and private kilns in Sarayama

Chamber no	1	2	3	4	5	6	7	8	Total
Cooperative Kiln	1.79	2.37	2.54	3.10	3.32	3.63	3.53	3.31	23.59
Private kilns									
Kaneichi	2.26	2.20	2.25	2.59					9.30
Yamani	2.75	2.89	3.33	3.43	1.50				13.90
Irisai	2.67	3.04	3.59	3.38					12.68
Yamaichi	2.07	2.80	3.05	2.43					10.35
Yamako	1.97	2.23	2.89	3.41	3.22	1.29			15.01

Table 4 Estimated annual income (in yen) of all potting households for the calendar year 1977

Household	Total kiln yield	Household share	Firings p.a.	Total annual income
Yamani	2,000,000		8	16,000,000
Yamako	2,250,000		7	15,750,000
Yamasai	2,800,000	1,400,000	6	8,400,000
Iriichi	2,800,000	1,400,000	6	8,400,000
Irisai	1,600,000		5	8,000,000
Yamasan	2,800,000	1,050,000	8	7,700,000*
Kanemaru	2,800,000	1,050,000	8	7,350,000*
Irisan	2,800,000	700,000	8	7,350,000*
Yamaichi	900,000		6	5,400,000
Kaneichi	800,000		5	4,000,000
Total annual income for all potting households				88,350,000

* In 1977, in the first three-household firing of the cooperative kiln, Yamasan fired chambers 1, 4, 8, Kanemaru 2, 3, 6, and Irisan 5 and 7. I have estimated the total annual income for these households on the basis of this order of rotation, whereby Irisan and Kanemaru thrice and Yamasan twice fired the two-chamber combination.

frequently amounted to two or three times that figure. Many of them also invested their accumulated profits in land holdings, and all but two potters increased their holdings of mountain land during the *mingei* boom (the two exceptions, Yamaichi and Kaneichi, having had to lay out capital on the building of independent kilns at the beginning of the 70s). At least three potters owned more than 50,000 square metres of forested mountain land at the time of my stay in the community.

Not all potters, however, invested in land. Some preferred to buy gold or purchase shares in a local silk factory, for example, or in a national automobile manufacturing corporation. That the potters had money to spare during this period can be seen in the way each household spent ¥850,000 in 1975 on the levelling of mountain land and its preparation into a softball ground for the hamlet of Sarayama (including Ikenzuru).[5]

The prosperity of the community in general may be gauged perhaps from the hamlet accounts. These showed that, on average, each Sarayama household spent, each year, six or seven times more than families living in the village of Shinohata, studied by Ronald Dore (1978:208). More remarkable, perhaps, were the annual accounts for the potters' cooperative. Here, annual expenditure for the ten potting households amounted to ¥1,406,220 in 1977. Entertainment alone amounted to approximately one-third of this figure.

Plate 48 Yamani drying yard, 1963

Conclusion

In this brief chapter I have given details of the way in which potters' incomes increased as a result of the *mingei* boom. I concentrated in particular on the economic development of one potting household, Yamaichi, and showed how the demand for pottery had enabled its head to pay for extensive renovations of his house and workshop, build a brand new kiln, and buy cars and other expensive items.

However impressive such expenditure may seem, it pales in comparison to what went on in nearby Koishiwara during the same period. It will be recalled that, in that community of Sarayama, there were nine potter households using water-powered clay crushers and two cooperative kilns, enabling a similar – though by no means identical – form of cooperative life to exist there as has been described for the potters of Onta. However, for a number of reasons that would take too long to describe here, pottery households in Sarayama Koishiwara decided to buy a clay pounding machine which, in the space of four hours, could complete work that, by means of a combination of the *karausu*, hand sieving and natural drying methods, had taken three weeks. Access to so much more clay enabled households to employ up to six apprentices working full-time at the wheel, and to build their own private wood-fired, multi-chamber climbing (*noborigama*), and gas-fired single-chamber updraught (*tangama*), kilns. The income generated from this considerable increase in each pottery household's output then permitted kiln operators to purchase land nearby the community bordering the main road that runs between the heavily-populated area of Kita Kyūshū and such tourist resorts as Hita, Hakutsuru and, further away, Yufuin, Beppu and Mount Aso in the centre of the island. There they set up large retail outlets which enabled potters to further increase their profits by cutting out the middlemen whom they had previously relied upon to handle their wares, as they sold directly to tourist buses and other traffic. The profits generated from such expansion were then used to rebuild homes and workshops on a much grander scale; to establish display areas, exhibition galleries and at least one museum; to purchase new equipment, cars, trucks, and vast amounts of land; to reinvest profits in *mingei* shops and restaurants of various kinds for tourists; and to set up younger sons – even the occasional apprentice – with their own homes, kilns and workshops. As a result, one Koishiwara potter was able to proclaim proudly that his annual income was more than that of all ten pottery households in Onta put together – a claim which backfired a few years later when the local tax authorities fined him for gross underpayment of taxes!

If we return now to Onta itself, we should note that Yamaichi's income was by no means the highest among Sarayama's potting households. Because of the potters' decision to specialize in the production of pottery, considerable variation

Plate 49 Iriichi concreted drying yard, 1979

150

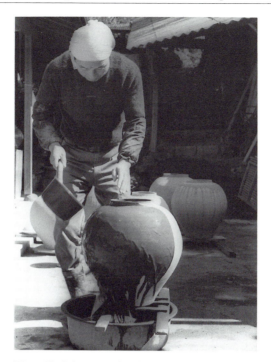

Plate 50 Sakamoto Shigeki glazing large jar, 1981

in incomes occurred. On the one hand, potters earned far more than non-potting households; on the other hand, increases among potters themselves differed greatly, firstly, depending on whether they had their own private kiln or not; and secondly, depending on whether they had an able-bodied father or son to help them throw pots at the wheel.

This kind of economic differentiation within the community only really started with the decision to stop farming and to go into pottery full-time. But, as with their decision to take advantage of technological advances and improved communications, potters' increased incomes from the *mingei* boom also led to further criticism of Onta pottery as those involved began to show their disdain for the success of Japan's overall economic development. Indeed, *mingei* connoisseurs' attitudes to consumerism in general may be summarized in the following passage from Mizuo Hiroshi's series of articles on handicrafts, where people and things are seen to exist for one another:

Someone who uses crafts also 'brings them up'. Although everyday articles are destined to be used in our lives and eventually to become too old or worn-out for use, handicrafts should not be seen simply as consumer items. People have to put their hearts into using things, to look after them

151

and to make sure that they do not get damaged in any way; they have to give things as long a life as possible. Obviously, one cannot deny that there is some economic reasoning behind this idea, but in the old days there was a seriousness about the way people used handicrafts that could not be neatly categorized as 'economic'. People did not treat things as material objects so much as things with life that needed their love. So were people at one with the objects they used.

(Mizuo 1974:6)

This extract shows quite clearly that critics do not blame craftsmen entirely for any perceived deterioration in their work. Yanagi himself distinguished between what he calls the 'first' and 'after' lives of a craft, between its production and its final use (Yanagi 1932), and present leaders of the *Mingei* movement have continued to emphasize that it is the methods of marketing – in particular of wholesaling – that adversely affect the quality of craftwork. After all, goes the argument, how can potters have a chance to look at their work and see how bad many of their pots are when dealers come up to Sarayama and take them all away while they are still hot from firing (Tanaka Takashi 1969:45)?

Ultimately, however, all fault lies with the potters, for it is they who allow the dealers to take away their pots, they who are ready to sell anything and everything. People in all walks of life frequently intimated to me during

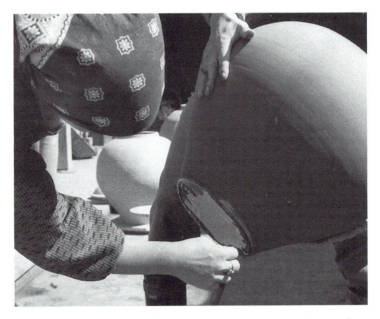

Plate 51 Shigeki's wife, Fumiko, cleaning glaze off the bottom of a large jar, 1981

Plate 52 Shigeki glazing a large plate, 1978

fieldwork that the richer potters became, the more their work deteriorated. Potters were seen to put profit before quality in their hierarchy of values, and this could only lead to 'pollution' in their work (Mizuo 1971:61; cf. Yanagi 1955a:130).[6]

> That demand for pottery should increase and the kiln as a whole flourish is excellent. That people should appreciate Onta pots and flock to buy them is not in itself particularly bad. However, once there is too much demand and commercialism gets the upper hand, the quality of the pottery produced has to be affected for the worse. This is precisely the evil afflicting Onta.
>
> (Mizuo 1972:106)

Folk art critics are not the only ones to suggest that artistic standards have declined as a result of the rise of industrial capitalism. We have already mentioned William Morris's hatred for 'commercialism and profit-mongering' and the opinion, pervasive among people like him in England at that time, that money and beauty did not make good bedfellows. Similarly, we find – at one extreme – an Indian philosopher arguing that good crafts cannot be created by industry where the love of work no longer exists (Coomaraswamy 1943:26), and – at another – a Mexican Marxist suggesting that the 'subjection of artistic creation to the laws of material production cannot help but have grave repercussions on art' (Vasquez 1973:179). Indeed, there would appear to be a pervasive idea among art critics and anthropologists all over the world that art is above such base considerations as money (Read 1936:2; Duvignaud 1972:37; Haselberger 1961:351). As Levin Schucking (1974:65) has observed, the currently acceptable view is that if something is liked by the public, it cannot be good. This leads to the function of criticism's consisting 'more in the correct interpretation of artistic creations . . . than in the formation of appropriate value judgments on their aesthetic quality' (Hauser 1982:471). Hence we find the use of words like '*pseudo*-traditional arts' and 'ethno*kitsch*' (Graburn 1976:6–7) to refer to those objects which, for one reason or another, are put on sale and purchased in mass consumer markets all over the world.

One problem here is that the (folk) art market is not a closed system, but a sub-system of a larger commercial system in which objects of all kinds are communicated. As a result, at least two 'aesthetics' have emerged in relation to art objects – one 'artistic', the other 'commercial' – with the former contained in the latter, even though the two are ideally separate (Thompson 1979:121–2). This separation of art from commodity is upheld by a notion of 'aura' (Benjamin 1969; Maquet 1979:12–13). Critics – and dealers (Becker 1982:110) – get hopelessly confused by these aesthetic and commercial values, so that in the end the market price of a work of 'art' comes to be seen as a reflection of its 'spiritual' value (Berger 1972:21). Once art works become saleable, once folk arts become *too* saleable, they lose their aura (Hauser 1982:516).

Thus with the appreciation of Onta pottery and folk arts generally, where the conflict between the various different values that are brought to bear on an art work becomes transparent. One such value is closely connected with aesthetics and may be called *appreciative value*; it is this which lies at the heart of the *mingei* philosophy put forward by Yanagi Sōetsu. Another stems from recognition of a financial value that derives from the fact that an art work is bought and sold on the market for a particular price: this may be termed *commodity exchange value*. These two values do not necessarily coincide, as the manager of Aboriginal Arts and Crafts Limited discovered in 1977 when attempting to sell Aboriginal art in New York. 'Authentic' art, he learned from the Australian Trade Commissioner in that city, was deemed to consist of only those works which were made for use and not for sale (Morphy 1995:215–6). In other words, as we have seen for *mingei* in Yanagi's concept of function, *use value* also comes into play in the determination of an art work's (aesthetic) quality.

At the same time, these values give rise to a fourth value, that of *symbolic exchange*, which enables people on the basis of appreciation (as well as *technical* and *social values* that I shall discuss later) to pay a certain amount of money for a particular art work. None of these values is ever fixed, though all of those involved in an art world may try to make them seem as stable as possible, in order to support their own independent positions in that art world. It is the *negotiation* of these values which is one of the fundamental tasks of members of any art world.

It is this kind of negotiation which has led, over the years, to Onta pottery being seen to be losing its qualities of 'craftsmanship' and 'healthy pricing' with the increase in demand for folk crafts, and to be moving away from the essential characteristics of *mingei*, which, critics claim, no longer exists in its original 'beauty' and 'honesty'. Those craftsmen who survive have to make the choice between two evils: whether to become individual artists or merely to turn out souvenir items (Mizuo 1966:84–85).

Which choice have the potters in Sarayama made? Have they decided to ignore Yanagi's ideals entirely and turn out kitsch? Or have they opted to be artist-craftsmen, and if so, what has happened to the ideal of community solidarity? What sort of pressures from outside are forcing potters to adopt one option rather than the other, and how do these pressures ultimately affect the potters' vision of Sarayama as a community? I shall try to answer these questions in the following chapters.

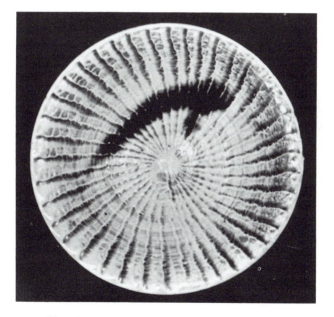

Plate 53 White slipped plate with *hakeme* brush
and brown *uchikake* overglaze decoration

155

Chapter Eight

THE DECLINE OF COMMUNITY SOLIDARITY

We have seen so far that economic development, along with improvements in technology and communication, has been largely responsible for the breakdown of social cooperation in Sarayama. I have inferred that the ideal of the 'community' is no longer as important as it once was, and that there has been a gradual decrease of what may be termed 'community solidarity'. People in Sarayama may say that they do everything together, but in practice they do not. At the same time, those who act as spokesmen for the *Mingei* movement tend to see such social changes in aesthetic terms. Because *potters* do not behave in the way that they once did, their *pottery* cannot be as good as it once was.

In this chapter, I want to take up the issue of community solidarity by describing the kind of arguments that used to break out among people living in Sarayama during my fieldwork there. My aim here is to show that dissension occurred in the community along two main axes in particular: firstly, between potting and non-potting households (i.e. between occupational groups); and secondly, between older and younger men, thereby upsetting the age-grade seniority system. Such dissension was caused, firstly, by an unequal accumulation of wealth as a result of the *mingei* boom; and secondly, by the external appraisal of Onta pottery. Within the context of Sarayama itself, the first served to differentiate one *household* from its neighbour; the second, one *individual* from his fellow.

Economic Differentiation Among Potting Households

Earlier, I argued that, ideally, economic equality among potter households in Sarayama derived from their use of the cooperative kiln. I have now shown that in practice potters have recently become comparatively wealthy and that there is a considerable difference in income levels between potting and non-potting households. At the same time, I suggested that there was also quite a wide range of income levels among the potters themselves. There are several reasons for this variation in wealth: the main one is the sudden, sustained increase in demand for folk craft pottery; others include the potters' decision to specialize

156

full time in pottery production, and the composition of each potter's household labour force at the beginning of the *mingei* boom.

Nevertheless, there would not have been such a difference in income levels among the potters if they had continued to fire the cooperative kiln all together. It is because five potters separated from the cooperative kiln and now fire independently that the increase in market demand and the decision to specialize in pottery full time took on such importance for community organization.

In 1962, during the early stages of the *mingei* boom, there was still not much difference in income levels among those firing the cooperative kiln and those firing independently. The head of Yamaichi reckoned that Yamani, which had just built its own private kiln – and to which he was himself apprenticed from 1952 to 1954 – averaged only ¥20,000 more per firing than his own household's ¥60,000–¥80,000.

So long as potters did not specialize in pottery, income levels among households in the community remained fairly standard. What really upset the financial equilibrium was their decision to give up agriculture. Potters were able to earn far more than those not potting – especially those potters who had sons working with them – for they were able to make and sell more than those working on their own or with ageing fathers. Yamani and Yamako were the first to step up production in the mid-1960s; Kanemaru and Yamasan followed them a few years later.[1] Other potters sharing the cooperative kiln and working on their own found themselves being asked to fire the moment one household had completed its quota of pots. Whereas, in the past, the schedule of the cooperative kiln had been geared to the pace of the slowest working household, it now proceeded at that of the fastest.

Once the operation of the cooperative kiln changed in this way, Yamaichi decided to separate and build its own private kiln in 1971; he could not maintain the speed with which the other potters worked. This left five households firing the cooperative kiln together. As I showed in the preceding chapter, the incomes of these five households (Yamasai, Yamasan, Kanemaru, Irisan, and Iriichi) have been fairly evenly balanced. There is, however, a wide variety of income levels among those firing independently. The cooperative kiln once effectively limited and standardized all potters' incomes and gave rise to financial equality in the community. Now that half the potters have built their own kilns and fire independently, they have widely varying incomes. Market demand for folk crafts also gives all potters incomes far exceeding those of non-potting households.

The breakdown of the cooperative kiln affected community solidarity in a less obvious manner, too. In the past, many households shared certain tasks precisely because they were working to the same schedule; now that they are firing independently, there is no need for them to continue such cooperation. A potter nowadays can start firing his kiln without the knowledge of other people in Sarayama; this would have been unthinkable back in the late 50s. The cooperative kiln was not just the potters' but the community's kiln. Every working man or woman in the hamlet would make some contribution toward a

Plate 54 Old slipped water jar with green *nagashi* trailing

firing, by preparing wood or by carrying pots back and forth as the kiln was loaded or unloaded. This is no longer the case.

The economic differentiation among potting households was aided in minor ways by potters' methods of wholesaling and filling in tax returns. Until the early 1960s, ex-kiln prices were fixed for the most part by the buyers who purchased from Sarayama potters. The *mingei* boom, however, created a demand that could not be satisfied by existing methods of production. Instead of buyers paying potters one-third the retail price of each pot, potters found themselves in the position of being able to ask for higher prices as they saw fit. Yamani, Yamako, and Yamasan took advantage of this new-found freedom and began charging much more than others in the community. Eventually, in 1970, when they realized the amount of money that these three households were making, Irisai and Yamaichi suggested that all potters fix a standard ex-kiln price for each type and size of pot. This proposal was met with approval by the majority of potters, and prices were fixed accordingly. Since then, therefore, Irisai and Yamaichi have been to some extent successful in checking the extremes of economic differentiation that occurred among potter households in the mid- to late-60s.[2]

As for taxation, until 1975 the potters' cooperative as a whole, rather than the individual households therein, was taxed each year. It was argued – mainly by Yamani, whose head was then leader of the potters' cooperative – that potters were not making much money, that they helped one another out with unfinished work, and that this *kasei* could not be reckoned in financial terms. This argument was accepted by the Hita tax authorities, who would proceed to bargain with the potters over the sum to be paid by the cooperative that particular year. The tax office in Fukuoka, however, insisted that there had to be economic differences between households, so that the Hita tax authorities told the potters to work out slightly differing income levels within the total revenue assigned the cooperative, before sending in their household tax returns.

In theory this was fine. Once potters got together, however, they found that it was impossible to fix income levels to everyone's satisfaction. This led to considerable resentment and friction among the heads of potting households. The major problem was that Yamani and Yamako were earning by far the most and yet wanted to report incomes that were the same as those firing the cooperative kiln. It was pointed out that their incomes were in fact very much higher, but the head of Yamani took advantage of authority conferred by his position as leader of the potters' cooperative to ensure each year that one of the households firing the cooperative kiln reported the same annual income as his own fabricated figure. He fixed a kind of rotation system among households so that each potter would come out at the top of the income bracket every five or six years. However, even then, it is said, he and one or two other older potters under-reported the income they had been assigned.[3] As a result, Yamaichi and Irisai once more insisted that they were going to keep proper household acounts so that they could present individual tax returns from 1975. Once two households refused to participate in the system, every other household was obliged to send in its own tax returns. Until the tax office decides to investigate these returns, however, there is little likelihood that the perceived offenders will be more honest about their incomes. Economic differentiation among potter households continues at that much greater a pace.

Potting and Non-Potting Households

Economic differentiation led to a greater concern with household than with community affairs. An indication of this is the frequency with which arguments used to break out between households. Yamasai, for example, laid plastic pipes to its clay crushers after a water channel caved in under the road through Sarayama and the prefectural authorities refused to let the household unblock it. In order to get the water to flow through the newly laid plastic pipes, Yamasai had to raise the level of the dam above its crushers by about fifteen centimetres. The head of Yamani, whose clay crushers lay immediately upstream of the dam, immediately objected that the higher water level had stopped his crushers from working properly. Potters quickly pointed out that this was not so at all, and public opinion ruled in favour of Yamasai.

Yamasai was also involved in another petty quarrel of this sort. There is a tiny patch of land in front of Irisai, which belongs to Yamasai, the main household.

159

The head of Irisai had long wanted to buy the land from his nephew in order to extend his drying yard. Even though the latter knew this, he decided to build a woodshed on part of the land, thereby denying his uncle the extra space he required and, incidentally, spoiling the view from the front window of Irisai's house.

Other arguments affected not just two, but all potting households. The head of Yamako, for example, incurred the wrath of all when he arranged for several extra truckloads of clay to be taken down from the clay deposit to his workshop one day, without bothering to ask the permission of any of his fellow potters. He thereby broke the rule that clay should always be shared equally.

One of the more violent rows among potting households that I experienced during fieldwork occurred over access to clay deposits situated in private land. It will be remembered that when the road between Sarayama and Koda was opened up, new deposits of raw clay were discovered and potters decided to dig from these rather than from the less accessible clay pits in the community-owned land behind Yamako. At first, they dug from land above the road, owned by Yamako and Irisan, but gradually moved away from Yamako's land into Irisan's. After the bulldozer had finished digging out another three years' supply of clay in 1975, the Koda road was asphalted by the city authorities. According to local government regulations, however, bulldozers are not allowed to operate directly from a metalled road, so that in 1978 it was necessary for some of Irisan's or Yamasan's land along the roadside to be cleared away, if potters were to go on supplying themselves with clay from this area.

A few months before the bulldozer was to be hired, however, the two heads of Irisan and Yamasan quarrelled over the use of a strip of land on the other side of the road. The branch house (Irisan) claimed that the main house was drying wood on its land and asked Yamasan to remove the wood – only to be met by refusal. Irisan's head then retaliated by saying that he would not let his main house have any clay from the deposit that he owned. This meant that all potters would have to get their clay from elsewhere.

After several arguments and considerable behind-the-scenes negotiating, Yamasai was persuaded to let potters take clay from *its* land adjoining Irisan's. However, to gain access to these clay pits, the bulldozer had to cross a small strip of land along the roadside, owned by Yamasan. Of course, the potters said, the head of Yamasan knew that his land would have been needed for the bulldozer to work from – even if Irisan had not refused to let potters have any more clay from its household land. And yet Yamasan went to the expense of clearing away a flat space and building a woodshed just where the bulldozer would have to manoeuvre. The simplest thing, perhaps, would have been for the potters' cooperative to have bought Yamasan's strip of land, but people were annoyed at the thought of having to pay out half a million yen extra to cover the cost of a woodshed that need never have been built in the first place. As it was, potters rented the land and pulled down the woodshed to make room for the bulldozer to pass into Yamasai's clay deposits. In a week or two the trees on the latter's land were cleared, and the topsoil was removed and deposited, for a sum, on a piece of Yamani's land.

When the bulldozer had finished, Yamasan began talking about rebuilding its woodshed. The potters objected. Were they going to have to pull down a woodshed every time they wanted to dig out clay? Yamasan's head was adamant; he needed a shed for his cardboard boxes. In the end, potters were forced to rent land nearby from a resident of Koda, so that the head of Yamasan could build his shed elsewhere. Costs for digging clay that year come to almost three-quarters of a million yen.

Much of the bickering that used to go on during my period of fieldwork was limited to potter households, but sometimes it affected the whole community. When this happened, potters often banded together against the remaining non-potting households in Sarayama. In fact, the argument over clay digging described above also illustrates the way in which the community could be divided into two factions.

When the bulldozer was hired to dig from Yamasai's land, it was discovered that it would have to manoeuvre, not just across Yamasan's strip with the woodshed on it, but on another, even smaller area of land owned by the whole community and on which one of the guardian deities, *Kompira-sama*, was housed. The potters decided that it would be best to buy the community-owned piece of land outright. They therefore called a meeting of the heads of all households in Sarayama to discuss the matter. The argument that followed was extremely confused. Kaneyo, which is not now a potting household, wanted the potters to pay the hamlet annually for digging rights. The potters retorted that in the past community-owned land had always been freely used, for thatch, fodder, wood, and clay; why should they now pay to rent the land? They were, however, prepared to buy it.

Most of the potters reckoned that the head of Kaneyo was trying to thwart them by keeping the *Kompira-sama* land in the name of the community, in case he ever tried to take up pottery again. If clay were then being dug from community-owned land, he would have an automatic right of admission to the potters' cooperative; if, on the other hand, clay were being taken from privately-owned land, his position would be considerably weaker. Eventually, Kaneyo gave in and said that the land could be sold provided that the money was used for some community project. However, potters offered what non-potting households thought was a minimum price for the land. The heads of Yamani and Yamasan, who were negotiating for the potters, wanted to protect their own household interests; they felt that if they offered too much for land from which clay could be dug, then Yamasai might ask for more than the fixed annual sum of ¥100,000 for the clay taken from its land. The heads of Maruta and Yamamaru, negotiating for the non-potting households, felt that if the potters were going to disturb community-owned land for the sake of their pottery, they ought to pay the going rate for the amount of clay in the piece of land. In the end, after a heated argument, the non-potting households gave ground, and the land was bought by the potters' cooperative for ¥150,000. The story did have a happier ending, however. A few months later, potting and non-potting households saw the wisdom of exchanging this piece of land for another, on which the Kompira deity was then rehoused.

Those households that do not pot – Yamamaru, Kaneyo, Maruta, and Yamamasu – all used to complain that potters behaved high-handedly: they did what they liked, how they liked, and when they liked to. Those who did not fire kilns were 'idiots'. And yet, if ever one of the non-potting households made any attempt at starting pottery, potters would protest bitterly. They have for the most part been successful in preventing an increase in their number. Although the head of Maruta began learning pottery from Yamasan, he stopped within a year. Yamamasu was said to have wanted to build a kiln some time ago, but was quickly dissuaded by its main house, Yamako. The head of Kaneyo had been prevented from potting because of illness, but once a healthy son-in-law married into the house, he was seriously thinking of taking up pottery once more. The only successful household has been Kaneichi, whose head drove a hard bargain when the potters tried to buy his land for a car park for the tourists. Yes, he would willingly sell them his land, but only if his son were allowed to take up pottery once more. Since Kaneichi had made pots in the past, the potters decided to let the household do so again, and a deal was made. Yamaichi sold one of its rice fields to Kaneichi, its branch house, so that the latter could install its clay crushers and build mixing and settling tanks for clay preparation.

But it was not just the non-potting households in Sarayama that regarded the potters as 'big headed'. People in the surrounding hamlets had the same opinion of them. These farmers may well have resented the fact that urban society paid such attention to a group of rural potters simply because they produced a kind of 'art' (cf. Graburn 1976:23). More probably, they resented the way potters had come into the money; certainly, they disliked the way in which, in regional matters, potters always put what appeared to be the interests of their community first.

But, in fact, potters' own interests were often put forward as 'community' interests. This was what made the non-potting households in Sarayama so unhappy. While they were out at work – sometimes as far away as Fukuoka – the potters could assemble at a moment's notice to make decisions that frequently affected the whole community. Potters were able to commandeer ¥150,000 from community funds to help pay for netting to be hung round the softball ground, and not one non-potting household was represented at the meeting. When potters decided to hold a ceremony for the *Kompira* deity after it was moved to its new sanctuary after the clay-digging episode, non-potting households were given only a few hours notice of this theoretically important community event. It was potters, too, who arranged to have the road widened along the ascent from the Ono valley to Sarayama. Sometimes, as in the last instance, the fact that the potters are a tourist attraction gives them a tool with which to turn the wheels of bureaucracy somewhat faster. Since communities down the valley had been waiting a decade to get a road put in and asphalted, the widening of an already

Plate 55 Main mouth firing of the cooperative kiln, with three small piles of purificatory salt, 1978

existing metalled road up to Sarayama was a luxury which, in their opinion, the potters 'did not deserve. Non-potting households in Sarayama did not object to the widening of the road; they objected to the fact that potters did not consult them before the decision was made. Although, theoretically, everyone was supposed to do things together, in fact the principle of cooperation by all households had once again been ignored.

It should be stressed that the division between potting and non-potting households was not an unbreachable rift of the kind described for another rural village by Robert Smith (1978:229–248). All fourteen households in Sarayama did – still do – participate in all sorts of activities together. However, potters all do the same work, they have the same technical problems with production, and they deal with the same buyers. They have to employ extra police to control traffic during their annual pottery festival, are asked by local authorities to contribute to exhibitions, and discuss their financial affairs together with the tax office. To repay favours done for them in business, they must entertain these groups, playing softball and drinking *sake*. So the potters have their own softball team, and they all spend a night out on the town together from time to time. People from non-potting households cannot participate in all these activities; hence they are very much aware of the differences between themselves and the potters.

Because potters produce *mingei* and *mingei* now is part of a national tradition, folk art groups, television crews, and newspaper reporters spend a lot of time

163

talking about Onta pottery and Onta potters; often they do not realize that the community of Sarayama actually contains four households that do not fire kilns. For instance, when Yanagi Munemichi was first appointed head of the Folk Craft Museum, he publicly expressed his earnest wish that 'everyone in Onta' would rally together, when he was in fact referring only to the potters' cooperative. Similarly, during my fieldwork, the Japan Broadcasting Corporation (NHK) put out a radio programme in the series *Country Villages of Japan* (*Nihon no furusato*), but the announcer limited his discussion to pottery and talked only to potters; when he staged a party to get the community together, only potters were invited. The potters did not take it upon themselves to ask non-potting households to go to the party with them, which suggests that they put their own group interests before those of the community as a whole.

The Appreciation of Individual Talent

In addition to the way in which an individual household or a group of households would put its own interests before those of the community as a whole, community solidarity has been weakened in another way: by the appreciation of pottery by outsiders. Methods of retail pricing, of promoting potters' names, and of exhibiting pottery have all served to emphasize the individual as an

Plate 56 Side mouth firing of the Yamani kiln, 1963

Plate 57 Sakamoto Haruzō, 1963

independent entity, rather than simply as a member of a small group such as a household or a community.

Shop owners and dealers fix their prices according to the perceived quality of the pots that they hope to sell; they must also take current market considerations into account. However, when a buyer decides that one pot is better than another, s/he is in fact suggesting that one potter may be better than another. Any differentiation in price thus becomes a differentiation in individual talent.

Buyers are interested in good pots: in other words, in pots that sell. But 'good' pots can only be made by 'good' potters, in their opinion, which means that dealers spend a lot of time trying to sell a potter since this will greatly enhance their profits. They therefore encourage customers to buy the work of certain potters whose individual names they do their best to promote. What buyers do not realize, and what potters theoretically cannot accept, is that within the sphere of the hamlet group all households must be more or less equal. If one potter is consistently picked out for what outsiders see as 'good' work, he and his household will gain status and thus destroy the non-ranking equilibrium of all households in Sarayama. So, by promoting the individual names of certain potters, and by pricing their work higher wherever possible, buyers are threatening the solidarity of the community. This means that, within Sarayama

165

itself, individual talent has to be denied unless it reflects upon the community as a whole. One of the reasons for potters' banding together to fix a standard wholesale price, therefore, was to provide some measure from within the community to counter the chaos of retail pricing in many Hita craft shops. Potters were in effect telling the outside world: 'you can retail pots at whatever prices you feel like setting. But here in Sarayama we don't admit to exceptional individual talent. Every potter is as good as another here'.

Onta pottery is generally marketed as such (*ontayaki*), and in theory at least, none of the potters in Sarayama signs any of his work with his individual name. Since the 1960s, however, buyers have encouraged potters to use special names for their tea ceremony bowls, since it is a 'name' that enables a tea bowl to be sold at a high price. The potters have been given 'tea names', and most of them sign their tea bowls with these names. They also comply – albeit unwillingly – with requests to write calligraphy on wooden boxes for these bowls.

But it is not just a potter's 'tea name' that buyers now try to sell. Many people ask for all pots to be signed in some way or other. Most of them want to give 'personalized' presents: one man, for example, may order 50 signed flower vases to be given to guests at his daughter's wedding; another may want signed plates for distribution by his company to customers to celebrate an anniversary; even the Oita prefectural authorities, who are in theory supposed to preserve the 'tradition' of Onta pottery, have been known to place orders through Maruta, which acts as the cooperative's retail outlet in Sarayama, asking to have the name

Plate 58 Sakamoto Masami and his mother, Matsue, 1963

166

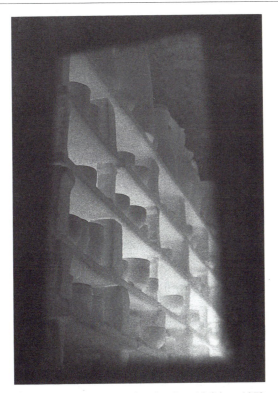

Plate 59 Yamaichi kiln chamber in mid-firing, 1979

of the maker of each pot written in pencil on its box. The authorities then arrange to have the craftsman's name written on the box in beautiful calligraphy in order to enhance the value of the gift.

As can be readily judged from their predilection for brand goods, Japanese consumers are very concerned with what they call 'name value'. Onta pottery has value in itself as a name, but since the mid 70s there have been indications that the pottery-buying public has become more interested in potters working in Sarayama than in Onta pottery as such, so that branding has shifted from a folk craft *community* to *individual* folk art potters. Although, as we have seen, buyers encourage the signing of pottery by individual potters in order to increase their profits, they are also trying to safeguard their own interests by making potters responsible for their work. At present, if a complaint is made about a purchase by a dissatisfied customer, the buyer cannot return the pot to the man who made it, since the latter will almost invariably deny that the work is his own. If potters were made to sign their work, however, they would have to take responsibility for its quality. This is the primary reason for the suggestion made by Miyake Chūichi of the Folk Craft Society that potters use household marks (*yagō*) on all

167

their pots, as Koishiwara potters usually do. But potters refuse to do this, even though they realize that some of their number are getting away with poor quality work, because they see the signing of names in any form whatever as endangering the community as a whole. Buyers would connect household marks with individual potters; but, within Sarayama itself, each potter acts as a member of his household, and each household is closely tied to the community. At the same time, by not putting his name on his work in some form or other, a potter avoids responsibility, and this can and does lead to the deterioration of the reputation of the community as a whole. This is a paradox that permanently bothers the more serious-minded potters in Sarayama.

Ironically, in view of the fact that *mingei* is supposed to be made by 'nameless craftsmen', the folk craft associations themselves have been largely responsible for the publicizing of Onta potters' names, although the media have tended also to make 'artists' out of craftsmen. The Japan Folk Craft Association holds an annual autumn exhibition at its museum in Tokyo, and Onta potters are asked to send in their pots. Although the Onta Potters' Cooperative as a whole was awarded the Museum Prize in 1968, potters have generally been invited to contribute as individuals and not as members of the cooperative. As a result, when making awards, the Japan Folk Craft Society has tended to give prizes only to individual Onta potters, rather than to the potters' cooperative as a whole.

In 1973, Onta potters were also encouraged by the Folk Craft Association to contribute to a biannual national exhibition known as the Japan Ceramics Exhibition (*Nihon Tōgeiten*) and sponsored by the Mainichi Newspaper Company. Exhibition regulations stated that only two pots could be contributed by any one individual or group. This meant that potters either contributed as individuals or chose two pots from among all their works and contributed as the Onta Potters' Cooperative. It is doubtful whether all potters were seriously interested in the exhibition, but the thought of having to decide whose work from ten households was good enough to be sent in to the exhibition was enough to stop them from contributing as a group. Instead two of them, Yamaichi and Irisan, contributed as individuals. Both had pots accepted, and Yamaichi was awarded one of the four major prizes at the exhibition (the Foreign Minister's Award, plus half a million yen).

The news of Yamaichi's success astonished everyone. The immediate reaction of the older potters was that his prize-winning lidded jar could have been made by any one of the other potters in Sarayama. The award was theirs as much as it was Yamaichi's (cf. Nakane 1970:83). In other words, they denied an individual's talent as recognized by the outside world. What was worse, however, so far as the older potters were concerned, was that the media paid so much attention to Yamaichi that his name became extremely well known among those interested in pottery and *mingei*. He was soon bombarded with requests to make this or that kind of pot, and anyone who had a query about Onta's history, its annual pottery festival, community life, the acquisition of materials, and so on tended to get in touch with Yamaichi instead of going through the official channel of the cooperative leader.[4]

Older and Younger Potters

The attention Yamaichi received because of his award highlights a further aspect of the way in which community solidarity has been affected in Sarayama. There was some resentment among his fellow potters because Yamaichi was called upon by *outside* forces to act as spokesman for *internal* affairs when he was still a comparatively young man in his mid-thirties. But it will be remembered that the appointment of the potters' official spokesman, the cooperative leader, was based on seniority of age. Thus, public evaluation of a single pot not only led to the acclamation of the individual who had made that pot; it also conflicted with the seniority system prevalent in the community in which that individual was living. So far as older men like the heads of Yamani and Yamasan were concerned, Yamaichi's position within the community had been strengthened and their own position weakened.

This was not the only occasion on which the Folk Craft Association's dealings with potters upset the community's gerontocracy. In 1962 one of the Folk Craft Museum employees was sent to stay in Sarayama and give advice to potters concerning what was and was not 'acceptable' *mingei* pottery. Over a period of ten years, this employee came down from Tokyo, staying a few days at a time in Sarayama, talking to potters, and making suggestions concerning the shapes, decoration, and glazing of certain pots. Her advice culminated in the distribution of an album to each potter household with photographs of what were considered by the Folk Craft Association to be 'old' and 'authentic' shapes and designs of Onta pottery.[5]

Undoubtedly, the employee's visits helped many of the younger potters who had very little idea of what Onta pots made half a century earlier looked like. Unfortunately, some of the older potters began to resent her appearance in Sarayama, for she posed a threat to the hitherto unquestioned assumption that the way in which they taught their sons to pot was the best possible way. As a result, the employee naturally found herself associating with those potters whose fathers were not working with them at the wheel – that is, with younger potters from Irisai, Yamaichi, Irisan, Yamasai, and Kaneichi. These men were able to look at their work differently, since they were not bound by loyalty to fathers who still oversaw their work.

Although the employee's consorting with younger potters was a natural result of the existence of Sarayama's household system, it led to the Folk Craft Association's public approval of the work of the younger Onta potters. This only annoyed the older potters more, since they sensed that their authority was gradually being whittled away. Younger potters appear to have been less conscious of the friction that the employee's visits generated, but the matter was then taken up by the dealer Mr T., who saw the elder potters' resentment as an opportunity for him to undermine the employee's position, both in the community and in the Folk Craft Museum itself. After all, she posed a threat to his own established position as general 'expert' on Onta's potters and pottery. For several years, therefore, Mr T. went around proclaiming that the employee concerned had 'broken up the community', that the potters were 'divided into factions'. As in the *Tale of the Heike*, he said, 'the proud must fall'; Onta's new found fame was but 'a puff of smoke in the blistering winds of history', and 'the greatness of its pottery is forever gone'. Here we have another example of the way in which social changes are seen to affect pottery aesthetically.

But there is a further way in which Sarayama's gerontocracy has been weakened, and this goes back to the discussion of the economic differentiation of households. I argued earlier that an unequal distribution of wealth brought about by the *mingei* boom led to a lessening of community solidarity and, in particular, to a division between potting and non-potting households. It happens that the wealthiest households in Sarayama are mostly those whose heads are the oldest men: Yamani, Yamako, Yamasan, and Kanemaru. They were able to work with their sons soon after stopping agriculture and thus take advantage of the *mingei* boom.

I have suggested that all households in Sarayama were of more or less equal economic standing, and this was indeed the ideal to which potters referred when they talked of the past. However, potters also admitted that some richer households provided for the welfare of all and expected a certain measure of obedience in return. Those who did not have enough money to contribute to community affairs were not expected to express their opinions in public. However, since the 1970s, this rule has no longer worked effectively, because, although there are differences in income levels among potting households, the enormous increase in their wealth has been enough to put them on an equal footing with one another. (At the same time, potters' newly acquired wealth separates them from non-potting households, which are expected to submit to potters' decisions.) In other words, there seems to be a minimal level of affluence above which everyone thinks he has a right to have a say in community affairs, and it is only since the *mingei* boom that potter households have risen above this threshhold.

Because all potters have a lot of money, younger men such as the heads of Yamaichi and Irisai could express their opinions in front of others in the community. But the wealthiest and oldest men (such as the heads of Yamako and Yamani) resented what they saw as unnecessary outspokenness. They objected to Yamaichi and Yamasai, not because the latter spoke up when they were not as wealthy as themselves, but because the two household heads were much younger. It was on the basis of this logic that Yamani, Yamako and one or two other households refused to give liberally on behalf of the whole community. Instead, they insisted that all households should contribute money equally, proclaiming that things should be done together 'democratically'. The ideal of 'everyone together' was thereby given a neat little twist. When it came to such contributions as netting for the softball ground, Yamani and Yamako refused to give any more than other households. This led younger potters with lower incomes to claim that if the head of Yamani and the others were really thinking of the good of the community they would arrange for those with higher incomes to pay more and those with lower incomes less. This would help redress the imbalance in income levels, and was the way in which things were then done in many other communities.[6]

Community Solidarity, 'Tradition' and 'the Past'

It can be seen that over the years community solidarity has been threatened in various ways. Firstly, within Sarayama a differentiation in wealth has led to the break-up of the cooperative kiln and to household individuation. Secondly, people have become increasingly conscious of the existence of two groups within the community: one, the majority, consists of potting households; the other, of non-potting households. Thirdly, the appreciation of pottery by outsiders has tended to emphasize the work and names of individual potters. Fourthly, the increased wealth of potter households and the external recognition of individual talent have been interpreted by some within the community as a threat to the seniority system of authority.

It is precisely because community solidarity is thus being weakened that two concepts were much referred to by residents. One of these – *mukashi*, the past – concerned the community as a whole; the other – *dentō*, or tradition – affected potters in particular. The first was unconsciously aimed at uniting all households within the community and hence at stemming the possible flood of resentment between potting and non-potting households. The second resulted from recognition of individual talent and was an attempt to bring all potters together and standardize their work so that they marketed a readily recognizable product known as *ontayaki*. Both reflect, in my opinion, direct or indirect assumptions that the way in which things used to be done was best.

The idea of *mukashi*, on which my 'model' of social organization was based, is probably prevalent throughout much of rural Japanese society – especially during the time that the country's postwar 'miracle' economy brought about major social and demographic changes. Ronald Dore (1978:65), for example, has commented on the way in which villagers of Shinohata frequently used to reminisce about the past. The themes are the same: the poverty of the past and the comparative luxury of the present. In Sarayama, anyone speaking to an outsider tends to talk of the way in which people used to lead their lives, of the hard times they had when there was not enough money to buy food or clothes, of the exhaustion of working in the fields and mountains. At the same time, the old way of life is viewed with a certain nostalgia, for villagers know that the 'good old days' of cooperation have gone forever. *Mukashi* is an important concept that is called upon, both to remind fellow residents of how things used to be and should be and to present a united front to the outside world.

Similarly, the concept of 'tradition' is also designed to maintain not just unity within the community, but the unity of the community as a whole *vis-à-vis* the outside world. Potters discourage one another, and are discouraged by leaders of the *Mingei* movement, from experimenting with clay texture, glazes, and designs. Onta potters all use the same glazes with more or less frequency; they

Plate 60 Yanase Asao unbricking the cooperative kiln, 1981

all decorate their pots in almost identical manner, limiting the number of designs they apply. There is a remarkable unity about Onta pottery that is not found so much in other folk potteries, such as Koishiwara, Tamba, or Mashiko.

Some potters want to experiment with new designs or glazes, but realize that, if they do so, they would be accused during the next drinking session of 'betraying the community'. On the purely technical level, Irisai has pointed out that one way of preventing bloating (a common trouble that comes from firing clay too quickly) would be to mix some grog into the raw clay and so raise its heat resistance. Every potter knows this; and yet nobody does it, because mixing clay with grog is considered to go against the grain of what constitutes 'Onta pottery'. From the point of view of design, Yamaichi remarked that in the past potters used to make a simple, white slipped rice bowl; and that nowadays they spent all their time decorating rice bowls with chattering, combing, or slip brushing. If he were to make a simple white bowl, he would be accused of imitating other pottery kilns – not only by potters, but by the dealer, Mr T., who, if he was the 'expert' he pretended to be, ought, in Yamaichi's opinion, to know better.[7] Here, we have an example of the way in which potters allow social and

172

symbolic exchange values to take on more importance than the technical values arising from their work.

'Tradition' would appear to have been adopted as a concept aimed at maintaining order within the community. It is unlikely that Onta potters had any understanding of what tradition meant until the term was 'invented' (Hobsbawm and Ranger 1983) by others, who could see in Sarayama's social organization and methods of pottery production a stability that was lacking in other sections of Japanese society. I suspect that the potters were made very much aware of the word when the techniques by which Onta pottery was made were designated an 'intangible cultural property' in 1970.[8] Nevertheless, I would also argue that the idea of 'tradition' could only come into its own only when community solidarity began to break down following contact with the outside world. Tradition is called upon precisely because the community is in many ways no longer traditional. It has become vital for potters to maintain a tradition in pottery, despite the number of minor innovations in methods of production, since this serves to reinforce an otherwise rapidly fading sense of community solidarity.[9]

At the same time, it should be pointed out that Sarayama potters – and only potters – can all recognize one another's work and can tell with fair ease who made what pot. In other words, potters are keenly aware of the stylistic differences among themselves, differences that they feel could be exploited by outsiders and be seen in terms of individual talent. I would suggest, therefore, that potters try to cover up their differences by stressing to the outside world that they all make the same traditional pots.

Plate 61 Kurogi Saihito unloading the cooperative kiln, 1982

173

Plate 62 Sakamoto Haruzō packing a jar in straw, 1963

In many ways, pottery is the idiom in which social change is expressed. For example, when a potter is accused of not making a traditionally-shaped teacup, he is really being accused of stepping out of line from the rest of the pottery households and attempting to go things alone. Again, a potter will explain that the potter's 'character' will remain in a pot if he uses a kick-wheel, but that it will be lost should he decide to throw on an electric wheel. What is actually meant is that by continuing to use a kick-wheel a potter is affirming the existence of his community, which would fall into total disarray should machinery be imported and each household start competitive production, as in Koishiwara. Another potter says that if you start studying really hard, you end up changing the shapes of pottery entirely. He was referring to the problem of coffee-cup handles that either are too small or make the cup warp at the lip, and the potter concerned said that in the end one would have to buy a new mould from Arita. But once you bought one mould you would buy others for other pots – pitcher handles, teapot spouts, or flower-vase grips, and so on – and in this way *ontayaki* would 'disintegrate'. Here technical values are emphasized to reinforce the social and symbolic exchange values of Onta pottery and Sarayama as a community.

So, changes in methods of production almost inevitably – in the eye of the potters – lead to social changes that affect the organization of their community. The adoption of moulds would lead to the purchase of machinery for clay preparation, to the building of new types of kilns, and to the employment of apprentices or professional workmen. Ultimately, not only the community but the household system itself would be threatened. If a glut of Onta pots were brought

174

about by overproduction, potters would have to sell their individual names or undercut one another in as many ways as possible in order to make a living. Sarayama as a community would no longer exist – at least not in the sense in which 'community' has hitherto been used. The potters' decision not to mechanize shows the importance that they still attach to the community as a whole.

Conclusion

In this chapter I have given an account of ways in which community solidarity may be said to have lessened in Sarayama. I do not, however, wish to give the impression that solidarity has disappeared entirely and that people now invariably put their own self-interests before those of the community. The ideals of harmony and all-together may not be lived up to all the time, but on the other hand, as Ronald Dore (1959:379) has said, 'Japanese villagers are not given to feuding as a pastime'. Indeed Sarayama, unlike many of its neighbouring hamlets, remains very much a community, in contrast to a place where several dozen people happen to live in close proximity to one another but

Plate 63 Haruzō's aged parents, Chūzō and
Hatsue, packing pots in straw, 1977

175

nothing more. People still share their lives; they still participate in communal events. Everyone turns out to help when it comes to building a new house, unlike – for example – the inhabitants of Kurusu studied by Robert Smith (1978:142). They all gather for frequently held community festivals,[10] and the purchase of a new car, the completion of building projects, or a man's forty-first birthday, are occasions for all households in Sarayama to celebrate (Moeran 1985:84–97). Programmes appear on each household's television screen by way of a common aerial. Although this might not seem to indicate community solidarity, in fact at the time of my stay in Sarayama three or four households forfeited the pleasure of being able to watch six different television channels obtainable on their own individual rooftop aerials; instead, they shared four channels with the remaining households, whose location in the narrow valley had not permitted more than the two NHK programmes to come their way until a high antenna was erected on the top of the nearest mountain.

On their monthly day-off from work, all men participate in softball games or archery contests before getting down to some fairly serious drinking in the late afternoon and evening. The exchanges of *sake* cups that flow so fast and furious are an important form of communication and serve to unite one man with his neighbour; indeed, the intensity of the arguments that accompany drunkenness reveals, paradoxically, how much each man values the ideal of a community transcending the individual (see Moeran 1984a). The trouble is that one man's ideal is not necessarily another's.[11]

So what Fukutake (1967:95) wrote of Japanese rural society in 1964 is still true of Sarayama: 'the hamlet imposed on its members an ideal of hamlet unity and hamlet harmony as the highest possible good, and although that ideal is losing its power to suppress individuality, it has still by no means disappeared'. There are cracks in the ideal, and without doubt the potters' vastly increased wealth is partly responsible for them. Higher income levels resulting from the decision to specialize in full-time pottery production have served to divide potting from non-potting households within the community and, as Nakano and Brown (1970:201) have observed in another context, 'economic diversification with the emergence of specialized interest groups also contributes to a decline in community solidarity'.

In my early discussion of Japanese rural institutions, I said that the hamlet (*buraku*) was an occupational and residential group. The relation between occupation and residence is important to our understanding of contemporary Japanese society. Fukutake (1974:57) has suggested that the 'community' does not necessarily depend on occupation, but rather on 'neighbourhood'. I have shown that almost all forms of social cooperation (particularly in the exchange of labour) in Sarayama depended on ownership of land and similar work patterns. When potters decided to give up agriculture, occupation became more important than residence. It would seem to me, therefore, that ownership of land and neighbourhood are only important to the hamlet as a community if all, or almost all, of its households are engaged in wet-rice agriculture. Once people start doing other kinds of work, or once they start specializing in different kinds of agriculture, the hamlet as such ceases to be either an occupational or a residential group (Johnson 1967:181). This is why Ariga (1956:25) stressed that one should examine the links between households forming an occupational group, rather than the hamlet itself, if one wants to understand the Japanese sense of community. The importance of occupation to the formation of a community may be seen in the way urban Japanese also give precedence to their place of work (which lawyers in fact refer to as their 'village', or *mura*) rather than to their local residential group (Nakane 1970:59–60).

Another point concerns individual and household status within the hamlet. In their discussions of hamlet organization, many scholars (cf. Fukutake 1967:138ff; Norbeck 1954:208) suggest that economic differences are primarily responsible for maintaining status differences. I suggested in my discussion of Sarayama's social organization that the age-grade system is important, for it provides an alternative to wealth in the determination of status. Seniority in age gives each individual (and household) authority in turn over other individuals (and households) junior to him. The system is ideally one of equilibrium in that a household retains its authority over other households only as long as its head is senior, but not senile. Once he is replaced by his son, his house will lose authority. In theory, therefore, every household in the community has the opportunity to rise to the top of the status system.

But the system of gerontocracy has been upset. We have seen that considerable conflict between older and younger potters has arisen from the accumulation of wealth and the public appreciation of their pottery. Although most older potters quickly observe that the 'artist' potter is a one-generation phenomenon, the appreciation of individual talent does offer an opportunity for one household that manages to produce successive generations of publicly-acclaimed potters to rise above, and hence perhaps rule over, other households whose potters remain very much run-of-the-mill. Whether this will happen in Sarayama remains to be seen, but it can be argued that talent is an alternative criterion to wealth and seniority in the determination of household status within the community.

The kind of data provided in this chapter as support for my thesis that community solidarity has been seriously undermined by the *mingei* boom is not wholly new. Other scholars have commented on the household's disengagement from the social sphere of the hamlet. What is special about Sarayama is that not only the household but the individual as well is affected by the appraisal of Onta pottery. By concentrating on the way in which the appreciation of individual talent affects household relations, I have presented a new angle from which the subject of community solidarity may be viewed.

Individual talent is an ideal to which the primary group in Japanese society appears to have some trouble adjusting. Shimpo (1976:104) has shown in his description of a village volleyball tournament that the group takes the credit for any of its members' successes. In the neighbouring pottery village of

177

Koishiwara, a case occurred in 1958 which was remarkably similar to that described above about Yamaichi's national award. A young potter, Ōta Kumao, had his work selected by Yanagi Sōetsu and sent to the Brussels Exposition, where it won the *grand prix*. Other potters in the community claimed that the prize belonged to all Koishiwara potters as a group and not to Kumao, since the pot had been exhibited, not under his own name, but under that of Koishiwara. The fact that *only* Kumao's work had been exhibited did not appear to worry anybody in Koishiwara except Kumao himself. As Arnold Hauser drily observes (1982:566), folk art is 'the creation of individuals and the property of many'.

The appreciation of talent, then, endangers the community which cannot *ideally* function as an egalitarian group if one of its members is consistently picked out for special praise. This point may be illustrated further by a weaving community in Amami Ōshima, an island situated south of Kyushu. More than two decades ago now, Hatae (1970:6) noted that in theory these *tsumugi* weavers should be designated, like Onta potters, holders of an 'intangible cultural property' for the tradition with which their work was done. However, at that time opposition came from the weavers themselves who feared that one or two of their number might consequently become 'national treasures' and collar the 'art' market. Other, less-talented weavers would then have to mechanize and shift to mass production in order not to go out of business; but by doing this, they would put an end to social organization in the community as it then existed.

The problem of talent in the craft world is by no means limited to Japanese society. Warren D'Azevedo (1973:141), for example, has noted that woodcarvers among the Gola of western Liberia 'claim that any special talent is looked upon with jealousy by others as a potential threat to the family in its efforts to develop loyal and dependable members'. It is not surprising, therefore, to find that Zuñi Pueblo Indian potters, like the potters in Onta, also claimed to be able to distinguish the works of their fellow potters (Bunzel 1972:64–65). Of course, the recognition of individual style does not have to be connected with the relationship between individual talent and the group, as discussed here. In communities like Sarayama there can be little anonymity, and 'most people would know the details of style, the aesthetic choices, and even the tool marks of their contemporaries' (Graburn 1976:21) as a matter of course.

'Anonymity' suggests the related problem of an individual craftsman's signing his name on his work. Nelson Graburn (1976) has argued that it was precisely to offset the growing lack of individuality in large-scale societies that the signing of art work was developed. In his book on ethnic and tourist arts, we find – as in Sarayama – middlemen and buyers doing their utmost to promote the names of individual artists, whether they be Seri woodcarvers, Navajo weavers, Pueblo potters, or Eskimo soapstone sculptors. Similarly, Dockstader (1973:119) mentions that the identification or hallmarking of their work by American Indian artists was brought about primarily by the Indian Arts and Crafts Board. Onta potters may well be confused about whether to sign their pots or not, but at least they have not so far reached the stage where, like some pottery vendors in central Mexico, they put fake names on their work in the belief that any name is better than none at all (Charlton 1976:142).

It is clear that – in the context of folk art generally – Sarayama's problems are by no means unique, and that the potters living there face the same difficulties as other craftsmen throughout the world. Local government authorities and the Folk Craft Association have tried to 'help' potters over the years by sketching designs, commenting on shapes and glazes, and even providing them with an album of photographs of old Onta pots. Ruth Bunzel (1972:88) has remarked on the mutation of style of Pueblo Indian pottery caused by the outside influence of white people, and Graburn's book (1976) has numerous examples of the way in which ethnic or folk arts all over the world have been 'interfered with' at the design level – for example, Hopi weaving and the Museum of North Arizona (p. 93), Navajo weaving and trading posts (p. 96), Aborigine bark paintings and a Methodist mission station (p. 274), and Yoruba dyeing and a representative from the Peace Corps (p. 309–310). As is customary in art worlds generally, patrons tend to play an active role in the planning and design of works in which they have an interest (Becker 1982:100–1).

Sometimes, 'help' is not limited to stylistic change, but includes complete innovations, so that traditions are invented in the arts as well as for political purposes (cf. Hobsbawm and Ranger 1983). Such apparently 'ethnic' arts as Eskimo soapstone carving and printmaking were introduced by a Canadian artist in the late 1940s and 1950s (Graburn 1976:42–43), and various forms of 'traditional' Indian art have been introduced in recent times by traders and curio makers (Dockstader 1973:116). It is thus not surprising to find people claiming that there is very little 'traditional' art being produced in the world today (Graburn 1969:458).

Comparatively speaking, Onta pottery's reputation for being traditional is perhaps fair. To a certain extent, potters embrace *mingei* aesthetic ideals by not experimenting with shapes and glazes. They turn down the numerous requests for this or that kind of shape, design, or colour combination, as buyers attempt to satisfy consumer demand for something different, something new. Potters do not experiment, because they know that Onta pottery would thereby lose its distinctiveness and, more serious, Sarayama would lose its consciousness of being a 'special' community that retains its distinctiveness precisely through its pottery. As with Pueblo Indian potters, Maori or Aboriginal 'artists', 'the survival of the craft indicates the survival of the people' (Brody 1976:76; cf. Mead 1976:291; N. Williams 1976:284). Like many makers of what Nelson Graburn calls 'Fourth World arts', Onta potters 'carry the message: "we exist; we are different; we can do something that we are proud of; we have something that is uniquely ours!"' (Graburn 1976:26).

Finally, let us turn to the relation between aesthetic criticism and social change. I have commented earlier on the way in which Onta pottery has been seen by *mingei* leaders to 'deteriorate' when production moves away from 'natural' methods that make use of local materials and when social cooperation breaks down as potters seek to benefit financially from the increase in market demand. I have also remarked on how the Folk Craft Association in particular has been responsible for some of the problems that have occurred in the social organization of Sarayama as a community. It is perhaps of interest to note here that, despite earlier criticism of Onta pottery, the Folk Craft Association has also acclaimed Sarayama's pottery as 'the best in Japan' (Tanaka Toyotarō 1966:11). Mizuo Hiroshi, who earlier wrote about Onta pottery's 'pollution' (1968:110), later re-evaluated his estimation and decided that pots had been bad only during the period immediately following Leach's visit to Sarayama, from about 1955 to 1962. By 1970 they were really quite good (Mizuo 1972:106–107) – thanks to the visits of one of the Folk Craft Museum's employees to Sarayama in 1962 (p. 111). The cooperative nature of the potters' work is emphasized by Mizuo along with their reliance on natural materials (p. 113). Nevertheless he makes the general point that the accumulation of wealth leads to ugliness in crafts, and – as we saw in the previous chapter – most *mingei* critics cannot accept the fact that Sarayama's potters are making a lot of money (cf. Tanaka Takashi 1971:24).[12] At the same time, consumer emphasis on individual names and the signing of work in pottery has meant that potters are no longer the 'unknown craftsmen' that Yanagi advocated they should be. In other words, as Howard Becker (1982:2) has pointed out, 'every way of producing art works for some people and not for others; every way of producing art produces work of every conceivable grade of quality, however that is defined'. In this respect, *mingei* connoisseurs can be said to provide 'a running revision of the value-creating theory which, in the form of criticism, continuously adapts the premises of the theory to the works artists actually produce' (Becker 1982:137–8).

Hitherto I have discussed the *Mingei* movement as it has affected the social organization of Sarayama, and tried to show how the critical appraisal of Onta pottery is closely linked to the *way* in which potters work, rather than to the pottery itself. While I have given examples of what folk art leaders and critics have had to say about Sarayama's potters, I have not given any details of what the potter themselves think about *mingei* and Yanagi's ideals. Do they agree with what Yanagi said about beauty and direct perception? Do they understand his moral philosophizing? To what extent do they accept his arguments concerning the beauty of local materials, of nature, of cooperation and self-surrender? Have the potters read any of Yanagi's works? Do they even know who he is? I shall now deal with these questions before going on to show how potters, buyers, and critics differ in their attitudes to the appreciation of pottery itself.

Chapter Nine

THEORY AND PRACTICE IN JAPANESE *MINGEI*

In Chapter One, I sketched the historical background to the Japanese *Mingei* movement and then described the main details of folk craft ideology as put forward by the movement's founder, Yanagi Sōetsu. I made a rough classification of Yanagi's thought into what I termed its 'moral' and 'utilitarian' aspects, and argued that Yanagi was more concerned with how crafts were made (the moral aspect) than with crafts as objects in themselves (the utilitarian aspect). I made it clear that, in spite of all that its leaders might have us believe, the Japanese *Mingei* movement is not an 'aesthetic' so much as a 'spiritual' movement. I showed how the critical appraisal of this pottery is based on the fact that ideally potters in Sarayama use methods of production that closely accord with Yanagi's theory: they use local materials for their clays and glazes; they do not rely on modern machinery, but are close to 'nature'; they are 'unknown craftsmen' who work in a spirit of cooperation with one another, without incentive for profit and personal gain.

With the recent sustained demand for *mingei*, however, potters have begun buying some of their materials from non-local sources; they have taken advantage of technological advances in the ceramics industry to purchase kiln shelving, ball mills, and belt-drive engines for their kick-wheels; they have made a considerable amount of money; they have stopped cooperating with one another; and they are beginning to be well known throughout Japan. As a result of these changes, their work has for a period been criticized by leaders of the *Mingei* movement. However, because social organization and the method of making pottery in Sarayama have remained relatively unchanged, compared with such other potteries as Tamba or Koishiwara, Onta potters' work is still seen to be the best example of '*mingei*' in Japan.

Now I should like to examine what the potters in the community think about the whole idea of *mingei*, and how they react to comments about their work by people who usually know little if anything about the problems involved in pottery production. I will also discuss what pottery dealers have to say about folk crafts in general and Onta pottery in particular, since my particular concern here is with the relation between production and marketing requirements *vis-à-vis* the theoretical concept of *mingei*.

Of interest to me as an anthropologist is the question of whether 'universal aesthetic standards' may be said to exist. Many would appear to aver with Herbert Read (1961:127) that 'essential aesthetic qualities' are 'universal and everywhere identical'. If by 'essential aesthetic qualities' Read wishes to imply that certain aesthetic phenomena are inherent in the objects to which they pertain, and that there is – in Janet Wolff's (1983) phrase – an 'aesthetic specificity' in such objects, I have my doubts. As Pierre Bourdieu (1984) has so cogently argued, any 'aesthetic disposition' is socially defined. If, on the other hand, Read means that all human beings have some kind of aesthetic sense of beauty, from the evidence of my fieldwork data I would not disagree. The problem is, do potters, buyers, and folk craft leaders all have the *same* aesthetic values? If not, why not? These are questions that I shall now try to resolve. Only by examining the 'total art processes' (Silbermann 1968:583) surrounding the production, marketing, and aesthetic appraisal of Onta pottery will I be able to consider how the notion of 'folk art' or its equivalent relates to society as a whole.

Mingei Theory: Potters' and Buyers' Views

The Japan Folk Craft Association has now published twenty volumes of Yanagi's *Collected Works*, in which all of his essays are published. There are also numerous articles in folk craft and other literary magazines about various

Plate 64 Dish with *nagashi* yellow and green overglaze trailing

aspects of *mingei*, as well as a wealth of lesser, perhaps more ephemeral, material in newspapers and popular magazines, dealing for the most part with particular places renowned for a '*mingei* style' of production.

During my stay in Sarayama, I talked with all the potters about problems arising from the existence of the *Mingei* movement. I also interviewed twelve dealers who bought and sold Onta pottery. Two of these men were from Tokyo, one from Kumamoto, one from Oita, and the rest from the local town of Hita. Three of these dealers sold Onta pottery as a full-time profession; the others ran their businesses as a sideline (cf. Yoshino 1971:14). Some of these retailers began to buy Onta pottery because they liked pottery as such; others because they were interested in the idea of folk arts and crafts; yet others because they were already involved in Hita's tourist industry in other ways. Both potters and dealers were questioned about each of the main points of Yanagi's theory.

All of the potters in Sarayama knew of Yanagi by name, and all those born before 1945 had met the man on one of his visits to the community. Of the fifteen potters working at the wheel in Sarayama during the period of fieldwork, five had not read one word written by Yanagi; eight had only glanced at the articles in which he wrote about Onta pottery in particular (Yanagi 1931; republished in booklet form, 1961). Two potters had read the first volume of his *Selected Works*, *The Way of Crafts* (Yanagi 1955a). Although they had found the style difficult, both of them thought the work educationally rewarding.

Although all potters receive copies of the monthly publications *Mingei* and *Nihon no Mingei*, only two claimed that they regularly looked at more than the photographs. Four potters said that they had read comments or articles by Hamada Shōji, the artist potter who was head of the Folk Craft Museum until just before his death in January 1978. Although Mizuo Hiroshi, editor of *Mingei*, had emerged as the movement's leading critic, not one of the potters expressed any great interest in his writings. Those who had tried to read his work regarded his style as 'academic' in the worst sense of the word; from hearing him speak, potters felt that Mizuo had nothing new to tell them about *mingei*; he was but parroting Yanagi's ideas.

Potters were not prepared to define the word *mingei* beyond calling it a 'popular craft' (*minshūteki kōgei*). Even though they had not read much of Yanagi's works, they had learned enough about *mingei* from the movement's leaders over the years to realize that both the word and the thought behind its coinage were too difficult for them to express clearly and concisely. The head of Irisai avoided the question by exclaiming that 'craft potters exist to make pots, not to understand theories'. His grasp of this ideologically important point made one suspect that he, and several other of the younger potters, knew more about *mingei* than they were prepared to let on. Although all potters had come to accept that Sarayama had become a 'folk craft kiln' (*mingeigama*), many of them would have preferred that the term not be used of the community; *mingei* had, in the potters' opinion, come to broaden and change in meaning since its original conception in the 1920s.

183

This view was shared by many of the dealers, who felt that the whole notion of folk crafts had been overused and that, consequently, Onta pottery should not be labelled *mingei*. Some even suggested that everyone would be better off if the whole idea of *mingei* was forgotten. Although potters did not themselves take this extreme view, they were aware that some of the pots that they regularly produced, such as flower vases and tea bowls, were not *mingei* items at all. This would suggest that they had a fairly clear understanding of what *mingei* was, so far as their pottery was concerned. Neither they, nor a majority of the dealers, professed to understand or to accept the spiritual aspect of Yanagi's thought.

Earlier, I explained that Yanagi was mainly interested in beauty and that, in his opinion, what he called 'direct perception' or intuition (*chokkan*) was the only means of understanding 'true' beauty. He argued that, in aesthetic appraisal, one had to put aside all concepts and allow a thing to be seen for itself. Direct perception gave rise to a standard of beauty which could be appreciated by anyone, regardless of education or upbringing.

The reaction of dealers and potters to Yanagi's concept of direct perception was interesting in that all of the dealers and many of the potters felt that *chokkan* was not simply an abstract, theoretical concept, but one which could be successfully practised. As a result, they accepted the idea that one should try to see a pot for what it was, 'directly'. However, neither dealers nor potters were prepared to accept that direct perception could provide a standard of beauty. Their disagreement with Yanagi on this point stemmed from their own experience in selling pottery. Potters, for example, often found that work they regarded as excellent would be entirely ignored by dealers or the general public; and what they thought were rather poor pots were frequently the first to be sold after a kiln firing. This suggests a lack of fit between potters' technical evaluation, and buyers' appreciation and commodity exchange evaluation, of their work.

One potter even contended that ten people would give ten different opinions of any one pot; in ranking ten pots in order of merit, they would give ten very different rankings.[1] The general opinion of both potters and dealers, then, was that there had to be, and was, individual interpretation in people's decisions as to what was and was not 'beautiful'. Many thought, as a result, that Yanagi's concept of direct perception was an ideal which only an enlightened few, such as Yanagi himself, Hamada, or Leach, could attain. For everyone else the appreciation of beauty would always be subjective, and potters remarked with some embarrassment that even the critics were not agreed about what made good pottery and what did not. They recalled that one autumn, Yanagi's son, Munemichi, had come down to Onta and personally picked out a couple of dozen pots which he felt were good enough to show at the Folk Craft Museum's annual exhibition. When the pots were judged by a panel of critics in Tokyo, all but one were rejected.

Potters also argued that if there was a 'standard' of beauty that could be shared by anyone using direct perception, everyone would, in theory, buy the same pots.

This, in fact, did not happen. They, and their buyers, were therefore convinced that direct perception could only provide a personal standard of beauty and that the appreciation of beauty depended entirely on the individual.[2]

Although Sarayama potters and dealers all talked about the concept of *mingei* and *chokkan*, they did not pretend to understand many other aspects of Yanagi's folk craft theory. Yanagi's argument that there was a close inverse connection between financial reward and quality – that the more interested craftsmen were in making money, the more their work deteriorated – was accepted by all potters in Sarayama regardless of their own particular economic level within the community. Thus the heads of Yamani and Yamako, who had both made a lot of money out of the *mingei* boom, agreed with Yanagi's idea. After all, they said, you have only to look at the quality of work in Koishiwara, where some potters were earning ten times as much as themselves, to realize that too much money leads to poor work. Other potters, such as the heads of Yamaichi and Yamasai, also agreed with Yanagi's inverse equation between profit and quality. But, instead of citing Koishiwara potters as examples, they told me to look at the pots produced by households like Yamani and Yamako to see what Yanagi meant.

Many, but not all, dealers agreed with the idea that craftsmen's work deteriorated the more interested they became in financial profit. There was a general feeling that newfound wealth did adversely affect the quality of potters' work, but that this deterioration was not a necessary consequence of financial success.

It is true that most outsiders regarded the whole community as having struck gold, but they failed to distinguish at what point precisely avarice took over to the detriment of the quality of one's work. Mizuo Hiroshi (1971:62), for example, accepted a certain amount of economic improvement, but not too much. Potters themselves were aware of the problem in distinguishing between necessity and luxury. Both Iriichi and Kaneichi remarked on the differences between rural and urban life-styles; in the country, they said, people had to spend a considerable amount of 'waste money' because of the network of personal relations (*tsukiai*) in which they were involved Thus, the subsistence level for a rural household had to be much higher than that for an urban one. This point was either not understood or not accepted by leaders of the *Mingei* movement. 'Just because money has come into our pockets, they say that our work has grown worse', moaned Yamako in exasperation. A remarkable comment was made to the head of Yamaichi by the former director of the Folk Craft Association, Tanaka Toyotarō: 'you Onta potters ought to start listening occasionally to what we tell you. After all, it is thanks to Yanagi's idea of *mingei* that you've got rich at all'.

Another of Yanagi's theoretical premises was that beauty derived from cooperation. None of the dealers expressed any clear opinion about this idea, although one of them in Tokyo thought that it may have been true of *mingei* in the past. About half of the potters in Sarayama accepted a connection between beauty and cooperation, but hedged their bets by adding that, though it may have been true of Onta pottery, they did not regard the idea as universally valid. Thus, potteries could produce good work even though cooperation may have broken down; conversely, a potter who had always been working on his own could still make beautiful pots. Potters were very much aware that their work was praised because they had in the past cooperated with one another, and they were therefore fairly keen on maintaining a 'united front' toward the outside world. But, as Iriichi pointed out, cooperation never worked out as well as one would have liked; in some respects, as I have shown, Sarayama's 'solidarity' was just for show.

Yanagi's argument that the environment in which the craftsman lived and worked was vital to the quality of folk crafts, and that beauty depended largely on the craftsman's 'closeness to nature', was also only partly accepted by potters. Many of them felt that the environment in which they lived did affect their work without their realizing it, but they did not always agree that their work was good *because* they relied on natural materials and on natural methods of production. After all, people who fired their wares in gas kilns or prepared their clay with pug mills could still make good pots.

Potters were aware that the word 'nature' was not easy to interpret, and they were not agreed that they could distinguish between the 'natural' and 'unnatural' elements of a finished pot. For example, when asked if they knew when a pot had been thrown on a kick-wheel ('natural') and when one had been made on an electric wheel ('unnatural'), they said they could not tell the difference. Similarly, very few potters thought that they could invariably distinguish between wood-fired and gas- or oil-fired pots. There was little agreement that they could distinguish between pots that had been glazed with natural materials and those that had been chemically glazed. It may be, therefore, that potters supported the equation between nature and beauty in folk crafts precisely because Sarayama was virtually the only pottery kiln in Japan still relying almost totally on 'nature' in its production.

Dealers were more adamant in their opinion of the aesthetic connection between nature and beauty. All but one were convinced that craftsmen made better work if they used natural materials. Some even said that Onta pottery would really go to the dogs if potters started using mechanical methods of preparing clay and gas- or oil-fired kilns. There was a close association in almost every dealer's mind between people's spiritual attitude, the nature of the environment in which they lived, and the quality of the work they produced. In particular, they envisaged craftsmen as living in secluded, beautiful surroundings undisturbed by the bustle and noise of urban life – a point to which I shall return.

Every potter believed that handicrafts expressed the craftsman's character and that they were therefore imbued with what was called 'heart' (*kokoro*). In this respect, potters agreed with dealers in believing that craftsmen's environment, as well as their tools, materials and methods, all affected the quality of their wares. Potters did not, however, think that beauty was born solely from the craftsman's 'heart'. They added – and this point echoes their criticism of direct perception – that what they saw in one of their pots and what a critic or buyer saw in the same pot were very different.

Although some of them were becoming well known as individuals because of their success in exhibitions, all potters in Sarayama stressed that they were craftsmen and not artists. They professed not to know anything about the relation between beauty and individualism, but disliked any word that smacked of 'art' being used of their work. They made 'pottery' (*yakimono*), not 'ceramics' (*tōki*), and they objected to people in the *Mingei* movement referring to their work as a kind of 'ceramic art' (*tōgei*). Art was for city, not for country, people.

They were also unhappy about Yanagi's idea that craftsmen should remain uncultivated and unlearned. They argued that, in view of the amount of time critics had spent telling them how they should be making pottery, it was impossible for them to throw pots 'unconsciously' any more. Potters said that they had learned to see their pots differently (i.e. they had been 'educated') and

Plate 65 Lidded pickled onion jar with *tobiganna* chattering and *uchikake* overglaze decoration

were now more conscious of their work; it was not surprising that people said it had got worse.

Aesthetic Appraisal and Pottery Production

Although Yanagi built his theory around the concept of *mingei*, which included a number of artefacts, from ('mud' or pastel paintings) through joinery to farmers' straw raincapes (*mino*), he was particularly interested in pottery. All the early leaders of the *Mingei* movement were potters and it would be fair to say that it is potters who have benefitted most from the *mingei* boom.

Yanagi has written one extended essay about what makes folk art pottery beautiful, and in it adopted a characteristically spiritual approach. Admitting that he knew little about either the historical or the technical aspects of Japanese pottery, Yanagi wrote of his love for the craft: 'I live with my heart steeped in its beauty, day and night. By looking at pots I am able to forget my self, to go beyond my self . . . For me, the realization of belief is also to be found in pottery' (Yanagi 1955b:372). He then argued that beauty could not exist without love. Beauty was born of the heart, therefore, and if a pot was 'unlovable', either it must have been made by a 'cold hand', or its appreciator had a 'cold eye'. Great works were produced when a craft potter's heart was filled with love. Yanagi visualized the potter alone at the wheel, intent upon his work, with no thought in his mind; he lived in the pot and the pot lived in him. They were at one; love flowed between them and beauty was born.

From this it may be seen once again that Yanagi was concerned not with pottery in itself but with how pottery was made. Although in evaluating individual pots he isolated such qualities as form, clay, colour, line, and taste, it was not the properties of these qualities so much as the way in which they affected the potter that Yanagi thought was important. For instance, clay was seen to be the 'flesh and bones' of a pot. But the quality of the clay was linked to the potter's spiritual attitude: for example, Japanese potters' choice of a softer clay than that found in Chinese porcelain revealed the 'soft' and 'pliant' nature of the Japanese people (1955b:342).

Like many art critics and anthropologists (e.g. Bell 1913; Boas 1955) throughout the world, for whom 'in one way or another, assessments of aesthetic excellence are concerned with the internal congruence of forms' (Maquet 1986:142), Yanagi regarded form (*katachi*) as the fundamental element determining beauty. Yet he thought that form was created by the 'heart' rather than by the hands. It was not technical accomplishment so much as a spiritual purity that gave rise to beauty. The form of man was to be found in the form of pottery (Yanagi 1955b:334–341) – a strange denial of the technical evaluation of pots so often practised by potters.

Form would appear to be the primary appreciative criterion by which the quality of pottery has been judged at the annual autumn exhibition held at the Japan Folk Craft Museum (Tanaka 1966:10). Since *mingei* is supposed to consist of functional objects for everyday use, it is not surprising to find that form – as part of use value – is emphasized by leaders of the movement. Good form results in good, functional pottery, and functional pottery is beautiful. The question is: to what extent do potters consider form when they make their pots? Do they make pots that are functional but not beautiful in form, or beautiful but not functional? Do dealers, and their customers in turn, purchase pottery because of its form? Or are they more concerned with other qualities such as colour and design? These questions need answers because ultimately they will reveal whether there is an aesthetic standard in the appreciation of *mingei*.

Function is often closely tied to form in crafts of any kind. This point has been made by art critics and anthropologists alike (e.g. Keesing 1958:350; Read 1936:126). However, while a basic form may be functional, non-functional embellishments may be added as craftsmen seek to make their work attractive to buyers. In the case of a pot, there may or may not be a foot-rim, and any foot-rim may be higher or lower, wider or narrower, according to potters' taste. They may choose to pull out the lip of a bowl or a plate to give variety to the curved body, or they may trim the belly of a bowl square rather than leave it rounded.

Plate 66 Old water jar with *nagashi* slip trailing

189

The exigencies of function do not, however, necessarily produce what a potter – from a technical angle – sees as a 'good' shape, so that folk craft leaders are indirectly criticized for relying on function as a basis for beauty. For example, when potters make a lidded jar, they say that if they are to take the pot's functional purpose into account, they should keep the mouth of the pot wide; the person using the pot can then easily put a hand in to get at its contents. But a broad mouth upsets the balance of the form below, so that in fact the mouth is kept fairly narrow. Similarly, an umbrella stand may look good if it is slender in form, but once it is filled with umbrellas, this shape becomes unstable, and so the pot needs to be swollen at the belly.

In other respects, potters are more faithful to the exigencies of function than their critics might suspect. For example, storage jars have shallow lids which merely cover the mouths of the pots; teapots have deeper lids to allow the pot to be tilted. A bottle-shaped *sake* pourer (*tokkuri*) should be made as light as possible, so that its user can judge how much wine is left. Such functional aspects of pottery do not appear in the outer form.

While form may be constrained by use, materials and methods of production also affect a pot's form (cf. Graburn 1976:54). Here I shall deal with the nature of the clay, glazing techniques, and methods of kiln loading as they affect Onta pottery.

One fundamental rule underlies the relation between form and function. This concerns the nature of the materials used in a craft, and is often ignored by Japanese folk art connoisseurs. The nature of Onta clay dictates to some extent the final form of its pottery, a form which cannot always be consistent with function. For example, to be functional, pickle jars should be made as cylinders. The pickles will then sink to the bottom of the pot, and they can be easily weighted down. However, Onta clay does not permit this shape for larger pots, for the clay tends to crack at the base. Consequently, most pickle jars must have a narrow base which, while it often gives the pot a streamlined shape does not guarantee stability in use. Similarly, plates more than fifteen centimetres in diameter cannot be made flat, but have to be curved, so that functionally they become dishes rather than plates.

Another way in which the nature of the clay affects potters' decisions concerning the shapes of their pots can be seen in the addition of foot-rims. According to buyers, *guinomi sake* cups and coffee cups should not have foot-rims at all. Potters prefer to give these pots foot rims, however, because small pots like these can easily become mis-shapen during firing.[3]

Their decisions about whether to give pots a foot-rim or not is often closely connected with their techniques of glazing. Sarayama clay does not permit a pot's total immersion in a glaze, and potters do not usually take the trouble to wax-resist those parts of a pot which they do not want glazed, since they find it too time-consuming to do so. As a result, it is much easier to glaze smaller pots if they have foot-rims. Larger pots are usually not trimmed at all, but some potters leave a ridge at the base of their flower vases. These pots can then be easily held upside down in the fingers of one hand, and glazing is much simpler.

Methods of kiln loading, too, result in various constraints on the form of pottery because potters try to make as economic use of kiln space as possible. The way in which pots are loaded into the kiln also affects the potter's overall decision about what shapes to make and fire. For example, although a potter might like making a rounded, jar-shaped flower vase, this shape can waste a lot of kiln space unless it is somehow counterbalanced by a narrow-necked vase with a fully curved body.

The best way to make maximum use of kiln space is by stacking pots on or in one another. The nature of the clay used in Sarayama permits piling in large quantities, but pots must be given higher footrims to ensure that they will not stick to one another if they become slightly mis-shapen – as they often do – during firing. The custom of stacking in quantity (made possible by the adoption of kiln shelving) has led to potters making their rice bowls and kneading bowls with straight rather than curved sides. They realize that, by doing this, they are making their pots 'colder' to look at and less suitable for the functions they serve. Ideally, both rice and kneading bowls should be slightly curved to make them easier to use.

Larger pots have always been stacked inside one another in a 'Chinese box' or 'Russian doll' type of kiln loading. In the old days, when the large pickling jars, water crocks, and pouring vessels were used by shops and farmhouses alike, potters were expected to adhere strictly to certain measurements. This meant that

Plate 67 Kiln loading technique with complementarily-shaped flower vases

most of the larger wares had to be of a fairly elongated shape if they were to be stacked inside one another as well as be functional. More recently, however, with the growth in urban demand for table ware, large pots have come to be made for decorative purposes only. Potters have stopped making their larger wares to measurement, and they strive to create new forms that 'look better' (cf. Lathrap 1976:202). These decorative forms are no longer functional and can be extremely unstable when given excessively broad shoulders.

Considerations of kiln space also affect potters' decisions about what glazes to apply to what pots, for certain colours only come out in certain parts of a kiln chamber. The glazes used in Onta pottery are composed of four or five materials: feldspar, wood ash, straw ash, iron oxide, and in some cases copper. Some of these materials are more heat resistant than others. A glaze which contains a higher percentage of materials that are more resistant to heat (e.g. green or white) has, therefore, to be fired at a higher temperature than glazes composed of materials with lower heat resistance (brown or yellow).

The nature of the climbing kiln is such that, at any given time, the temperature inside a chamber during firing will vary along three axes: from side to centre, from front to back, and from top to bottom. Consequently, potters must load their kilns in such a way that they can, at least partly, control the melting point of the various glazes during firing. None of the kilns is quite the same as another, and potters say that each kiln has its 'characteristic' so far as glaze colouring is

Plate 68 'Russian doll' style of kiln loading

concerned. Some kilns with humidity produce really good colours; others do not. The cooperative kiln is said to be best for brown and transparent glazes; Yamako's produces a good green; Yamani's, green and black; Yamaichi's kiln is remarked for its brown, green, and white glazes, while Kaneichi's is good for all colours except green.

Thus, to cite one example, when loading one of the chambers of his kiln, the head of Yamaichi places pots glazed with green and black at the very front of the shelves, copper and transparent over white slip at the back of the front shelves, light green and brown at the front of the back shelves, and brown at the very back of the chamber. On the vertical axis, he cannot place green-glazed pots at the bottom of the chamber, because the flames there during firing are extremely 'fierce' (*hageshii*), and the temperature fluctuates to such an extent that if the front of a pot did come out green, the back would remain a greyish black where the copper had failed to melt.

The glaze order outlined here differs from chamber to chamber within a kiln. In one chamber, for example, brown comes out very nicely near the edges, as well as along the rear of the back shelves. Yamaichi has learned from experience that white and green do not come out at all well in the bottom chamber of its kiln, but will do so best in the second and fourth chambers respectively. Similarly, potters sharing the cooperative kiln know that green does not come out at all well in the bottom four chambers, but it does in the top four, while black works in precisely the opposite way.

All of this may sound too technical for a social anthropological study. But these details of the problems faced by potters in firing their kilns are pertinent because buyers consistently order all sorts of different colour combinations. Potters may be asked to fire pots glazed with colours that, given the limitations of the climbing kiln, cannot be combined. Or they may be asked to fire an impossibly large quantity of one or two colours only. They point out that technically they cannot meet such requests, but buyers tend to think that this is another lame excuse and that the potters are being high-handed now that there is so much demand for their work. Not surprisingly, relations between the two groups are not improved by such misunderstandings.

Aesthetic Appraisal and Pottery Marketing

One major source of conflict between Onta potters and leaders of the *Mingei* movement stems from their different viewpoints in appraising pottery. While connoisseurs are concerned with the appreciation of beauty ('a practical mastery which . . . cannot be transmitted solely by precept or prescription' [Bourdieu 1984:66]), potters are trying to make a living from their work. Critics look at the potter's wheel and the *art* of his kiln (*yōgei*) (Yanagi 1955b:365); potters look to their kilns for *economic* survival. Even if potters agree with the idea that their work deteriorates if they are too interested in profit, there comes a time when they themselves have to put economic interests before personal aesthetic preferences. However *mingei* connoisseurs may evaluate their work, potters must consider market demand and the interests of their buyers.

When Yanagi first discovered Sarayama, the potters made a selection of wares that were used for the most part in farmhouses round about. These wares consisted mainly of large pickle jars, water crocks, containers for homemade wines and soy sauce. They also made bottles in which *sake* was sold from shops in Hita, and large, elongated lavatory bowls. Some smaller wares were made – notably teapots like the one that first attracted Yanagi's attention in Kurume – but the emphasis was on big pots.

Since the Pacific War and Japan's rapid economic development in the 1950s and 60s, there has been a radical change in market demand. The development of plastics, for example, put an end to the use of really big pots, while rapid urbanization led to consumer demand for much smaller items that could be used in the modern, often westernized, home. Onta potters found that they had to adapt to the new, postwar demand if they were to survive; *mingei* connoisseurs, on the other hand, have been primarily interested in the wares that potters produced to meet pre-war demand.

This is revealed by the fact that folk craft leaders do not regard many of the pots now being made in Sarayama as truly traditional Onta wares, and they urge potters not to make flower vases, tea bowls, coffee cups, and so on, because they are not traditional. Potters are inclined to agree with their critics on this point, but they add that it is precisely these items that sell well. They thus have little alternative but to continue making such pots. They admit, however, to not knowing what sort of shapes to make. In the past, they relied on dealers to help them, and they also copied photographs of pots from books and magazines (cf. N. Williams 1976:271). Some buyers have on occasion sent potters sketches of shapes that they want made, but potters point out that dealers have often tried to order shapes that cannot possibly be made with Onta clay.

To a certain extent, potters put personal preferences first when they decide on what shapes to throw. For example, although told that a tea bowl should not have a high foot-rim but should 'sit low', they feel that such a shape is entirely unsuitable to the nature of the clay that they use. Hence they continue to give their bowls higher foot-rims than tea 'experts' demand.

Over the past twenty years or so, potters have been helped both by local government officials and by folk craft leaders in the design of their pots. The Hita Crafts Institute (Hita Shikenjo) drew some flower vase designs for potters soon after Leach had visited the community (Leach himself taught them the medieval English pitcher shape); some of these were later adapted by a member of the Folk Craft Museum. Potters all feel that the shapes they were asked to make were pretty odd and suggest that the schools of flower arrangement must be in a bad way to be advocating such poor vase forms. Instead, they make vases that are fairly straight, tall, and thin in order to facilitate maximum use of kiln space, or rounded with a narrow mouth, so that misshaping is not noticeable.

As noted earlier, almost all the demand for *mingei* pottery comes from urban

Plate 69 Small lidded pickle jar for urban use

areas. This means that potters not only have to make completely new types of pots, but have to make pots that are specifically for town rather than for country use. For example, there is now an increasing demand for *guinomi sake* cups instead of the much smaller *sakazuki*, although both types have been made in Japan for a long time. People living in urban areas tend to drink *sake* either on their own or from just one cup when in the company of others; they find a small cup troublesome to fill time and again. In the country, however, nobody drinks *sake* on his own, but almost invariably participates in an exchange of cups with friends and neighbours. For this purpose, the smaller *sakazuki* is deemed far more suitable, since the larger *guinomi*, favoured by townspeople, only hastens alcoholic incoherence and spoils the party.

Potters also find it hard to keep up with the urban demand for coffee cups. They find it too time-consuming to make and attach handles individually to each cup. In the late 60s, Miyake Chūichi, leader of the Folk Craft Society, arranged for handle moulds to be made for Onta potters, who have for the most part used them ever since, fixing them near the rims of the coffee cups. Over the years, the demand has been for increasingly smaller cups, and potters now attach handles to the rims. When the cups are fired, however, they become misshapen.

Obviously, potters could pull their own handles or order new, smaller moulds. The fact that most of them do neither shows that at the moment they are more concerned with economics than with aesthetics as such. Similarly, a potter whose

195

household does not have a large labour force may refrain from making teapots at all because it takes too much time to make and apply the parts (spout and handle grip). In the 70s, demand for Onta pottery allowed the potters considerable choice of what to make and what not to make. It was such economic freedom that critics have resented.

But if potters must make a lot of new shapes that are patently not traditional, they have also been extremely clever at adapting old shapes to new purposes. The pre-war water crocks, for example, have been slimmed down slightly into umbrella stands; the big ash-burning *hibachi* hand-warmers have been shrunk into ashtrays; and small pickled-plum jars have had spout and handle added to convert into *kyūusu* teapots.[4]

Both dealers and private individuals ask potters to make shapes that may fail to meet their personal or *mingei* aesthetic demands. Sometimes potters can refuse to make certain shapes with the excuse that they do not suit the nature of Sarayama's clay (a ploy used by Aborigine carvers in Arnhem Land [cf. N. Williams 1976:283]). At other times, potters are not really interested in the form of a pot, because, as the dealers say, it is not form so much as the colour combinations brought out in pattern and glaze designs, which give a pot its market appeal.

Of 24 dealers retailing pottery in northern Kyushu and Tokyo, sixteen said that they placed primary emphasis on glaze colouring and on pattern or design when choosing pottery. Only six said that they chose pottery because of its form. The remaining two men (both with close ties to the Folk Craft Museum) said that

Plate 70 Slipped white teapot with *uchikake* splashed green overglaze

196

they use 'direct perception' to select good pots. Of those dealers who placed primary emphasis on form, three were affiliated to one or the other of the two folk craft associations. One of these dealers, who has been buying Onta pottery for more than 30 years, argued that there was no standard by which colour could be judged, but that there was so with form. Another man who expressed a preference for form over colour in choosing pots added that this was no more than personal preference; the general public was, in his opinion, more likely to buy pottery because of its colour.

During fieldwork, I asked quite a lot of visitors to Sarayama what had made them buy the prticular pots they had bought. If no immediate answer was forthcoming, I asked whether their purchases were easy to use, of pleasing design, nicely glazed, or well shaped. Of the 235 people interviewed, 160 answered that they were primarily influenced by colour or pattern; only 32 cited form as their criterion of choice.[5] Potters are, naturally, aware of this market demand for good glaze colouring and intriguing patterns, and they decorate almost all their pots with *hakeme* brush strokes, *tobiganna* chattering, or *uchikake* and *nagashi* methods of glaze application, which have all now come to form Onta pottery's hallmark of recognition.

Primarily because they realized that they could apply thicker glazes and hence improve colours, potters started bisque firing in the 1960s. In the past, all pots were 'raw' glazed, but now many of the smaller pots, and some of the larger ones as well, are fired to a low temperature before glazing. In theory, the bisque firing is done in order to minimize losses during the main firing, and it is true that customers tend to complain if a pot is mis-shapen or in some way blemished by firing. In practice, however, potters know that they can apply a greater number of, or thicker, glazes to a bisque-fired surface than to an unfired one. They are thus able to provide a range of colour combinations that help satisfy market demand.

Good glaze colouring is a result of the careful preparation of raw materials and the way in which the kiln is fired. Potters admitted that they tend to ignore personal aesthetic preferences in deciding what glazes to apply to what forms. Yamasan, for example, dislikes yellow, but argued that it was the only glaze that comes out well at the back of its kiln chambers; the head of Iriichi at one stage glazed a lot of his pots black because of the poor quality of wood ash in his transparent glaze. He said then that he would prefer to glaze his slipped pots with the transparent rather than the black glaze, which he did not see as being part of Onta's 'tradition'.

Retail Pricing and the Concept of *Mingei*

Earlier I noted that Onta pottery is sold all over Japan, but that the majority of pots are bought by dealers retailing in and around the neighbouring town of Hita. Their customers are primarily tourists who buy Onta pots as gifts for friends and relations back home. It will be remembered that Yanagi was convinced that 'true' folk crafts should be made in large quantities and sold cheaply. One of the reasons Onta pottery used to be appreciated and bought by local farmers was its extreme cheapness. However, over the years, prices have increased considerably. In 1971 Miyake Chūichi, director of the Folk Craft Society, warned that if prices were to be raised any further, Onta pottery would be in danger of becoming an art craft (*bijutsu kōgeihin*), rather than simply a folk craft (*mingei*). Since then, wholesale prices have gone up more than half a dozen times. Is Miyake's criticism justified and, if so, on what grounds?

Potters in Sarayama do not make any attempt to cost their work by the weight of clay used, kiln performance, fuel prices, or labour input (cf. Cardew 1971:232–233). Their system of wholesale pricing is therefore 'natural' rather than 'just', and there is little rationalization in the fixing of prices. Dealers complain that some pots – coffee cups, for instance – are much too expensive, and that it is therefore almost impossible to retail them at anything more than a marginal return. In private, they also admit that some pots are comparatively cheap wholesale; on these they can make excellent profits.

Even though the price of Onta pottery went up considerably during the 60s and 70s, and even though the potters were earning vastly increased incomes, it is the dealers' retailing – rather than potters' wholesaling – practices that led to Onta pottery's ceasing to be cheaply priced folk crafts. The fact that Onta pots are bought by tourists as gifts undoubtedly helps the dealers set high retail prices; people would think nothing of paying ¥5,000 for a really nice tea bowl if it were boxed and wrapped – at a time when, according to a representative of an Oita department store, the average expenditure on gift pottery was about ¥10,000 per person.

Other factors have influenced dealers' decisions to retail Onta pottery at very high prices. In the first place, production in Sarayama is limited. Only about 45–50 kiln firings take place every year and these yield pots worth (in 1980) about ¥90 million. In Koishiwara, where apprentices are employed, potters will fire their climbing kilns six times a year and their gas kilns between four and six times a month. Dealers are ensured of regular supplies and can therefore afford to retail at reasonably low prices, although they may well employ a different marketing strategy. Onta potters, however, have not been able to produce enough pottery to meet demand, because they have not modernized production methods. There are too many dealers trying to buy too little pottery, and the only way the potters can survive financially is by retailing at very high prices or by branching out into other lines of business.

Secondly, there is a demand not just for folk crafts but for *handmade* folk crafts. It is because potters in Sarayama do not use up-to-date machinery, and because they stick to methods of production that are seen to be old-fashioned and traditional, that people want to buy Onta pots. They are also prepared to pay a lot extra because the pots are hand, and not machine, made.

Thirdly, dealers know that their customers have individual taste and that direct perception does not lead to a standard of beauty. They can therefore take advantage of their different tastes, knowing full well that even if twenty, 50 or 100 people think that a pot is too expensive, someone will eventually like it so much that s/he will pay the sum demanded. The fact that many of the dealers trade in Onta pottery as a sideline allows them to pursue a strategy of selling small amounts of pottery at fairly high prices. This in itself helps raise Onta pottery from the category of 'folk craft' to a higher 'art' level.

One way in which dealers will take advantage of individual taste is by not putting any price at all on some pots. Customers are left to name their own prices, and these may often exceed the maximum a dealer would have thought acceptable. One shop owner told me that a customer had once bought a tea bowl for ¥30,000, when she would never have charged more than ¥20,000; another said that he had sold a lidded vase for ¥50,000 when the going price was between ¥30,000 and ¥40,000.[6]

Finally, retailers can and do take advantage of the *social* value of pottery. Although potters in Sarayama do not rationally calculate ex-kiln prices on the basis of time, labour, and material costs, they tend to price pots according to size and to ignore their purpose. Dealers do not overlook the way in which a pot is used in the home, and to set their retail prices accordingly. For example, an umbrella stand is more expensive ex-kiln than a plate 40 centimetres in diameter – mainly because it uses more clay and takes up more kiln space. The dealer can, however, sell the plate at a much higher retail price, since it will be 'used' as a decorative piece, probably placed on a stand in the *tokonoma*, the sacred place of any Japanese household. The umbrella stand, on the other hand, will be filled with umbrellas, golf clubs, and children's toy rifles and placed 'down below' in the hallway (*genkan*) of the house. Similarly, flower vases can be retailed at fairly high prices, not only because they will be placed in the *tokonoma* but also because they are an essential part of the aesthetic theory of flower arrangement (*ikebana*), so popular in Japan. Once pots come to be used for artistic rather than everyday purposes, they can be sold at very high prices (for example, ¥6 million for a tea bowl by the former 'national treasure', Arakawa Toyozō). Bowls used in the tea ceremony are a good example of the way in which dealers take advantage of a popularly practised 'art' form. Potters sell their bowls for ¥1,000; they think this is too high a price for the amount of work involved and clay used in making a tea bowl; they also know that they have no idea about how a tea bowl ought to be made and copy shapes from photographs in books. However, when visitors come up to Sarayama, they often refuse to buy tea bowls because they are too *cheap*. Dealers in Hita and other towns in Kyushu retail tea bowls at from five to 100 times their wholesale price.

The problem here is that potters are primarily concerned with their image as producers of *mingei* pottery. If they sell tea bowls at too high a price, in market terms their work will cease to be folk craft, and there is a danger that they themselves will be seen not just as craft potters but as artist craftsmen. Dealers, however, are interested, not in Onta pottery as *mingei*, but in the tea ceremony as an 'art' form and the fact that a lot of people believe that the more they pay for a pot, the better it must be 'artistically'. To their credit perhaps, those dealers close to the *Mingei* movement – Takumi in Tokyo, for example – have never bought pottery that can be used in such popular 'arty' pastimes as flower arrangement and the tea ceremony. They have, instead, fallen in line with Yanagi's argument that 'men of tea' can ruin folk crafts (cf. Yanagi 1961:4).[7]

Conclusion

In this chapter I have discussed some of the practical aspects of folk art theory, and have outlined what both potters and pottery dealers think about Yanagi's concept of *mingei*. My main aim has been to find out whether there exists an aesthetic standard accepted by, and common to, potters, dealers, the general public, and leaders of the *Mingei* movement of the kind argued for by Arthur Danto, for example, when he writes: 'it seems clear that some members of the language community one may refer to as the artworld do not merely tend to share the values that words express, but would seldom disagree among themselves as to whether a given term applies to a given work' (Danto 1981:155). In showing how different people attribute different values to *mingei* pottery, depending on whether they are potters, dealers or folk craft connoisseurs, this chapter has undermined both the philosophical and anthropological (cf. Maquet 1986:138) belief that beauty is not only in the eye of the beholder, but inherent in the object. It also supports Arnold Hauser's contention (1982:473) that there is no single permissable and acceptable interpretation of any work of art; rather, there are numerous interpretations, each one of which hints at – and, of course, contributes to – one or another of an art work's possible meanings. This is as true of anthropologists' as it is of art critics' apparently detached pronouncements.

Three main points may be made on the basis of the material presented here: one is concerned with the existence of different types of value discussed in Chapters 7 and 8; a second concerns the concept of 'direct perception'; and the last the problem of whether Onta pottery is an art or a craft form. Let me deal with each of these in turn.

First, at the end of my discussion of the *mingei* boom and the consequent economic development of Onta potter households, I suggested that a number of different values are brought to bear on works of art generally and that these values are always in a process of negotiation among all those participating in an art world – artists, critics, collectors, dealers, auctioneers, media representatives, and so on. Those values that I focused on then were called *use, appreciative, commodity exchange*, and *symbolic exchange values*, but I also mentioned two others – technical and social values – to which I promised to return at a later stage in the book. Although they have been introduced during the course of an earlier chapter, it is now time to discuss this system of values in greater detail.

Technical values derive from the processes of production of every art work – in this case, from potters' personal knowledge and understanding of the work that they do. For example, during the course of these pages, it has become clear that potters disagree with critics about the relation between form and function because of their own experience in making pots – an experience which is not shared or understood by folk craft connoisseurs, who tend to be more concerned with the appreciative values of a particular pot. Thus, potters will talk about the 'plasticity' of the clay that they use and the effect this has on pottery forms, and will put forward technical arguments about why particular pots have particular forms (a footrim or base ridge, for example, to assist in the process of glazing), or a particular combination of glazes (dependent on their location in the kiln). Such technical values are extremely important to our understanding of aesthetics since they are not always part of an art world's conventions. That they are by no means the *only* values can be seen from our discussion of the way in which critics and connoisseurs generally give preference to a set of appreciative, and dealers to commodity exchange, values in their appraisal of Onta, and other folk craft, pottery.

One other general category of evaluation, not yet discussed, that comes into play in the definition of what makes 'good' or 'beautiful' *mingei* (and, indeed, of art in general) are *social values*. Social values derive from a number of different factors. For example, a potter's work can be held up for public esteem because the potter concerned happens to be close to a particular critic or collector. Thus both Hamada Shōji and Bernard Leach became extremely well-known in Japan, not just because they made good pots, but because they happened to be close to two other potters who themselves became famous – Tomimoto Kenkichi and Kawai Kanjirō – as well as to Yanagi Sōetsu himself, who earned *his* reputation in part from his affiliation to leading writers of the Shirakaba group. There is, then, a rubbing-off effect whereby potters, and artists in general, become well-known for the company they keep (and the masters to whom they have been apprenticed), while their art works increase in value because of their makers' personalities.[8]

But social values, as we have seen in this chapter, can also stem from other factors. For example, the social use to which a particular pot may be put – whether as an umbrella stand in a hallway, or decorative plate in a *tokonoma* sacred alcove – also affects its symbolic exchange value. Sometimes, it is careful manipulation of such potential social and symbolic exchange values – as when an ordinary Korean peasant rice bowl is transformed into a tea bowl to be used by an elite *samurai* lord in Japan – that raises an object socially from mere artifact to art. In many ways, the whole philosophy of *mingei* as espoused by Yanagi Sōetsu stems from a set of premises which – in their focus on hand rather than automated work, and on natural rather than artificial materials – totally overturns currently accepted social values stemming from the practices of industrial capitalism. At the same time, as suggested at the end of Chapter 7, social values are closely intertwined with use, technical, appreciative, commodity exchange, and symbolic exchange values, all of which together interact and are actively manipulated and negotiated by those participating in the *mingei* art world, as well as in other art worlds which thereby set themselves apart from one another and form exclusive, 'unique' social groups formed round similarly 'unique' art works.

And now let us move on to my second point. Although Yanagi argued that in theory 'direct perception' gave rise to a universal standard of beauty (a vision shared by the anthropologist, Jacques Maquet [1986]), we have seen that in practice neither potters nor dealers were prepared to accept this premise. Although both groups agreed that direct perception was a useful way of appreciating beauty, from their own experience in selling pottery, potters and dealers both felt that different people had different tastes. In their opinion, direct perception could only provide a personal standard of beauty. Although, with Bourdieu (1984), we could probably argue that such a standard was in fact shared by a number of people with the same educational and cultural 'capital' – people who thus formed the narrowly-defined art world of *mingei* – on the basis of evidence cited here, I would agree with Forge (1973:xxi) that the existence of a universal human aesthetic is very much 'a matter of faith'.

This difference in attitude towards 'direct perception' is of interest in that it shows how the aesthetic practice of *mingei* parallels the social practice of the potters' ideal of 'community'. I have argued, in my discussion of the social organization of Sarayama, that ideally the individual is not as important as the primary group to which s/he belongs – that is, to the household or hamlet in Japanese rural society. We have seen, however, that in fact the marketing of pottery has made the household more important than the community, and the individual more important (to outsiders at least) than the household. Individuals do not always put group interests first; they can and do manipulate group ideals to their own personal advantage. Although they are bound to some extent by the social ideals of 'harmony' and 'all together', individuals engage in bitter fights to satisfy their self-will. Thus the social ideal is not matched by social practice – a point which anthropologists of Japan have finally grasped in their general pronouncements on the group organization of Japanese society (cf. Befu 1980; Krauss *et al.* 1984).

I have also pointed out that, according to folk craft theory, the determination and understanding of beauty is neither arbitrary nor subjective. If someone surrenders his self, he can create beauty; if she rids herself of prejudice and uses direct perception, she can appreciate beauty. Beauty is available to all, regardless of rank or education. But potters argue that in practice the appreciation of beauty is always individual, that what is beautiful for one person is not necessarily so for another. Thus the aesthetic ideal is not matched by aesthetic practice either.

This latter argument has been supported by a more detailed discussion of the aesthetic appraisal of Onta pottery. I noted that although leaders of the *Mingei* movement were mainly interested in the form of pottery and the way such pottery was used by the consumer (appreciative and use values), potters in Sarayama were perhaps more concerned with technical considerations (or values) arising from methods of production – in particular, with how the nature of the clay encouraged some forms and discouraged others, and with ways in which glazing and kiln loading also affected their decisions about what forms to throw.[9] We also saw that, although critics may have based their appraisal of Onta pottery on its form, buyers and the general public were primarily interested in glaze colours. This preference for colour over form in the selection of Onta's pots is similar to that expressed by buyers of Shipibo pottery in Peru, who purchase wares that rely on large blobs of contrasting colours for visual effects (Lathrap 1976:204).

Potters do not, of course, disregard either form or function entirely when they make their pots. But they do have to contend with a predominantly urban demand and way of life which, as rural craftsmen, they do not fully understand. Form may thereby be affected. This problem is faced by many folk artists all over the world. Graburn (1969:426), for example, has discussed the way in which Eskimos in Alaska have had to simplify the design and shape of their carvings in response to demands from their North American buyers, who favour objects that are easier to dust! Abramson (1976:256–257) reports on changes in the size and design of Iwam shields in New Guinea when they cease to be used in war and become objects of commerce. Onta potters may not have such problems of hygiene or warfare. They do, however, have to produce for an urban market that increasingly looks upon *mingei* pottery as decorative rather than as purely functional.

The increasing interest of the general public in *mingei* pottery for its decorative rather than its functional aspects brings me to my third point: that Onta pottery, and *mingei* pottery generally, is gradually coming to be seen by the public as a form of decorative *art* – a trend which shows how criticism in general not only trans*lates*, but trans*forms*, an art work (cf. Hauser 1982:472). One indication of this trend may be seen in the extreme concern of customers with the superficial appearance of Onta pottery. In the days when pottery was made to be used, people did not worry if pots were slightly mis-shapen or bloated from firing, so long as they fulfilled their function. Nowadays, precisely because many examples of Onta pottery are no longer used in everyday life but only on special occasions, people complain if pots are not perfect.

However, the main reason for Onta pottery coming to be seen as an art form lies in the fact that potters in Sarayama have for the most part chosen to retain traditional methods of production that are 'close to nature'. This accounts for the massive amount of media attention to *mingei*. On the one hand, the general public wants handmade things because they are novel and comparatively rare; on the other, dealers take advantage of the public's demand for novelty, and of potters' inability to produce in quantity, to retail pottery at comparatively high prices. They are able to do this precisely because of their awareness that all individuals have their own differing tastes, and that someone will therefore eventually pay the prices they demand. Consequently, Onta pottery is no longer bought for daily use by the common people, as Yanagi advocated was necessary for *mingei*. Instead, it has become a luxury item to be used, if at all, on special occasions only. As Beardsley (n.d.:31) noted of Tamba pottery, 'it is hard to escape concluding that Tachikui ware and work from certain other similarly known areas have edged into the elite collector's domain'. High retail prices, together with the use of individual 'tea names' by potters, have led to many people's seeing Onta pottery as an art rather than as folk craft. Other indicators of Onta pottery's increasing aesthetic value include its designation by the Japanese government as an intangible cultural property, the display of select items in museums in Japan and overseas, and its first fakes (cf. Thompson 1979:32).

Potters find themselves in a slight dilemma. Market demand is always changing, and dealers expect potters to introduce new shapes and designs to meet changing tastes and needs. *Mingei* leaders, on the other hand, disapprove of novelty and change, and want potters to throw traditional pots. In other words,

> Craftsmen [are] encouraged to follow traditional modes and to avoid being innovative, and contemporary artists are encouraged to change to find newness. The mechanism of pressure is simple and universal: the stick and the carrot. Innovative craftsmen and conservative artists are punished in material losses and failure to achieve prestige and reputation; conservative craftsmen and innovative artists are rewarded in material gains and reputation.
>
> (Maquet 1986:205)

Folk craft potters are treated in much the same way as Eskimo carvers who have to produce 'authentic', 'identifiably Eskimo' works for their buyers (Graburn 1969:459; 1970:336). Onta potters know that they cannot entirely ignore what folk craft connoisseurs tell them, even though there is currently enormous demand for their work, because it was their critical appraisal of Onta pottery in the first place which led to such demand. Potters have, therefore, followed one or two pieces of advice given them by the Folk Craft Museum: for the most part they have stopped making incense burners and dragon-embossed vases; they have also almost entirely refrained from using the *yuhada* (yellow) glaze to which critics for some unknown reason took a violent dislike. Many of the younger potters also copy old Onta pottery forms from the photograph album which the Folk Craft Museum made and distributed to every pottery household in Sarayama. There is, then, considerable stylistic conservatism in the *mingei* art world.

In view of the fact that critics regard the old Onta pots as best and tell potters not to make non-traditional wares, it is perhaps ironical that the folk craft associations have helped redesign the shapes of the old storage jars and *unsuke* pouring vessels, and have given advice about how to create new forms for pitchers, flower vases, and other pots not originally in the potters' repertoire. Paradoxically, by giving help in decorative designs, folk craft leaders have contributed to the so-called 'degeneration' of the crafts that theoretically they are trying to preserve, in that *mingei* ideals stress that pottery must be used if it is to be really beautiful.

This chapter has merely served to emphasize Arnold Hauser's point (1982:242), therefore, that: 'the evaluation of market conditions and the relationship of artists to . . . their patrons and customers . . . is never completely independent of the economic interests and the social views of the people who have to make the judgment'. So, the relationship between Sarayama's potters and the leaders of the *Mingei* movement is in many ways one continuous set of paradoxes. Onta was discovered by Yanagi Sōetsu in 1931; it was made famous by Bernard Leach's visit to Sarayama in 1954. Onta pottery was the perfect example of *mingei*. Yet, over the years, everything that had made the potters' work so 'beautiful' has been altered by the existence of the *Mingei* movement: pots are no longer cheap, nor purely functional, nor used by local people in their everyday lives; potters are no longer 'unconscious' craftsmen who know nothing of the vice of money. It is sad to relate, but, in a way, *mingei* connoisseurs have been indirectly responsible for almost all the ills that they have come to bemoan.[10] Their only consolation, perhaps, is that this is not the first time such a thing has occurred, as the following conversation between the anthropologist Edmund Leach and Herbert Read highlights:

Plate 71 Spouted vessel with brushed slip and
uchikake splash decoration

205

Read: Any decay in art, any kind of stylistic decadence, to put it more simply, is due to the artist becoming self conscious or, if you like, conscious of elements and styles which are not spontaneous.

Leach: Surely this has the implication that the art critic is the destroyer of contemporary art because he makes the artist conscious of what he is doing.

Read: Yes, I would accept that. The art critic only appears in decadent periods of art.

(Marion Smith 1961:112)[11]

Meanwhile, potters do their best to hold both connoisseurs and buyers at a respectable distance. They cling to the concept of tradition both to please the folk craft leaders and to counteract the market demand for novelty and innovation. Dealers always want something different: a coffee cup with combing instead of *hake* slip decoration; a teacup with green overglaze at the lip instead of the customary transparent glaze; red overglaze on a flower vase; a pitcher half brown or black and half green – the requests are endless. In the days when pots did not sell well, potters had to comply with requests like these. But now that the *mingei* boom has improved their economic conditions, potters can call on the concept of 'tradition' to combat the chaos of market demand and refuse some of the stranger orders, such as those for statuettes of drunken badgers or for double-spouted teapots!

Potters stick to their traditional methods of production and remain acceptably close to nature because their pottery is all the more appreciated by the leaders of the *Mingei* movement. If – like potters in Koishiwara – they were to mechanize techniques, take in apprentices, and increase production, not only would their social organization disintegrate entirely, but Onta pottery would almost certainly lose its good reputation. Yet the longer they remain close to nature, the more highly their work is appreciated. It seems inevitable that potters will in the end be acclaimed as 'artist craftsmen'. And yet, ironically, such acclamation would also lead to a disintegration of the community (as I have hinted is already happening). Whatever potters should decide to do in the future, the nostalgia for a 'community', which so pervaded their conversations during my stay in Sarayama, will probably never be realized.

Chapter Ten

FOLK ART, INDUSTRIALIZATION AND ORIENTALISM

Social and Aesthetic Ideals

This book has concentrated on the relation between ecology and the social organization of a Japanese pottery community, and on the interpretation of that relationship in the context of the Japanese *Mingei* movement. I have shown that the social organization of Sarayama has to some extent depended on certain environmental limitations. The ways in which agricultural crops were grown and local raw materials were prepared for the production of pottery were seen to bring about cooperation among all households in the community. My description of social organization was partly idealized, since it also depended on an image of the past which those living in Sarayama wished to present to the outside world, and in this respect can be said to parallel general interpretations of Japanese society (e.g. Nakane 1970). At the same time, this social ideal closely corresponded to an aesthetic ideal. Yanagi Sōetsu, founder of the Japanese *Mingei* movement, put forward a theory suggesting that the quality of folk crafts derived from 'closeness to nature' and a 'sense of community'. Beauty depended on the natural environment in which the craftsmen lived, and resulted from cooperation among those producing folk crafts.

We have seen that in Sarayama individuals were expected to subordinate their personal interests to those of the household and community to which they belonged. People were expected to live in harmony with others. At the same time, according to *mingei* theory, not only is beauty divorced from all idea of individualism and the individual artist, but there is a standard of beauty which can be appreciated by all people, provided that they make use of 'direct perception' in their judgement of folk crafts. Beauty is seen, moreover, to result from the mutual cooperation of a *mingei* object's creator, admirer, user, and critic (Yanagi 1932). Thus, according to both social and aesthetic ideals, society is a harmonious entity in which individuals should surrender themselves to the ideals of 'community solidarity', on the one hand, and 'beauty', on the other.

However, neither social nor aesthetic ideals have been lived up to in Sarayama. First of all, social organization has been affected by various changes in the community's relation to its natural environment. For example, potters took advantage of improved communications to stop using some local raw materials and devote themselves to full-time production of pottery. They also made use of such technological developments in the ceramic industry as kiln shelving, the adoption of which led to the breakdown of most forms of household cooperation and to the economic individuation of potting households. The increase in potters' wealth made possible by the purchase of kiln shelving and by an increase in market demand for *mingei* pottery brought about a division within Sarayama between potting and non-potting households.

Secondly, the community's social organization has been upset by potters' contacts with the outside world. I argued that *mingei* leaders' interest in Onta pottery not only re-enforced an emerging division between potting and non-potting households in Sarayama, but strengthened the position of younger potters *vis-à-vis* their elders, thereby upsetting the community's age-grade system of gerontocracy. The situation was further complicated by the fact that the aesthetic appreciation of Onta pottery focused on individual potters' talent; and yet the community was an egalitarian group of households which, ideally, could not admit to individual talent if it was to operate as a real 'community'. Thus the community as a whole, and the seniority system by which Sarayama had hitherto been run, lessened in importance as ideals, and individuals were freer to take advantage of opportunities to further their own ends. In this respect, Onta potters and their fellow inhabitants of Sarayama had embarked on those processes of change that are the stuff of ethnography all over the world. As Arnold Hauser has put it:

> The conservatism of rural strata of people is uncommonly resistant, just like their instincts and inclinations. However, if the rural population once comes into contact with forms of life which are easy to come by and apparently more comfortable, then their loyalty to innervated customs, traditions, and mores collapses astonishingly quickly. Nor is there any trace of the romantic nostalgia with which higher cultural strata cling to their lost tradition.

> (Hauser 1982:557)

Just as the collapse of traditional loyalties can upset anthropologists intent on recording 'traditional' cultures, so did changes in Sarayama's social organization affect the critical appraisal of Onta pottery by leaders of the *Mingei* movement. In other words, the failure by potters to meet a *social* ideal became simultaneously a failure to meet an *aesthetic* ideal. In Chapter 1, I pointed out that, in Yanagi's opinion, beauty could be adversely affected if craftsmen relied in production on modern technology rather than on local natural materials; if they put their own interests before those of the community in which they worked; if they became too interested in financial reward and increased production beyond a given point of 'equilibrium'; if prices were not held at a reasonably low level; and if *mingei* became decorative rather than purely functional, and thus folk 'art' rather than folk 'craft'.

We have seen that Onta potters did make one or two technological innovations, and they did stop relying altogether on the use of local natural materials – though not as much as folk art potters elsewhere in Japan. Their newly acquired wealth also prompted them to give priority to individual rather than to community interests. Leaders of the *Mingei* movement interpreted this as meaning that potters were too concerned with financial reward, and argued therefore that Onta pottery had recently deteriorated because of the commercialism surrounding the potters' work. Moreover, because of the demand for folk crafts in general, potters had been able to increase their wholesale, and buyers their retail, prices above what was considered acceptable by *mingei* connoisseurs. As a result, although folk crafts were in theory to be used in people's everyday lives, a lot of Onta pottery had come to be used only for special occasions. Some wares were no longer used at all and served a purely decorative purpose. Strictly speaking, therefore, Onta pottery could not be as 'beautiful' as it once was, because it was no longer purely functional.

Finally, I discussed the perception of 'beauty' itself. Yanagi argued that there was a standard of beauty which could be appreciated by anyone in Japanese society, regardless of his or her rank of education, provided that s/he made use of what he termed 'direct perception'. Fieldwork investigations revealed that this was an ideal which could not be put into practice. Although both potters and dealers thought that direct perception was a useful method of appreciating *mingei*, from their own experience in making and selling Onta pottery they stressed that different people had different tastes. They consequently argued that the use of direct perception could give rise only to a personal, rather than universal, standard of beauty.

Throughout this book, then, I have shown that there is a close parallel between the social ideal of how Sarayama should be organized and the aesthetic ideal of how *mingei* should be made. Any social change necessarily brings with it a corresponding change in aesthetic appraisal. If potters remain close to nature, their work 'improves'; if they fail to cooperate, their work 'deteriorates'. So-called aesthetic *mingei* ideals are in fact no more and no less than prescriptions for the organization of Japanese society. *Mingei* is in this sense 'the autobiography of society' (Mukerjee 1948:57); like all things, it has its 'social life' (Appadurai 1986).

Folk Arts and Society

The argument between potters and *mingei* leaders concerning the standard of beauty that is provided by use of direct perception now leads us to a more general discussion of the relation between folk arts and society, and thus of what James Clifford (1988:222–6) refers to as the 'art-culture system'. After all,

The problem which has to be solved, even if it can hardly ever be solved satisfactorily, consists in answering the question as to how it is that everything connected with art is invested from the outset with a sociological significance and assumes a particular place not only in the art historical process but also in the sociohistorical one.

(Hauser 1982:203)

We have seen that Yanagi and the present leaders of the Japanese *Mingei* movement have taken the view that beauty is absolute and can be objectively perceived. Potters have countered by arguing that beauty is a subjective state of mind which is relative to the individual. Clearly, neither the absolute nor the relative view of beauty is tenable. The former is impossible to prove; the latter is overly subjective. At the same time, aesthetic standards cannot be purely individual for they represent group values instilled in individuals making up a group (Tomars 1940:396) of people to whom I have referred as an 'art world'. The question is not 'what is good *mingei*?', but 'what is *mingei* that is good for whom, accepted by what sort of people, and on the basis of what criteria?' In speculating about some of the answers that might be given to this question, I will adopt a position that is neither 'absolute' nor 'relative' but socially relative, and thus hopefully maintain a kind of 'methodological atheism' towards what Alfred Gell (1992:41) has rightly called 'the religion of art'.

It has been argued that folk arts and crafts tend to emphasize their communality, which distinguishes them from the arts of other local or national communities (Graburn 1976:4; Tomars 1940:55). We have seen earlier that pottery could be an idiom in which community social relations were discussed. The concept of tradition was important to those living in Sarayama in that it served to give Onta pottery its distinctiveness; if Onta pottery was distinctive, then Sarayama as a whole was a special community which maintained its identity precisely because of its production of pottery.

This point has been made for other societies facing the sort of external pressures that have affected Sarayama's social organization (cf. Brody 1976:76; Gill 1976:113). Nelson Graburn (1976:5) has pointed out that what he calls 'tourist' or 'airport' arts externally define an ethnic boundary with the outside world, while internally they help maintain ethnic identity and social structure. For Sarayama's potters themselves, Onta pottery is not tied up with problems of ethnic identity as such, although it has become an idiom by which local group identity is fostered and expressed and by which the community of Sarayama, the minimal section in Japanese rural society's system of interlocking groups (cf. Nakane 1970:94), is defined.

At the same time, as part of the genre of *mingei*, Onta pottery can be seen to serve an 'ethnic' function at a national level. Yanagi and his followers have often emphasized that the concept of *mingei* is uniquely Japanese and they have been concerned that local traditional handicrafts are dying out because of the Japanese people's demand for western products. In Chapter 1, I mentioned the relation between Yanagi's ideals and Confucianism in the pre-war period in Japan. Here we might note that *mingei* first became popular – and thus a 'movement' *per se* – in the 1950s and 60s, when Japan was going through one of its more fervent periods of Americanization, and that its 'boom' period coincided with an overall Japanese nostalgia for tradition and the countryside at the very end of the 60s and early 70s (Ivy 1988). It would seem, therefore, that just as Onta potters make use of the idea of tradition to protect their community from many of the outside influences upsetting their social organization, so have the Japanese as a whole gone back to their traditional arts in order to preserve a national identity in the face of cultural innovations from the west. The fact that the Japanese government now bestows such titles as Intangible Cultural Property, Traditional Craftwork, or Award of Cultural Merit on individual craftsmen or craft communities is an indication of the importance attached by the authorities to the maintenance of a specifically Japanese image, which sets Japan apart from other highly industrialized western nations.

Although, in this instance, the concept of *mingei* has come to be put to parallel social uses both by craftsmen living in a rural community and by their public living in predominantly urban areas, a distinction needs to be made once more between producers' and appreciators' overall views of, and participation in, folk crafts. As we have noted, the concept of a 'folk' art or craft that emerged in the nineteenth century was a means of identifying the arts and crafts of a lower class, which was generally rural and non-literate and followed local traditions. These folk arts were seen to be communal by nature and in direct contrast to the urban, literate, upper-class, fine arts (cf. Tomars 1940:46). So, folk arts or crafts are at first generally appreciated as *art* by people living in the 'outside' world, and not by their producers. The attitudes adopted by each of these groups towards what they both come to term folk art or its equivalent usually differ to a considerable degree – and so affect the overall amalgam of values that I have outlined here as a means of going beyond an anthropology of aesthetics *per se*.

One such difference concerns the nature of the art or craft in question. To the potters in Sarayama, *mingei* was not a folk 'art' but a folk 'craft' (indicating their emphasis on use and technical values). In this respect they came close to adopting the purist view of *mingei* espoused by folk craft leaders. At the same time, the term *mingei* has come to be seen by many members of the general public (who are generally more concerned with appreciative, commodity and symbolic exchange values) as more closely approximating 'art' than mere 'craft', and *mingei* connoisseurs (who tend to be suave manipulators of appreciative, social and symbolic exchange values) are themselves in part responsible for this shift in perception. Various reasons underlie this difference in opinion, and people's notions of what constitutes beauty or art clearly derive from their social environment.[1] As far as *mingei* is concerned, there are clearly certain dichotomies in the life-styles of those who make and those who buy, appreciate and discuss folk crafts. Although none of these dichotomies is entirely independent of the others, they may – I think – be broadly categorized as natural/industrialized, rural/urban, handmade/machine-made, and individual/anonymous. It is with the effect of these dichotomies on people's appreciation of *mingei* (and thus with the construction of appreciative values) that I shall now deal.

We have seen that Onta pottery came to be seen specifically as an art rather than a craft form because potters remained close to nature and did not use modern machinery. In considering the concept of closeness to nature which Yanagi argued was a fundamental source of beauty, it will be remembered that both *mingei* critics and buyers tended to have an image of Onta potters working alone in undisturbed peace, at one with their natural surroundings. In actual fact, this was hardly the case: potters were constantly interrupted by tourists and other visitors; they spent most of their time 'drowning' the silence outside with their radios, and one young man actually threw all his pots at the wheel while watching television. To rural craftsmen, then, nature is not something to be contemplated aesthetically in a detached manner. Rather, it is the environment in which they have to survive; it provides the materials with which they work; it is the source of their success and of their fears (Tomars 1940:390).

Clearly, people idealize nature only when they are not directly involved with it in a struggle for survival – which is probably why the concept of 'nature' so often forms part of the appreciative values of philosophers and anthropologists alike (cf. Shelton 1992:229). In this respect, we can surmise that the aesthetic ideal which associates the quality of folk arts with closeness to nature derives primarily from urbanization (Tomars 1940:391). Urbanization, usually – though not necessarily – depends on industrialization. The nostalgia for a return to nature arising from urbanism in Japan may be seen not only in modern *mingei*, but in the painting and poetry practised by an urbanized aristocracy during the Nara and Heian periods (710–1185). It may also be found in the aesthetic philosophy of Zen Buddhism, by which Yanagi himself was influenced (cf. Leach 1978:81), and which came into its own with the construction of the castle towns in the sixteenth century, emphasizing simplicity and quietism during one of the most lavish and turbulent periods of Japanese history. In Europe, landscape painting was to a large extent created by painters of the urbanized Low Countries, while the literary convention of the pastorale developed among writers living in the growing cities of Europe (Tomars 1940:390–391). The painting of Constable and Turner also came just at the time the English countryside was being polluted with the smoke and dirt of the first industrial towns (Mukerjee 1948:210–211). In one sense, then, the 'grounding' of aesthetic theory in the concept of beauty may be said to derive from the destruction of nature which has hitherto accompanied urbanization and – since the eighteenth century – industrialization (cf. Okada 1976:171).

People who buy Japanese *mingei*, then, use the concept of 'nature' – perhaps unconsciously – as a means of measuring just how far Japanese culture has progressed (cf. Graburn 1976:13–14). Certainly, when I interviewed 100 visitors to Sarayama about the relation between nature and beauty in *mingei*, a large majority (70 per cent) believed not only that the potters in Sarayama made good pots *because* they used natural materials and means of production, but that potters *ought* to continue to rely on nature and not yield to economic considerations. Thus the moral tone found in Yanagi's concept of nature, and adopted by present *mingei* leaders, would appear to extend to a large section of the Japanese public. Potters in Sarayama work in a way in which almost the whole of Japanese society once worked; now that Japanese industry has made such advances, people like to look back and see how far they have progressed. They want potters in Sarayama to stay the way they are, so that they can measure their own and the nation's prosperity. In exchange, they are prepared to accord potters the honour of acclaiming their work as 'art'.

Coincidental to the main argument presented here, but connected with urban attitudes toward nature, is the relation between art consumption and gender. Two Japanese 'arts' currently popular and closely associated with the Zen Buddhist appreciation of nature are the tea ceremony and flower arrangement – both of them now largely practised by women. I have noted that women are the main purchasers of *mingei* in general and, in particular, of the tea bowls and flower vases made by Onta potters. This would seem to support Adolf Tomars's theory (1940:388–389) that in a competitive business society women form the leisure class, which performs the social prestige function of art consumption. Thus with Japanese *mingei*: not only are women the major purchasers, they also form a large majority of the membership of the two folk craft associations. They are thus extremely active in the negotiation of *mingei*'s appreciative values.

This is, perhaps, to be expected. After all, folk crafts are domestic utensils to be used in people's everyday lives; women, especially married women, are thereby more likely to appreciate something like Onta pottery. But although strictly 'non-*mingei*' items such as tea bowls and flower vases are also bought by women, the really large decorative wares tend to be purchased primarily by men, so that it is they – and not women – who are most active in the manipulation of commodity and symbolic exchange values.[2] This shift from female to male control as an object climbs from 'rubbish' to durable art has also been noted by Michael Thompson (1979:33). Evidence from this study of Japanese pottery, therefore, can give no more than partial support to Tomars's theory that women are the main art consumers in a competitive business society.

Nevertheless, this itself raises a second general issue regarding the relationship between *mingei*, art, craft and gender. It is now accepted that the gender of an artifact's maker – together with other social values such as where something is made and for whom (Parker and Pollock 1981:70) – can greatly influence whether that artifact is seen as an 'art' or 'craft'. Thus, as Roszika Parker and Griselda Pollock point out in their exploration of women's place in the history of western art, embroidery, quilting, and other arts that adorn people and their domestic environment have been stereotyped as 'feminine' and 'craft', in contrast to the 'higher' and more 'masculine' Art of (nude) portrait painting and sculpture (see also Nochlin 1973). In other words, craft is distinguished from art by *who* makes it *for whom*, as well as by *what* it is, for *what purpose* it will be used, and *where* it is made (in the home or studio). Under such limiting

213

conditions, stoneware pottery made out in the rural sticks of Japan by country farmers for use by urban housewives would not seem to stand much chance in the aesthetic hierarchy of taste that constitutes Art (with a capital A). Despite their overt display of Kyushu masculinity – or chauvinism, depending on your outlook – Onta and other *mingei* potters would appear to be 'feminized' by the arbiters of taste in contemporary Japanese society.

But are they? Both the British Arts and Crafts and Japanese *Mingei* movements have put forward an 'aesthetic' ideology which is anti-capitalist and anti-industrialist, and thus in many respects anti-*masculine*. If certain works within the *mingei* genre come to be accepted as 'art', therefore, they can be said to constitute an 'anti-aesthetic' (Foster 1983) in the sense that they form an alternative evaluation of hitherto-held ideas about art. Moreover, in that Yanagi Sōetsu espoused an approach to beauty and (non)-creativity which, in *chokkan*, was anti-intellectual and anti-verbal, it can be argued that his *mingei* philosophy also supported a 'feminine' aesthetic, since it is women who are usually seen to be 'emotional', 'non-verbal', 'intuitive' and so on. And yet, as Lee Hall notes (in Hess and Baker 1973), Art itself (the capital A variety) is also believed to be a non-verbal, non-intellectual activity, so that here, too, the 'feminine' ideals of *mingei* and arts and crafts form a kind of counter-aesthetic to prevailing norms – in much the same way that Onta potters by their very lifestyle contradict all the norms of capitalist production in contemporary Japanese society.[3]

Let us now turn to the relationship between art, beauty, and mechanization. The first point to note here concerns the way in which handmade goods are usually extolled by those living in highly industrialized societies. Machine-made goods generally serve their purpose extremely well; they are functional, efficient, and cheap. At the same time, their low price makes them available to everyone in society. Even though the fact that they are mass-produced by industrial methods does not in itself disqualify them from being 'aesthetic' (Maquet 1986:196), their consumption here is not – to use Veblen's terms – 'honorific' so much as 'common'. Handmade goods, on the other hand, are not produced with such efficiency; they cannot compete in either quality or quantity with machine-made goods, so that they 'usually fail to achieve sharpness in lines, symmetry in shapes, regularity in textures, and uniformity in hues and brightness to the same degree that machine-processed objects do' (Maquet 1986:198).[4] Yet, precisely because of this, they are seen by some to be 'more serviceable for the purpose of pecuniary reputability; hence the marks of hand labour come to be honorific, and the goods which exhibit these marks take rank as of higher grade than the corresponding machine product' (Veblen 1925:159).

The notion of 'honorific consumption' affects aesthetic taste in two ways. On the one hand, people place appreciative value on the quantitative aspect of handwork. Because handmade things are not generally produced in large numbers, they are comparatively expensive. Veblen (1925:128) argued that people tended to judge a thing's beauty by the amount of money they had to spend on its acquisition – a point borne out by dealers' comments on some of those who purchased Onta pots which could be retailed at comparatively high prices because it was coming to be seen as decorative rather than strictly functional ware. In other words, people sometimes regard Onta pottery as beautiful *because* it is expensive; conversely, at other times, they do not think it beautiful *unless* it is expensive (as in the case of the women who thought Yamaichi's tea bowls were beautiful until they learned how cheap they were). On the other hand, people are attracted by what they see as the qualitative aspect of handwork. They decry as 'unaesthetic' any form of mechanization, any new technological device that might interfere with the 'beauty' of hand labour (cf. Tomars 1940:200–201). We have seen this kind of attitude adopted by leaders of the Japanese *Mingei* movement toward Onta pottery. Yet, it might be argued that because most forms of art are in fact handmade, anything that is handmade – or made by some other form of obsolete technology (cf. McLuhan 1964:ix) – may well come to be seen as 'art'.

Veblen argued that the qualititive aspects of handwork most appreciated were 'commonly, if not invariably . . . certain imperfections and irregularities in the lines of the hand wrought article, showing where the workman has fallen short in the execution of the design' (1925:159). He further suggested that the thought and ideas of people like Ruskin and Morris, who exalted the defective and propagated a return to handicraft and household industry, would have been impossible in an age when the more nearly perfect goods were also more expensive (Veblen 1925:162; see also Hauser 1982:213–4). Although Japanese folk crafts usually do contain some slight imperfection of form, it should be realized that the aesthetic attitude which praises the irregular in Japanese art is many centuries old (Keene 1971:18ff). Thus, the notion in Japan that beauty derives from imperfection and irregularity (cf. Yanagi 1955a:53) was not conceived in – although it may be strengthened by – modern industrial society's reaction to the perfection and regularity of machine-made things.

Although Yanagi himself did not object to slight imperfections in *mingei*, he was at pains to stress that individuality was irrelevant to the appreciation of folk crafts which were to be made by and for ordinary people. Paradoxically, nowadays many Japanese see an expression of craftsmen's individuality in the imperfection of their work. In my survey of visitors to Sarayama, I asked 100 people if they thought that handmade, not machine-made, objects expressed their maker's character. Every person interviewed – remarkably, without a single exception – agreed with the idea. It can be concluded, then, that there is a strong association in most Japanese people's minds between handicrafts, imperfection, and individuality, on the one hand, and mechanization, perfection, and impersonality, on the other.

But the idea of individuality connotes again the concept of art. It appears that individual craftsmen come to be praised because industrialization has given rise to what the majority see as an impersonal and anonymous social environment (Nisbet 1976:134). When people are forced to live in large-scale urbanized societies, they begin to realize, perhaps for the first time, the meaning of anonymity – an anonymity often attributed (e.g. Vasquez 1973:177) to the growth of the capitalist market.[5] Then there is a tendency for the individual craftsman to be publicly proclaimed an 'artist'. Nelson Graburn (1976:21–22) has noted that the signing of art works in general was encouraged to offset an increasing impersonality. Although I agree with this argument, I think that the notion of 'honorific consumption' should also be taken into account in any discussion of the signing of art work – which, so far as Japanese pottery is concerned, is an art form in itself (Moeran 1990).

There is a concluding parenthetical note to be made to Graburn's comment (1976:21–22) that 'the world has now become so homogenized and self-conscious that the most folksy arts and crafts are soon identified, glorified, preserved and stultified'. As James Clifford (1988:238) has pointed out, over the course of this century, two parallel but complementary systems of classification have been developed by art and ethnographic museums whose practitioners now act as *flâneurs* 'delighted, amazed, but also troubled by the chaos of simultaneous possibilities'. The former save artefacts, the latter customs, in a kind of temporal limbo as both seek to cope with the ever-changing 'categories of the beautiful, the cultural and the authentic' (Clifford 1988:229). Thus, much of the individualism and the glorification of artisan work as art has been fostered by anthropologists, museum curators, art historians, or collectors (cf. Brody 1976:75), who seem intent themselves upon acquiring the prestigious status normally associated in the west with the words 'art' and 'artist'. This may be seen most clearly when anthropologists frame their discussions of Lega baskets, Kwakiutl masks, Navajo blankets, Tikopian headrests, Trobriand gardens, and so on and so forth in the context of an 'anthropology of art' (e.g. Layton 1991 among many). How infinitely superior to a mere 'anthropology of craft' or – with apologies to Danny Miller (1987) – 'anthropology of material culture'! It is because of the potential self-gratification inherent in any anthropologist's ethnocentric notion of art that I sympathize with the call by Jeremy Coote and Anthony Shelton for an 'anthropology of aesthetics' (e.g. Coote and Shelton 1992). All the same, the use of the word 'aesthetics' in English also smacks of elitism – especially since it tends to preclude the commodity exchange value which is attached to all works of art and which, together with those other (use, technical, social, and symbolic exchange) values that anthropologists do tend to mention (albeit in an unsystematic way), contributes to their overall appreciative or 'aesthetic' value. This is why I have tried to go beyond an anthropology of aesthetics by proposing a less value-laden 'anthropology of values'.

As I have pointed out in the Introduction, the category of the 'aesthetic' *per se* is problematic in many ways. What I have tried to show throughout this book, therefore, is that the aesthetic constitutes a number of different values which interact with one another and together define whether an object is, or is not, art. To recap: the first of these is use value (*jitsuyō kachi*). As we have seen in critics', potters' and buyers' discussions of what makes 'good' *mingei*, pots are 'beautiful' if they are made for use and are 'properly' used – although, in fact, *any* use gives an object use value, regardless of how closely that use may approximate to the folk craft ideal. Thus, a 'tea' bowl has use value whether it is used for drinking tea, eating rice, displaying flower-petals in water, or storing paper clips.

At the same time, the way in which potters' own attitudes towards what makes 'good' Onta pottery are influenced by considerations of clay texture, kiln-loading methods, and so on shows that there is also an important technical value (*gijutsu kachi*) that comes into play in aesthetics (but which may not be appreciated by *mingei* connoisseurs, or indeed by collectors, buyers and the general public). This technical value may, or may not, be part of an overall appreciative value (*hyōka kachi*) which, in the *Mingei* movement, has been monopolized for the most part by folk craft critics, but which can still be applied and negotiated by potters, dealers and consumers generally. Closely connected with such appreciative values are social values (*shakai kachi*) where what constitutes 'good' *mingei*, for example, depends on how potters cooperate with one another and live in social harmony with the environment, but which may also be utilized in teacher/apprentice (*sensei/deshi*), potter/buyer/collector, potter/critic, critic/collector and other relations.

At the other end of the production/consumption continuum, we find that dealers and the public bring commodity exchange value (*shōhin kōkan kachi*) into play when deciding which pot to select for purchase. Onta pottery may meet all other requirements, but unless it is priced in such a way that, as a commodity, it can be equally exchanged for all the use, technical, appreciative and social values perceived to exist therein, it will not be purchased. Finally, in this respect, precisely because *mingei* is *hand*-made, with *natural* materials, in *cooperation* with others, it takes on a symbolic exchange value (*shōchō kōkan kachi*) that interacts with all other values and so adds to, and is part of, its commodity value.[6]

It should be clear from the above that I do not intend the anthropology of values to concentrate on the study of 'art' objects alone. It can equally well address itself to the arts of 'exotic' or 'primitive' peoples – to woodcarving, weaving, metalwork, and so on – as it can to those of our own industrialized societies (including 'primitive art in civilized places' [Price 1989]). But it also covers all other fields in which values of the kind illustrated in this book prevail. The anthropology of values is thus that branch of sociology or anthropology which deals with punk, not just classical, music; with science fiction and *manga* comics as well as with Literature (with a capital L); with film, and with dance. More important, its methods can be used to study fashion, certain types of sports (for example, gymnastics, diving, or synchronized swimming), advertising, wine, antiques, landscape gardening, architecture, jewellery, and cuisine, as well as the intricacies of Arab race horse breeding, or the colours of cattle among Nilotic peoples (Coote 1992). In short, the anthropology of values avoids the definitional problems of both 'art' and 'aesthetics' and reaches out to all those other aspects of culture which we have come to link with notions of beauty or taste.

Mingei and the Marriage of East and West

In *Lost Innocence: folk craft potters of Onta, Japan*, as a gesture to Alfons Silbermann's demand (1968:587) that the sociology of art develop laws of prediction on the basis of analysis, I made a hypothesis about the relation between folk art and social organization: in any highly urbanized and rapidly industrializing society, such as those of northern Europe in the nineteenth and Japan in the twentieth century, I suggested, an aesthetic philosophy of the kind put forward by William Morris or Yanagi Sōetsu was likely to be adopted within that society at some stage fairly soon after industrialization began; further, I continued, it would 'boom' once a large consumer middle class emerged. Despite appearances, this hypothesis was not intended to be a further contribution to economic or historical determinism so much as to indicate the reciprocal dependence that I perceived as existing between certain kinds of social and artistic phenomena (cf. Hauser 1982:192–3). Clearly, by the turn of the twentieth century, developments in communications were making the internal nurturing of independent aesthetic ideals subject to numerous external influences, both in Japan and elsewhere – as Nelson Graburn's book on ethnic and tourist arts so aptly illustrates.

Such influences were certainly far from absent in the development of the Japanese *Mingei* movement, and it is these that I wish to address now. There was one person in particular who, by making known the ideas about arts and crafts of William Morris in Japan, had a major influence on Yanagi Sōetsu and his concept of *mingei*, and who then acted as cultural intermediary by ferrying the Morris-imbued notion of 'folk craft' back to England, from where it was disseminated throughout the western world. I am referring, of course, to the English potter, Bernard Leach.

Bernard Leach was born in Hong Kong in 1887, and then almost immediately was taken to Japan to be brought up by his grandparents after his mother died. There he spent four years before returning to Hong Kong, Singapore, and eventually England, where he attended school from 1897. He went on to study art, before returning to Japan in the spring of 1909[7] and bringing with him an etching press. Among those who came to his etching classes were several members of the newly formed Shirakaba artists and writers group, including Mushakoji Saneatsu, Shiga Naoya, Kojima Kikuo, and Yanagi Sōetsu (Kojima 1933; Shiga 1933).

Leach and Yanagi seem to have become close friends very rapidly. Yanagi had studied English so that he spoke, read and wrote with some fluency, and Leach himself was picking up enough Japanese with which to get by. The Englishman told the Japanese about William Blake (on whom Yanagi was later to write a voluminous tome), and the Japanese for his part introduced the Englishman to the work of mystics, both of east and of west, as well as to Van Gogh (Yanagi 1954:78–9; Leach 1978:74–5). Leach contributed etchings to the Shirakaba group's art exhibitions, designed one of its magazine's covers, and wrote the first article on Blake ever published in Japan (Azuma 1980:136).

It was at about this time that Leach met somebody else who was to revolutionize his life: Tomimoto Kenkichi (1884–1963), a young Japanese artist who had gone to London in 1908 and studied stained glass at the Central School of Arts for a term in 1909. Again, the two men hit it off at once and Leach (1978:63) later described Tomimoto as being 'nearer the English temperament than any Japanese I have met hitherto, yet he remains Japanese'. Their friendship was important for three reasons: firstly, they 'discovered' pottery; secondly, they discovered 'oriental' crafts – in particular Korean ceramics – at the Colonial Exposition (Takushoku Hakurankai) of 1911 (Leach 1978:56, 64; Tomimoto 1981a);[8] and thirdly, between them they introduced William Morris's ideas to Japan.

This is something not generally admitted in the Japanese literature (see, for example, Mizuo 1978:20). Yet it is clear that both Tomimoto and Leach were interested in William Morris and talked about his ideas (Leach 1978:66). Tomimoto himself had spent a lot of his time in England sketching various crafts in the South Kensington (now Victoria and Albert) Museum (Tomimoto 1981b), and proceeded to published a long article on Morris (the first in Japanese) soon after his return to Japan (Tomimoto 1981c).[9] Leach seems to have introduced him to Yanagi just after this, sometime early in 1912. Given the intensity of the relationships between these three men, it seems highly unlikely that Yanagi could have remained ignorant of the work of William Morris until, as has been claimed, after he had published his first work on crafts in 1926. The evidence suggests, then, that he probably took more of Morris's ideas than his supporters and scholars in Japan would like to admit.

At the same time, Yanagi's ideas were also different from Morris's – particularly, in the way that he focused primarily on Japanese and east Asian crafts. But, interestingly, it seems to have been Bernard Leach who prompted this focus by going to live in Beijing in 1914 to pursue his interest in Chinese art. There he was visited by Yanagi, who discovered for himself the beauty of Korean crafts *en route*, persuaded Leach to return to live with him in Abiko on the outskirts of Tokyo, and wrote in *Shirakaba* about the need to introduce oriental (*tōyō*), and not just western, art into Japan (Mizuo 1978:94). That Leach did not altogether approve of the way in which Yanagi and other members of the Shirakaba group devoted so much of their time to foreign art was clear from his own article a couple of years later (Leach 1978:124),[10] and it is noticeable that from about 1919–1920, *Shirakaba* gradually started to focus on oriental art and literature (cf. Kishida 1920:27). By 1920, when Leach decided to return to England with Hamada Shōji to start up a pottery at St. Ives, Tomimoto Kenkichi was able to write:

Even in the chaotic condition of present Japanese fine art, something solid seems to have begun to move in the depths. For the sake of mere convenience I gave this something the name of Neo-orientalism. Or I might have called it the revival of Orientalism. Anyhow it is to be born out of two vital forces, that is, the full understanding of Occidental art as a subordinate factor and the spirit inherent in our country as the chief moulding power. This is precisely what has been attempted by many, and often fancied accomplished. But to my mind we have as yet to start from the very beginning and the attainment entirely belongs to the future.

(Tomimoto 1920:38)

Whether that attainment belongs to Yanagi is probably a moot point, but in 1922 he published the first of his writings on craft, 'The beauty of ceramics' (*Tōjiki no bi*) (Yanagi 1982b), dedicated to his two friends Tomimoto and Leach (Mizuo 1982:694) and designed to accompany a publication on Korean art.[11] He then began his discovery of Japanese crafts in Kyoto, coined the word '*mingei*' and made plans to establish a Japanese Folk Craft Museum. At the same time, he began his first book-length work on crafts, each chapter of which he would read out aloud to Kawai Kanjirō and ask his opinion about (Mizuo 1982:704). With Leach back in England, revitalizing the remains of the Arts and Crafts Movement and imbuing it with the 'spirit of the east',[12] and Hamada back once more in Japan, having been most impressed by Ethel Mairet, Eric Gill and the craft community of Ditchling, Sussex (Leach 1976:58–61, 80), it must have seemed that the attainment referred to by Tomimoto was only just around the corner, and that the 'first complete, round, human society' (Leach 1920:41) was indeed in the making.

Folk Art, *Japonisme* and Orientalism

This discussion of the possible influence of Bernard Leach on Yanagi Sōetsu's development of the Japanese *mingei* ideal has revealed a number of themes that I shall now pursue in the wider context of *Japonisme*, or 'a taste for things Japanese', and what Edward Said (1978) has termed 'Orientalism'. Clearly, we are not just dealing with the ways in which William Morris's ideas were carried to Japan, and Yanagi Sōetsu's back to England, but with an ongoing and long-term discourse between east and west about the meaning of modernity. As John MacKenzie (1995:106) has pointed out, by the second half of the nineteenth century, 'it was a major preoccupation of the avant-garde to break down the distinctions between fine and applied arts, to elevate the craftsman to equal status with the artist, and to assert the need for artists also to be craftsmen'. This preoccupation was connected with three things: a decline in art/craft values following industrialized mass production; a quest for the integration of all arts to create a 'total art'; and a shift in emphasis to simplicity as the prime criterion of internal design (cf. Sato and Watanabe 1991).

The attempt to break down the distinction between arts and crafts (by whatever name), and to introduce, through simplicity, a new criterion of taste, coincided with both a re-evaluation of eastern designs and an appreciation of the work of Asian craftsmen, together with the social institutions in which they produced their work (MacKenzie 1995:118). It was out of this, as well as out of a fear of standards being 'debased' that the 'cult of Japan' grew – nurtured first and foremost by the International Exhibition held in London in 1862, and then by other expositions in Paris (1867, 1878 and 1889), Philadelphia (1876) and Chicago (1893, see Harris 1990) and elsewhere (MacKenzie 1995:124).

In other words, in mid-eighteenth century Europe, two parallel developments were taking place. Firstly, critics like Ruskin and Morris were looking to their own medieval past for inspiration; secondly, others such as Christopher Dresser, Sir George Birdwood and Walter Crane discovered in Asian (middle eastern, Indian and Japanese) crafts their sources of aesthetic delight. In other words, 'the Gothic soul' and 'orientalism' are two sides of the same artistic coin (cf. Conant 1991:79–80). While Yanagi and Morris focused on the role of popular art within their own societies, others looked outside their own cultural environment and cited Japan as a country whose arts and crafts were perfectly merged into a single unity. Siegfried Bing, for example – who is said to have 'effectively created *Japonisme*' (Wichmann 1981:9) when he started the magazine, *Le Japon artistique* – wrote in May 1888: 'this art is permanently bound together with ours. It is like a drop of blood that has been mingled with our blood, and now no power an earth is able to separate it again' (Wichmann 1981:12). Others, such as Baron Hubner, homed in on what they saw as an apparent lack of distinction between an elite group of artists and privileged patrons, as well as on artistic worth being appreciated among the lower, as well as the higher, classes of society (Evett 1982:72). Meanwhile, in his *Of the Decorative Illustration of Books Old and New* (1896), Walter Crane had this to say:

> There is no doubt that the opening of Japanese ports to western commerce, whatever its after-effects – including its effect upon the arts of Japan itself – has had an enormous influence on European and American art. Japan is, or was, a country very much, as regards its arts and handicrafts with the exception of architecture, in the condition of a European country in the Middle Ages, with wonderfully skilled artists who were under the influence of a free and informal naturalism. Here at least was a living art, an art of the people, in which tradition and craftsmanship were unbroken, and the results full of attractive variety, quickness, and naturalistic, force. What wonder that it took western artists by storm, and that its effects have become so patent.
>
> (quoted in Wichmann 1981:8)

This blending of European medievalism and orientalism towards the end of the nineteenth century is also seen in Jackson Jarves's account of his visit to Japan in the mid-1870s:

> In looking back on Japan, we get a general likeness to what must have been the dominant passion of Europe during the Middle Ages for ornamental art; for until yesterday, there obtained in this country a kindred

feudalism and division of society into castes, ranks and guilds, and an average instruction of the people, almost identical in direction and quality with what prevailed in Europe before the Renaissance.

(Jarves 1876:100)

This comparing of Japan to a 'medieval court'[13] is hardly surprising, since the country was only just beginning to open its doors to foreigners after more than two centuries of self-imposed isolation. At the same time, though, it had a major – albeit accidental – effect on European perceptions of art, thanks to its participation in many of the international expositions taking place in the latter half of the nineteenth century.

> The wisdom of separating and ranking the fine and applied arts was questioned implicitly by the World Expositions where the contemporary fine arts of Europe were displayed separately from the European decorative arts, but where the products (both high and low) from other countries were grouped together. Despite their separation in the European sections, the industrial and applied arts received a new emphasis that pointed to changing attitudes about their stature and importance . . .
>
> The appearance of Japanese Art in the context of the world expositions may have predisposed people to think . . . in these terms and its great popularity may have depended on the way it appeared to embody this idealistic goal of the expositions. Its association with these aspirations and its link with medieval art in this respect emerged most clearly in the Exposition of 1878, where the art of the Middle Ages and Japan shared center stage.
>
> (Evett 1982:75–6)[14]

Attitudes displayed towards Japan's 'popular arts', then, reveal many of those themes discussed at length in this book. Just as Morris tried to return to his 'garden of childhood' (Lindsay 1979:9), so for those interested in Japanese art, was Japan an 'Oriental Garden of Bliss' (Miner 1958:51), an Eastern Eden or 'Arcadia' (La Farge 1986:16), with the 'Japanese artist as a kind of Adam before the Fall, playing like an innocent child . . . at one with himself and nature' (Evett 1982:43). There was a sense of humility, in which artists and writers like John La Farge (1986:96), Lafcadio Hearn (Miner 1958:93), and Bernard Leach (1978:62) who visited Japan during the Meiji period sought to deny their 'self', to live 'in harmony with nature' and to make their art subservient to it, while striving for the 'Absolute'. They were also convinced that 'a beneficent universe preserved the original childlike innocence of its people' (Evett 1982:44). Not only was the Japanese artist like a child (La Farge 1986: 97, 107), but we ourselves had to become like children, if we were to appreciate beauty (Leach 1914:15).

Here we find an image that brings us close to Yanagi's concept of direct perception, or intuition, which – as we have seen – both allows us to enter into an object and to communicate with it immediately, without the intellect's impeding our perception in any way, and which in many respects defies 'logical explanation' (Yanagi 1932:52–60).[15] Not only do we find here the common opposition between eastern intuition versus western reason that has characterized much writing about Japan (e.g. Leach 1920:42) and indeed about the 'orient' as a whole (Said 1978:40);[16] Yanagi's idea of 'pure gaze' complements the notion of a visual naiveté of childhood and the creation by the Impressionists of a 'natural eye' which was believed to receive 'impressions without being influenced by the artistic conventions that shape and direct modes of seeing, just as the infant's perception has yet to be affected by preconceived notions of how things should look' (Evett 1982:105).

The irony, in the context of Yanagi's promulgation of *mingei*, is a double one that nicely illustrates a less polemical aspect of Said's thesis (1978:2) that 'the Orient is an integral part of European material civilization and culture': not only is Japan seen by Europeans to be 'childlike' (cf. Moeran 1993); 'folk art' itself is regarded as 'primitive' and 'childlike'. By promoting *mingei*, therefore, Yanagi merely reinforced European stereotypes of Japan and of folk art.

By Way of Conclusion

This last point brings me to a few comments on 'Orientalism' by way of conclusion to this book. They will concern specifically *Japonisme* and Japanese views of the west, and act as a coda to various conclusions drawn by Edward Said in his work on Orientalism. Although the latter's focus is on the 'near' rather than 'far' orient, and although, as a result, Japan is given no more than seven cursory mentions in a book of more than 300 pages in length, Said's general argument about hegemony and Orientalism would seem in some respects to hold good for interpretations of Japan – whether in art or in anthropology.

Let us start with the relationship between the Arts and Crafts movement, *Japonisme* and Orientalism. We have seen that western views of Japanese society and art during the last decades of the nineteenth century bore an uncanny resemblance to those put forward by William Morris in his description of how his own society's art ought to be.

> The Japanese approach to nature as the main topic of discussion and the avenues taken to explain it were both based on general western perceptions of Japanese civilization and the spirit of the Japanese people. Long-standing myth, often reinforced by biased travellers' reports but nurtured mostly by an escapist longing for the opposite of advanced, complex western civilization, perpetuated a vision of the Japanese as simple, innocent, primitive people living in blissful harmony with gentle, nurturing, benign nature. The Japanese pictorial image of nature seemed in turn to confirm this picture, and an intricate set of intertwined observations and explanations of Japanese art and the people who created it produced a general view that the Japanese civilization had been arrested

223

in permanent infancy. Unlike the west, it had not experienced progressive development and had remained fixed in its original state. That meant that the Japanese were like early man, living simply and in primitive, childlike rapport with nature.

(Evett 1982:xiii)

Evett's point is that the dominant European image of the Japanese was of a 'primitive' people, and that *Japonisme* was 'a unique expression of a general primitivist sentiment that has long been recognized . . . as a key motivating force in the major art movements in the late nineteenth and early twentieth centuries' (Evett 1982:xv). *Japonisme* certainly had a profound effect on English and French artists such as Whistler, Burne-Jones, Tissot and Manet, who made use of Japanese compositional devices, as well as artifacts as props in their paintings – and on other artists (including Bernard Leach's teacher, Frank Brangwyn) who all began to adopt Japanese compositional devices, perspective and colouring (MacKenzie 1995:126).[17] In short, *Japonisme* 'became an essential ingredient of Victorian painting' (Sato and Watanabe 1991:25) and was also 'an important phase in, rather than prelude to, the primitivist strain in modern art' (Evett 1982:xvi) – a strain which, in anthropology, has been seen as related somehow to virtually every 'non-western' art form *except* Japanese art (e.g. Clifford 1988:189–251; Coote and Shelton 1992). Modernism in art did *not* begin with the discovery of African sculpture and other ethnographic objects languishing in the museums of Europe; it began in the west when Van Gogh and Gauguin decided to make Japanese *ukiyoe* woodblock print artists *their* predecessors and so to deny the previous history of western art (Danto 1992:125–8).

Given that we can distinguish two strains of 'primitivism' at work (Miner 1958:29), it would seem to be a mistake to try to separate the ideals of Morris, Yanagi or *Japonisme* from one another. As we have seen, the first is *cultural* and relates Europe to Japan *synchronically*, although it also suggests that Japanese art is characteristic of a previous European 'golden' age. The second is more specifically *historical* and anchors Japan *diachronically* to an ideal, and primarily mythological, past that sets the country off from the rest of the world in cultural isolation. These two strains of primitivism, one of them focusing on space and the other on time, would appear to follow the more general practices of Orientalism:

There is no doubt that imaginative geography and history help the mind to intensify its own sense of itself by dramatizing the distance and difference between what is close to it and what is far away. This is no less true of the feelings we often have that we would have been more 'at home' in the sixteenth century or in Taihiti.

(Said 1978:111)

This brings us to the problem of whether, in the context of Orientalism, *Japonisme* should be seen as part of, or separate from, what Said argues is the typical pattern of hegemonic relations practised by the west in its dealings with the Orient. Cannot the 'oriental', or 'medieval', aesthetic (in other words, 'cultural' or 'historical' primitivism) be seen to question the relationship of power seen to pertain between Occident and Orient (Said 1978:5)?

There are two points to make about this supposed hegemony. Firstly, in the arts the fascination with Orientalism arose out of opposition to, rather than a consensus with, established power structures. In their attack on commercialism, the division of labour, mechanization, environmental pollution, individualism, and all the other 'ills' of industrial capitalism, both Morris and Yanagi questioned the basic premises on which their respective societies were founded. The appeal to Japan and other easts (the Middle East, India, China), as well as the recreation of 'a feudal, chivalric, pre-industrial world of supposedly uncomplicated social relations and retributions, heroic connections with the environment, a supposedly appropriate separation of gender spheres, and enthusiasm for craft production' (MacKenzie 1995:209), all brought into question the hegemonic discourses of both western art and western politics. Thus, as we have seen in William Morris's political agenda for the Arts and Crafts movement,

> The arts of eastern traditions were [also] being used as a weapon to attack the productive processes of industrialism, its resultant social relations and its shoddy products. By the end of the century, perceptions of eastern artistic canons were being used to mount a full-scale radical assault on western convention.
>
> (MacKenzie 1995:212)

Secondly, despite Said's essentially static and politically dichotomous viewpoint, Orientalism is never fixed, but is always on the move, always in a process of change. Nowadays, power no longer emanates – if ever it once did – from a single geographical and cultural centre. Rather there are multiple centres (Clifford 1988:272) which include an emerging China and, most famously, Japan. The Japanese are no longer simply subject to a western hegemonic discourse; they themselves participate in and actively manipulate the ever-shifting developments, backtrackings, tangents, twists and turns of Orientalist practices – whether they be part of a philosophy of business management, group organization or aesthetic ideals – often converting them in the process into Occidentalist self-imaginings (cf. Carrier 1995). Thus, we find British Arts and Crafts concepts transformed into 'Japanese' *mingei* ideals which then influence craftsmen and women in Europe and the United States, and so provide a good example of how a cultural or historical primitivism becomes transcultural or panchronic – a little like those ads for an Irish stout which claim that it is 'good for you', whoever or wherever you may be.

Here we face the problem of synthesis between western and Japanese artistic notions, frequently called for by Leach and other 'Japanofiles'. Are Japanese *mingei* ideals ultimately little more than a form of western 'aesthetic imperialism' (Albrecht 1970), or do they derive from an independent Japanese aesthetic tradition? In other words,

> Can the artistic norms of one culture retain their integrity, if not their actual identity, if they are combined with aspects of artistic expression of a completely different culture? Is it possible to actually assimilate elements of a foreign aesthetic, or does appropriation amount at best to a gross, awkward grafting of the alien element onto the native species? Which attributes of a foreign mode are most attractive to adoption – those bearing the most affinity to, or those differing the most radically from, the characteristic assumptions of the receiving aesthetic? Does the relative 'success' or 'failure' to appropriate foreign notions depend on any far-reaching comprehension of the different meaning, intent, or purposes of the alien creations?

(Evett 1982:100)

In partial answer to this question of 'creolization' in 'transnational connections' (Hannerz 1996), it should be pointed out that Yanagi's admiration for nature is typical of Japanese aesthetics in general (Warner 1958; Katō 1971); that his notion of *chokkan* owes something to the Tendai Buddhist and Japanese literary tradition of spiritual meditation (or *shikan*); and that his concepts of function (*yō*) and *getemono* beauty were developed within the context of the Japanese tea ceremony.[18] Moreover, it is to the tea ceremony that one or two other Buddhist ideals in *mingei* (such as *tariki*, 'other power', for example) may be attributed.

And yet, at the same time, a number of these ideals are also to be found in European thought. We have seen that urbanization has often had a tendency to encourage aesthetic philosophies that focus on nature; that scholars from Thomas Aquinas to Harold Osborne have examined the relationship between perception and beauty; and that 'function' is very much a part of western 'intuition' and pragmatics. This would appear to suggest that western interpretations of *Japonisme*, for example, did not necessarily *create* Japan (*contra* Said 1978:158), but that the Japanese had their own set of aesthetic norms to which they could turn when in need. If Japan was, indeed, as Oscar Wilde suggested, 'a pure invention' and the Japanese people 'simply a mode of style, an exquisite function of art' (Sato and Watanabe 1991:40), then both that invention and style were mutually conceived (MacKenzie 1995:210).

It is here, of course, that we come face to face with the weakness of Orientalist arguments which, like Said's, do not admit the possibility of a genuinely authentic cultural tradition, or of a non-hegemonic interaction between different traditions. The trouble is that no cultural tradition can ever be pristine, ever be pure. As I have shown in this book with Yanagi's concept of *mingei*, total aesthetic independence is, in the long run, virtually impossible.

The same can be said of Orientalism itself. Just as Yanagi and his followers refused to admit the influence of Morris on his thinking about crafts, so nowadays do Japanese businessmen and academics make use of techniques hitherto practised exclusively by western Orientalists – a splendidly monolithic

226

view of the west, for example, together with the conception of humanity in large collective terms and abstract generalities (cf. Said 1978:154). At the same time, as I mentioned above, these myths – generally subsumed under the heading of *nihonjinron* (or what it means to be 'Japanese' [Dale 1986]) – have put forward as positive features precisely those facets of Japanese society enthused upon by Japanologists and anthropologists alike: harmony, nature, tradition, collectivity, dependence, familial relations, the Japanese 'spirit', and so on and so forth. Such visions of the Japanese by both Japanese and westerners partly confirms the way in which Japan, like the Orient in general, is contained and represented (Said 1978:40), but they also contain and represent the Occident, and so show how this discourse has shifted with the emergence of Japan as a major world power. It is with these different styles of Orientalism, or different orientalisms, in mind that anthropologists of Japan should henceforth frame their apparently endless debates over 'group' and 'individual', 'harmony' and 'conflict', *uchi* (inside) and *soto* (outside), and so on and so forth.

In the meantime, Bernard Leach's cry (1920:41) will continue to echo in this chorus of confusion that accompanies all these images of 'Japan':

I have seen a vision of the marriage of East and West, and far off down the Halls of Time I heard the echo of a childlike voice. How long? How long?

Plate 72 Bernard Leach in Barbara Hepworth's garden, St. Ives, May 1974

Afterword

THE ART WORLD OF JAPANESE CERAMICS

When I had finished and written up my research into the production, marketing, and aesthetic appraisal of *mingei* pottery, I began asking myself another set of questions – this time about pottery as an Art form (with a capital A). How did a potter like Hamada Shōji succeed in having bestowed on him the Award of Cultural Merit (*bunka kunshō*), or in being designated the holder of an 'Important Intangible Cultural Property' (*jūyō mukei bunkazai*) – the highest accolades available to craftsmen in Japan? The answer to this question could be simply put: it was through exhibiting their work that potters came to be accepted as artists, and by selling their work and winning prizes at exhibitions that they might eventually be designated a 'national treasure' (*ningen kokuhō*) (to use the popular phrase).

At the time, I naively assumed that it was the quality of potters' work which won them the ultimate accolade, but by the end of a second period of fieldwork in Japan (between January 1981 and July 1982), I had come to realize that a national treasureship was as much related to the nature of potters' social relations as to their technical accomplishments.[1] In this Afterword, I will describe the art world of contemporary Japanese ceramics, by examining first and foremost the structure of pottery exhibitions in Japan. This will then enable us to understand some of the social mechanisms that surround the production, marketing and critical appraisal of ceramics, and so provide us with a more complete view of the artworld of Japanese ceramics as a whole.

Exhibitions can be neatly divided into one-man shows, on the one hand, and competitive exhibitions which are juried and have prizes attached, on the other. One-man shows are generally held at galleries and department stores.[2] Although a small handful of prestigious galleries in Tokyo (for example, the Kuroda Tōen in the Ginza, or the Green Gallery in Aoyama) are attractive to the socially ambitious potter, it is in the art galleries of the country's numerous department stores that most potters try to exhibit and sell their work. There are several reasons for this preference. In the first place, prestigious galleries are comparatively few and far between. Hence it is not easy to gain access to them, unless the potter happens to have some kind of personal connection with those involved in their management.[3] Second, not that many people visit galleries, and since one of the potters' stated aims is to have people look at and evaluate their work, department stores appear to provide more suitable surroundings for a show. After all, on an average shopping day, between 5,000 and 8,000 people walk into a Tokyo department store, while 3–4,000 will visit stores in the larger provincial cities. Clearly, not all of these will go to the stores' galleries, but potters are more likely to attract an audience there than in the private galleries, which are rarely visited by more than a couple of hundred people a day.

The third reason for potters' preferring to exhibit in department stores is connected with the 'quality', rather than mere 'quantity', of an exhibition's visitors. Those who visit private galleries tend to be a dealer's 'clientele', rather than people merely walking in off the street. In this respect, there is a greater probability that they will buy a potter's work, whereas visitors to a department store show are more likely to 'browse' without buying. But department stores also have their own clientele whom they will inform of any exhibitions being held in their art galleries. This clientele consists of art connoisseurs of all kinds, is thus larger than that of a privately run gallery, and can run into several hundreds, even thousands.[4]

Given that department stores offer Japanese potters the best forum in which to exhibit their work, it is hardly surprising to find that they do their best to hold at least one one-man show there every year. What happens during these shows will be described below, but, first, it should be pointed out that there is a hierarchy of stores in Japan and that this hierarchy automatically affects potters' decisions about where, or where not, to hold their shows. The criteria used follow well-worn lines: first, that the capital is always superior to the provinces; and second, that 'industrial gradation' applies as much to department stores, and hence to the quality of 'art', as to large corporations such as Mitsubishi or Marubeni. In other words, the close qualitative alliance made in people's minds between stores and potters – and, indeed, among other institutions in the art world – is similar to that more generally prevailing between top corporations and their employees in Japan's status gradation of industry (Clark 1979:72–73).

In other words, so far as potters are concerned, any exhibition that they put on in Tokyo will always be 'better' than one held anywhere else in the country. At the same time, in the capital itself, stores are ranked according to criteria which may differ from one potter to the next, but which almost invariably place Mitsukoshi at the top, closely followed by Takashimaya, Seibu, and Isetan. This ranking is carried down to the smallest provincial department stores, so that effectively potters are almost always trying to climb the marketing status ladder and to exhibit their work in what they see as 'better' stores.

Competitive Exhibitions

The Japanese art world in general is somewhat unusual in that one of the main forums for the exhibition of art works is the department store. The underlying philosophy behind such exhibitions is by no means new. From the end of the

Meiji period, for example, stores such as Mitsukoshi and Shirokiya attempted to provide their customers with entertainment as well as to sell them goods, and modern stores have continued to flavour their commercial practices with cultural ingredients.[5] In addition to their pre-war policy of renting out space to artists wanting to show and sell their work, department stores have, since the beginning of the 1950s, put on a series of major exhibitions of – predominantly Western – art. These exhibitions have frequently been 'sponsored' by newspaper companies, and – when successful – have attracted vast crowds. For example, 8,462 visitors a day were recorded at Asahi/Mitsukoshi's first exhibition of Soviet Russian Art Treasures in 1975; 9,220 visitors at the Mainichi/Daimaru Sao Paolo Museum of Art Exhibition in 1978; and 10,487 at the Mainichi/Matsuzakaya special Renoir exhibition in 1967. The highest number of visitors recorded at a department store 'blockbuster event' is that of the 14,629 people who queued up daily outside the Seibu Department Store in 1971 to see another Renoir exhibition, sponsored this time by the Yomiuri Newspaper. The all-time record is held by the Mona Lisa exhibition, shown at the Tokyo National Museum in 1974. Total attendance was 1,505,239 at a daily average of 31,359 visitors (Asano 1981).

Department stores' interest in art as a whole has been of considerable benefit to potters, and a number of major ceramics exhibitions have been instituted over the past three decades. Probably the most important of these are the Traditional Crafts Exhibition (Dentō Kōgeiten), sponsored by the Asahi Newspaper and held at Mitsukoshi Department Store's headquarters in Nihonbashi every autumn, and the biannual Japan Ceramics Exhibition (Nihon Tōgeiten), sponsored by the Mainichi Newspaper and held at Daimaru Department Store, above Tokyo Station. Each of these exhibitions is then shown at department stores around the country, as is the Japan Arts Exhibition (Nihon Bijutsu Tenrankai, or Nitten for short) which, although shown at the Metropolitan Art Museum in Tokyo, is often put on at department stores in the provinces. Important local ceramics exhibitions include the Chūnichi Newspaper-sponsored International Ceramics Exhibition (Kokusai Tōgeiten), held at Mitsukoshi in Nagoya, and the Nishi Nihon Newspaper-sponsored West Japan Ceramic Art Exhibition (Nishi Nihon Tōgei Bijutsuten), shown at Iwataya in Fukuoka every year. To all of these exhibitions, potters contribute works which are judged by a jury of potters, and/or critics, and/or museum curators, and prizes of up to ¥2 million (or US$20,000 at today's exchange rates) are awarded to 'outstanding' works. Recipients of such prizes find that they become the focus of considerable media attention, and that prestigious department stores will clamour at their workshop door, begging to be allowed to put on their next one-man show. In this respect, competitive exhibitions can provide a springboard to success, and can considerably aid a potter's progress toward the top of the one-man show status ladder. They thereby contribute to the elevation of ceramics as Art (with a capital A) in much the same way that the world fairs of the late nineteenth century helped raise pottery from a craft to an art form.

Newspaper Companies

As we have seen, mass media have been closely involved with department stores in the promotion of large-scale art and ceramic art shows since the early 1970s. Almost every big exhibition is officially sponsored by one of the national newspapers – in particular, by the Yomiuri, the Asahi, the Mainichi, and the Nihon Keizai – and local newspapers will also sponsor cultural exhibitions within their own areas.[6] These organizations actively promote shows by writing about them in their columns, by arranging for their affiliated television stations to film them, and by producing lavishly illustrated, but reasonably priced, catalogues.[7]

Such promotion is, of course, expensive. In the 1980s, the cost of a domestic art exhibition, such as the Nihon Tōgeiten, came to approximately ¥30 million (US$300,000), although it could rise to four times that amount. Exhibitions of art brought over to Japan from Europe or the United States cost from somewhere between US$0.5 and $1.5 million. In 1980 the Asahi had an annual budget of about US$10 million for the sponsoring of its art events, and Havens estimates that the Japanese press as a whole sponsored 'art exhibits and performing-arts productions at a level of $45 to $50 million a year' (Havens 1982:138).

One question that immediately arises concerns how the newspaper companies can afford to spend so much on art and cultural activities. The invariable general answer comes in terms of readership circulation: by sponsoring major shows such as the Japan Ceramics or the Venus de Milo exhibitions, a newspaper like the Mainichi or the Asahi is able, or hopes, to increase its circulation. At a more specifically detailed level, since they promote shows to which admittance fees are charged, newspaper companies are usually entitled to a percentage of the box-office receipts. They will also be responsible for the production of catalogues and expect to make a profit from their sale at the museums or department stores holding the exhibitions that they sponsor. It is from these three sources, and – in the case of juried exhibitions – from processing fees, that newspaper companies theoretically recoup their costs.

However, although the national and local newspapers would appear to be funding Japan's quest for art and culture, this is not in fact so. Since the 1970s, there has been a tendency for newspapers to sponsor major exhibitions in name only, and to leave the main financing in the hands of the department stores. This means that a newspaper will often claim credit for a show's success, but disclaim the responsibility that goes with sponsorship if an exhibition does not meet with public approval. In other words, there is a tendency for newspaper companies to be interested primarily in making the Japanese public think that they really are interested in art, when in fact they are more concerned with the promotion of their 'cultural image' and with the status that each organization feels is vital within the media's 'industrial gradation'. It is perhaps significant that the sales of the Asahi have fallen, while those of the Yomiuri have risen, in almost direct proportion to the degree to which they have participated in the sponsorship of blockbuster art exhibitions during the 70s and 80s.[8]

231

This point raises a further question: if it is the department stores that are really providing the money necessary for such exhibitions, why do they bother to ask the newspaper companies to act as sponsors? One answer, of course, is connected with readership. Newspapers not only carry advertisements at especially reduced rates for the department stores; they provide free coverage of an event in their columns, and hence help draw the hoped-for crowds. Department stores are interested primarily in attracting people into their buildings, since this increases their overall sales. At the beginning of the 1980s, for example, it used to be said that when the Nihonbashi branch of Mitsukoshi put on a major art show that attracted some 10,000 visitors a day, its daily revenue would increase by as much as ¥100 million (US$1 million at today's exchange rates). If this figure is then multiplied by the number of days during which the exhibition continued, it can be seen that the initial outlay quoted earlier is not that poor an investment.

Another reason for department stores' allowing newspaper companies to act as 'sponsors' revolves around the old problem of the extent to which art should, or should not, be overtly involved with money – a problem that we came across in our discussion of Onta potters and *mingei*, and to which we shall in due course return. Department stores are primarily profit-making concerns. They thus lack the status necessary for them to be able to approach museum curators and ask for the loan of works of art to be shown on their premises. This problem is all the more apparent in their dealings with the international art world. It is here that the newspaper companies can be extremely valuable allies, for they generally have the personal contacts, and display the seemingly disinterested credibility, necessary to successfully borrow important art works for exhibition in Japan.

There are both advantages and disadvantages in having a newspaper company sponsor ceramics exhibitions. One of the advantages is that, since pottery is not an enormous money spinner, when a newspaper does decide to take on a show, it generally does its best to produce a good one. A major disadvantage, however, is that if one newspaper decides to sponsor an exhibition and to advertise it in the usual manner by devoting a lot of space to it in its columns, its major rivals will often ignore the show entirely. This means not only that some members of the general public may be unaware of an exhibition's existence, but that it is very difficult to get a balanced view of its merits and/or demerits. Finally, it should be noted that there is a tendency for certain newspapers to form close alliances with certain department stores – alliances that are not always seen to be in the best interests of artist potters.

Potter Organizations: The Nitten Group

My discussion of the structure of pottery exhibitions has touched upon a number of formal and informal relations which make up the ceramic art world. The first of those with which I shall now deal concerns potter organizations. There is a tendency for potters everywhere in Japan to form loosely-affiliated groups based on residence, and/or type of ware made, and/or teacher/apprentice relations. Very often, the main objective of such organizations is to hold their own group exhibitions at department store galleries, but members also get together to discuss their work and, occasionally, to have it criticized by senior potters and/or critics. Such 'criticism' usually centres on whether a particular potter's work is good enough to be passed by the jury of a forthcoming competitive exhibition, and the senior person called in to pass judgement is in such cases almost invariably a member of the jury concerned.

Two major associations of potters are those centering around the Japan Arts (Nitten) and Traditional Crafts (Dentō Kōgeiten) exhibitions. It is not just potters who form these groups, but all kinds of artists and craftsmen, ranging from painters and sculptors at one end of the spectrum to dyers and basket weavers at the other. Several hundred potters, too, are members of these two associations and their organization needs commenting upon, since the structure of each exhibits many of the classic features of Japan's vertical society (*tate shakai*) made known to us by Chie Nakane (1972).

Nitten is an abbreviation of the Nihon Bijutsu Tenrankai. It was started in its present form in 1946 and is now a private corporation. To some extent, however, it still shelters under the organizational umbrella of the Japan Arts Academy, by which it used to be officially sponsored until 1959.[9] The organization consists of a number of ranks through which all potters – or, indeed, all contributing artists – must pass if they are to attain the final accolade of the art world. The lowest of these ranks is that of 'associate member' (*kaiyu*), which is attained by a potter's having had his work accepted in the exhibition a minimum of three times. Next, there are 'full members' (*kaiin*), each of whom must have had his work exhibited ten times and have been awarded a prize. Then there are 'jury members' (*shinsain*), who are appointed by an 'executive' (*riji*), the latter himself being one of between two and four members of an executive committee, headed by a chairman (*kaichō*). In all probability the chairman of an executive committee will be elected, at the end of his term of office, to membership in the Japan Arts Academy, and in due course – if he lives long enough, has the right contacts, and is prepared to pay out enough money – will have bestowed on him the Award of Cultural Merit (Bunka Kunshō).[10]

The whole system depends to a very large extent on an *iemoto*-style hierarchical structure based on teacher/apprentice relations (O'Neill 1984), and – as intimated above – a member of the panel of jurors will preside over preview sessions where aspiring potters will present a selection of their works for 'advice'. In exchange for a suitably deferential attitude and an undisclosed fee, the juror will then advise his colleagues about which potters' works should be voted for in that year's exhibition, and he himself is advised about which of his colleagues' adherents he should vote for.

Needless to add, perhaps, this system of 'give and take' (*gibu-ando-tēki* in Japanese English) does not end there. Any juror owes his position to one of those on the executive committee – a position for which he has himself paid in one way or another over the years. Continued allegiance and deference to his immediate senior in the vertical structure may in the end lead to his being elected as a member of the executive committee.

The trouble is that, with so many former pupils competing for the favours of an eminent potter in the Nitten group, there is no guarantee that such loyalty will in the end be rewarded. This means that the Nitten organization is always subject to factionalism, when somebody finally becomes alienated from the group's constraints. As with all patronage of this sort, a leader has only so much in the way of privileges and rewards to distribute to his followers. Thus, when a following gets too large and the leader is unable to secure access to new sources of 'funds', the teacher/apprentice kind of vertical relationship is doomed to disintegrate. Clearly, a talent at pottery has only a certain amount to do with one's position in the artistic hierarchy in this kind of organizational structure, so that it is probably patience, rather than technical mastery, that finally allows certain potters to get to the very top of the pyramid-like structure of the Nitten pottery world.

Potter Organizations: The Dentō Kōgeiten Group

The Dentō Kōgeiten is an annual exhibition of 'traditional crafts' held at Mitsukoshi Department Store every September. In it are included pottery (which occupies the larger part of the exhibition), lacquerware, metalwork, bamboo objects, dyed and woven fabrics, and one or two other things that come under the rubric of 'traditional craft'. The Traditional Crafts Exhibition was first started in 1954, following the government's decision to institute a system of 'intangible cultural properties' (*mukei bunkazai*) after there was an outcry over the loss of a number of art treasures in the Hōryūji Temple fire of 1949. Almost two dozen traditional craftsmen were appointed the holders of intangible cultural properties and were invited to show their work at a special exhibition arranged by the Agency for Cultural Affairs at Mitsukoshi. These craftsmen included such well-known potters as Arakawa Toyozō, Kaneshige Tōyō, and Katō Tōkuro.

In the following year, the present system of 'important intangible cultural properties' (*jūyō mukei bunkazai*) was established. The first potters designated what have popularly been called 'national treasures' were Ishiguro Munemaro for his *tetsuyu*, iron-glazed wares; Arakawa Toyozō for his Shino and Seto wares; Tomimoto Kenkichi for his overglazed porcelain: and Hamada Shōji for his *mingei*, or folk craft, style. People with 'traditional skills', such as the thirteenth-generation potters Kakiemon and Imaemon – both overglaze enamel porcelain-ware potters – were asked to contribute to the 1955 exhibition.

It was in the same year that the Japan Crafts Association (Nihon Tōgeikai) was formed. Its members' work was to centre on 'traditional work' (*dentōteki na shigoto*) and in this respect it directly opposed the individual 'creativity' (*sōsaku*) of Nitten artists. In 1956, members of the Nihon Tōgeikai were permitted to exhibit in the Dentō Kōgeiten, and the year after that the exhibition took on its present form when contributions were solicited from craftsmen all over Japan.

The system as it stands is that any craftsmen or women who have their work accepted for exhibition once are elected an 'associate member' (*junkaiin*), and three more times a 'full member' (*kaiin*). However, in the Dentō Kōgeiten, unlike the Nitten exhibition, full membership does not automatically ensure selection of craftsmen's work each year in the national exhibition, although it usually does for regional shows. Thereafter, each step up the hierarchy of the Nihon Tōgeikai is much the same as it is for the Nitten group – with influential ranks of 'judge' (*shinsain*), 'executive' (*riji*), and 'executive chairman' (*kaichō*) all subject to delicate negotiation.

All in all, however, it is probably fair to say that the organization of the Nihon Tōgeikai is not quite as in-bred as that of the Nitten group. Factionalism does exist, however, and it is still virtually impossible for anyone to get to the top of the hierarchy on the basis of talent alone. Some of the more pressing problems stem from the facts that teacher/ apprentice (*sensei/deshi*) relations are still strong (so much so that at one stage it became possible to talk of a 'school clique' [*gakubatsu*] between students of the Tokyo University of Art and their professors, Fujimoto Nōdō and Tamura Kōichi); that 'local' networks have an important part to play in which works get selected to the exhibition, in that potter jurors tend to choose works by potters living in their own region of Japan;[11] and that the panel of jurors at the Traditional Crafts Exhibition is not limited to craftsmen, but includes one or two critics as well. This is beneficial in that their presence prevents craftsmen from forming cliques that are too intense. However, it is just as easy for critics to form their own factions of craftsmen, and to do their utmost to pass the work of their followers into exhibitions (as we saw earlier in discussion of potter organizations' prejudging' sessions). Potters themselves actively participate in such practices by taking their work along to critics on the jury of the Dentō Kōgeiten and asking for 'advice' on which pots to submit. Although there is no guarantee that the 'thank you' envelope passed across the *tatami* will lead to a potter's work being accepted (cf. Rosenberg 1970:389–90), in general the evidence suggests that the part played by critics in the selection of what is seen as 'ceramic art' is not unimportant.

Critics

In general, critics are extremely powerful in the Japanese art market (Havens 1982:125), and the ceramics art world is no exception to this rule. In many respects, the English term 'critic' is a misnomer, for those whose business it is to write about art in Japan rarely say anything critical. Instead, as the Japanese word *hyōronka* implies, critics merely 'appraise' work being exhibited in galleries and department stores.

One of the more remarkable features of contemporary Japanese ceramics is the background of those who in the early to mid-80s were seen to be the country's leading critics. A number of critics were employed in art museums and universities, but there were others whose main specialization was in philosophy, design, civil engineering, or amateur archaeology. Hardly a single one among those men called upon to act as interpreters of ceramic art started out his career as a pottery specialist, and very few were full-time professional critics. Primarily specialists in other aspects of Japanese art, they had over the years found themselves being asked to appraise pots because of the boom in department store exhibitions, and because of the burgeoning art publication business that had accompanied these exhibitions.

One of the more important qualifications for a successful critic would seem to consist of an ability to speak fluently and knowledgeably about contemporary ceramics. In other words, critics are expected not merely to comment upon some aspect of the pots before them, but to phrase their comments in terms that reflect present-day cultural preoccupations.[12] Opportunities to do this are not infrequent, since critics are invited to give advice to potters' groups, accompany collectors on tours of potters' kilns, lecture the general public at exhibitions, and write down their thoughts in exhibition catalogues, newspaper articles, and longer art publications. However, it is in the system of 'references' (*suisenbun*), written on behalf of potters, that the critics probably have the most immediately effective influence.

Suisenbun are used on invitation cards to one-man shows, are hung on wall placards at the entrance to a gallery, and are included as a Foreword to any catalogue that a potter might have printed. Precisely because critics here act to 'explain' a potter's work to the public (Schucking 1974:60–1), we find that they do not attempt to give an 'objective' view of a potter's work, but instead provide a 'subjective' discussion of the potter concerned: in particular, of his or her private life, technical skills, and kiln tradition. In general, it is not *what* a critic says about pots so much as *how* he talks about potters that is important.

In the 1980s, critics were paid up to ¥100,000 for a 'reference' – possibly more if the reference was then published in a widely-circulated newspaper or journal (Havens 1982:125–6). A popular critic would write as many as fifty or sixty references a year – good business when it is remembered that payment is in cash, and probably slips by the eyes of the tax authorities. In such circumstances, it would clearly be counter-productive for a critic to be 'objectively' critical, since he would find the demand for his *suisenbun* falling off. At the same time, because critics very often are given pots by grateful potters, it helps to write appreciatively about the latter, since they can then enhance the value of their own rapidly growing collections, while passing off as 'gifts' to their own friends and acquaintances the works in their possession by potters who, for one reason or another, do not become famous in the course of time.

Critics' real power comes more perhaps from their social contacts than from their writings, and critics make sure to keep in touch with a number of collectors since it is the latter who, by purchasing pots, validate a critic's claims about a potter's work. Some of these collectors, like the potters themselves, live far from

236

Tokyo, so that critics in many respects act as mediators between the capital and the rest of the country, between urban and rural values. They tell both potters and collectors what is up-to-date, fashionable, and 'aesthetically' pleasing, and – like *yakuza* or politicians – make sure to carve out 'territories' of their own. Thus, in the past, the Seto/Mino area was said to be 'owned' by the renowned – and important – critic, Koyama Fujio. In the 80s, it was suggested that the district of Hagi 'belonged' to the tea ceremony specialist, Hayashiya Seizō, while Kyushu potters were gradually becoming affiliated with Yoshida Kōzō.

Critics also make use of these contacts to initiate business deals with department stores and galleries in Tokyo.[13] The latter, always eager to find new talent, will ask critics to help them out and very often it is the latter who end up arranging potters' one-man shows. At the same time, because of their connections with the media, critics are frequently invited to participate in some new publishing venture involving ceramics, and they tend to make sure that one or two or their own 'favourite' potters are included. Perhaps not surprisingly, in the ceramics art world there is unanimous disapproval of the critics – mainly because it is clear that their position on a number of exhibition juries enables them to wield enormous power – a power that is frequently resented by those unable to combat or take advantage of it.[14]

Potters and Department Stores

Mention of critics' relations with department stores brings us full circle to our starting point: potters' one-man shows. Precisely because the critics are unable, or unwilling, to publicly criticize contemporary Japanese ceramics, potters have found that the single criterion by which 'aesthetic' value has come to be determined in present-day Japan consists of total sales figures at their one-man shows. Primarily because potters exhibit their work in department stores, rather than in low-turnover galleries or museums of art, they find themselves faced with a conflict between appreciative value and commodity exchange value. While potters are concerned with the quality of their work, department stores are interested in its sales potential. The higher the total sales, the greater the stores' intake, based on a twenty to forty per cent commission.

This focus on sales as a means of determining artistic worth partly explains the hierarchy of stores alluded to earlier. A store like Mitsukoshi or Isetan is placed at the top of the prestige ladder because it has a far better sales potential than – say – Matsuzakaya, although Tokyo stores in general offer greater possibilities than provincial stores. Successful potters find themselves exhibiting at successful stores, but the final onus falls on the potters' ability to sell their work. It is this which finally determines their rankings in the ceramics art world.

In the 1980s, it was more or less assumed that any potter in the country could earn somewhere between one and two million yen in a six-day one-man show in a department store gallery.[15] Rankings can be thought to begin, therefore, once a potter sells more than ¥2 million. All in all, my informants suggested that there were about five classes, with one superclass, based on the following sales figures in Tokyo during the early to mid-1980s.

Class 5	¥2–5 million
Class 4	¥5–10 million
Class 3	¥10–30 million
Class 2	¥30–50 million
Class 1	¥50–100 million
Superclass	¥100+ million

To some extent, these figures suggest that Japanese department stores provide potters with a form of patronage which in our own society might be provided by government. There is, however, more to these figures than first meets the eye. So concerned are potters with sales as a gauge of success that they frequently call upon their (former) apprentices to come to their show to buy one of their works. It is said that in exchange for this favour, they will do their best to influence members of the jury at the next major competitive exhibition. Not only this, but in some cases, when it is becoming apparent that their sales are going to be down from the previous year's total, potters will telephone dealers and ask them to buy up several large and expensive pots. After the show is over, they are generally obliged to supply the dealers concerned free of charge three times the value of pots purchased at their one-man show.[16]

Department stores, for their part, have a habit of approaching potters after a successful exhibition and obliging them to buy extremely expensive antiques worth several million yen. If the potter concerned refuses to avail himself of what is usually put across as a 'unique opportunity' in which to pursue his 'research', he soon finds that he is not asked to hold any further exhibitions at the store in question. It is hardly surprising, perhaps, to hear one skeptical dealer comment as follows:

> These potters may look as if they're making an awful lot of money, but things aren't quite what they seem, you know. For a start, of course, there are production expenses to take into consideration: the materials needed to make and fire the pots, for example – not forgetting running costs, apprentices' salaries, packaging, boxing, advertising, and so on. Then the potter has to come up to the capital with his wife and stay in Tokyo at a hotel that's flashy enough to suit his successful image. And while he's here, he has to wine and dine the critics who've been writing up his show in one or two of the art magazines. Nor must he forget to get in touch with his favourite collectors and 'encourage' them to come and buy his work. He also has to make sure he butters up the Art Section employees in the department store, by taking them out for a couple of long nights' drinking during the course of the show. And they, of course, respond by asking him to buy up some ancient Persian pot, or something, so that in the end the poor potter hardly has enough with which to pay the return fare home. But,

if he hasn't earned himself any money, he has at least earned himself a name. That's what pottery exhibitions are all about.

This form of sales technique is referred to in Japanese as *oshitsuke*. It has not only been practised on potters, but also on department store suppliers. For example, I once came across a set of Hamada Shōji dishes at a Tokyo auction house where the auctioneer told me that this was not the first time that these particular pots had been through his hands. This time they had been brought in by someone who supplied a leading department store with a rather special brand of *sake*. Unwilling victim of the store's *oshitsuke* practices, the *sake* brewer found that his original purchase price of ¥1 million could not be matched at the auction, where the dishes were sold for just over ¥200,000. The buyer was none other than a representative of the same department store that had originally disposed of the dishes. Marx, if he were alive today, would no doubt be surprised at this novel interpretation of his notion of the 'circulation of commodities'!

Although *oshitsuke* as such is illegal in Japan, other department stores in Japan have practised, and still practise, a form of 'obligation purchasing', or what Ronald Dore (1983) more charitably calls 'goodwill marketing', which is not dissimilar to the more damning '*oshitsuke*'. A dealer friend put it this way:

As you know, I often act as go-between and put on pottery shows in local department stores' galleries. At the end of last year, one of the stores concerned invited me along to their new year party. That was to be expected, I suppose. After all, we'd done business together. But what I didn't anticipate was suddenly finding myself being asked to purchase a suit from one of a number of cloth retailers lining the way out of the building. '*Tsukiai de katte kure*' (buy it because of our personal connection) was the way the Executive Director put it, and I had little choice but to accede to his request. A suit was cheap at the price, though. Friends of mine have been obliged to buy jewellery and fur coats for their wives. All one can do is knock it off as 'expense account' costs.

Conclusion

This has been a brief account of some of the more informal relations which exist among those connected with the contemporary ceramic art world in Japan. I have only been able to focus on those most closely involved in the production (potters), marketing (department stores and newspaper companies), and aesthetic appraisal (critics) of contemporary Japanese ceramics, and have ignored the part played by the media, dealers, auction houses, collectors, government officials, politicians, and even the imperial household. For example, some of those involved in the propagation of contemporary Japanese ceramics have included senior members of foreign legations in Tokyo who, in order to enhance the value of their own private collections, arrange for exhibitions by favourite potters to be put on at prestigious institutions in their home countries. I hope, however, that this Afterword will have afforded my readers a reasonably clear idea of the way in which the ceramic art world functions in present-day Japanese society.

My aim here has been to show that, although contemporary ceramics may not be appreciated as highly in the United States or Europe as they are in Japan, there appears to be nothing that makes Japanese ceramics peculiar in the context of art worlds in general. This is not to suggest that the mechanisms supporting similar art institutions will themselves be similar – one need only look at the relationship between art patronage and the tax structure in the United States and Japan to realize this – but comparisons may usefully be drawn. Some of these I have already remarked upon in the endnotes, but there is one in particular that is quite striking: the close parallel between the Nitten exhibition structure and nineteenth-century Parisian Salons.

It will be recalled that the organization of the Japan Art Exhibition displays the kind of hierarchical pyramid-like structure that has come to be seen as being typical both of *iemoto* artistic groups and of Japanese society in general. However, it should also be recognized that this same organization bears remarkable similarity to the external system of painting in France during the mid- to late nineteenth century. There we find, for example, that: an artist first had to enroll in one of the studios of the Ecole des Beaux-Arts, where he was obliged to paint in an acceptable style subjects that were deemed 'proper' by his teachers; he then strove to have his work accepted by a jury for display at the annual or biennial state exhibitions, known as 'salons'; if his work received an honourable mention or prize, he could expect to be awarded the Prix de Rome, allowing him to study in Italy for a year; as a successful artist, he would then have his work purchased by the state; he would proceed to receive commissions for works that were to be placed in state buildings; he might then go on to achieve the pinnacle of success by being elected to the Academy of Fine Arts, and/or by being awarded the ribbon of the Legion d'Honneur (Rogers 1970:195–6).

In his fictional account of the Parisian art world in the 1860s, Emile Zola (1968, especially Chapter Ten), depicts a large number of minor details that I frequently encountered during the course of my own fieldwork in Japan: the successful artist who finds himself suddenly wealthy, not knowing what to do with easily-made money, and besieged by other artists and would-be artists who come with requests that he help them pass into the Salon; the faked sales designed to keep up inflated prices; the jurying of the exhibition 'complete with all the ambitions, cliques, intrigues and chicanery that have brought polities into such disrepute'; the hostility of critics at loggerheads over which pictures to accept, and trading votes for each others' proteges; saying what they think when first glancing at an art work before them and then eating their words when they decypher its signature; the vast crowds that swarm through the exhibition halls; the minor artists always complaining about the way their work has been displayed; above all, perhaps, the maliciousness of the gossip on which the art world thrives.[17]

The simplest explanation for the parallels to be found between the Nitten and Salon systems suggests that critical attitudes toward art are a product of certain historical conditions. Just how and why they may be so, however, is rather more difficult to pinpoint. Rogers accounts for the influence of the state on French art in the following manner:

> The deleterious effects of this tight State control of the art of painting were exacerbated by the political upheavals experienced by France during the first half of the nineteenth century, which had particularly affected the nobles, traditional patrons of the arts. To make up for the loss of this market, artists were turning to the new bourgeoisie, which was quite willing to buy paintings but lacked training in taste. Only through the Salons could this public be educated to appreciate new works of artistic merit and thus enable young artists to achieve a reputation and persuade this growing, prosperous class to invest in their paintings. But that public regarded honours, medals and prizes won at the Salons as proof of an artist's merit and so it bought only the works of the docile pupils.
>
> (Rogers 1970:196)

Clearly, there are several respects here in which early twentieth-century Japanese society was not unlike French society of a century before: the final break with the feudal past in 1868, the gradual demise of the *samurai* class, the emergence of a new bourgeoisie lacking training in taste, the education of this public through state-run exhibitions which themselves acted as a focal point for artists to express their ideas. It is more than likely that the Nitten has inherited its present structure from its forebears, the Bunten and Teiten exhibitions, but why it should have continued in such rigid form for so long in a society that has in general shown extreme fluidity and change over the past 50 years, I cannot tell. Perhaps it could be argued that Japan's defeat in the Pacific war brought about the rise of yet another bourgeoisie equally lacking training in taste; that the establishment of the government-run system of important intangible cultural properties merely served to reinforce the pre-war exhibition system; and that, as a result, the public still regards honours and prizes as more or less the only proof of an artist's merit.

All of this remains speculative and needs to be considered in much greater depth, but if these similarities in forms of aesthetic *appraisal* between French and Japanese art worlds were found to be more than superficial, it might then be possible to add a further hypothesis in the light of my own general theoretical argument concerning aesthetic *production* put forward in the Conclusion to this book. There I suggested that phenomena such as urbanization, industrialization, and consumerism had given rise to a folk art aesthetic ideal that explicitly joined the 'creation' of beauty to certain forms of social behaviour (community, selflessness, being close to nature, and so on). Here it might be added that a certain set of social conditions may give rise to a certain way of understanding (or, in this case, of not understanding) art, and that this aesthetic attitude itself encourages the formation of a certain type of art world. In other words, as we have seen in my description of Bernard Leach's influence on Yanagi Sōetsu and Japanese artists and writers in the years leading up to the discovery of '*mingei*', the relationship between society and aesthetics is very much a two-way process.

Plate 73 *Ame* brown sake bottle dipped in *yuhada* yellow glaze, with *nagashi* trailed motif

NOTES

Introduction

1 Witness the interminable discussions among anthropologists, art historians and museum curators about the status of 'primitive' art (e.g. Hiller 1991). For a brief description of the adoption of ethnographic artifacts by European artists and their assimilation into the category of primitive art, see Maquet (1986:65–76). The classic account is by Goldwater (1967). Note, however, the limited view of non-western art forms taken by anthropologists who totally ignore the role of Japanese art in the development of European aesthetics (see Chapter 10).

2 In anthropology, the institutional definition of art has recently been narrowed down to the marketing of art objects and the 'abstract processes of value creation' that occur therein (Morphy 1994:651), on the one hand, and allied to an 'interpretive' approach (Gell 1996:36), on the other. Danto himself (1992:89–112) has tried to come to terms with the metamorphosis of ethnographic artefacts into artworks by indulging in a skillful – but extremely problematic (Gell 1996) – invention of 'a plausible anthropology for a pair of African tribes' (Danto 1992:95), known as the Pot People and Basket Folk, whose baskets and pots become 'art' when imbibed with what he refers to as an 'Absolute Spirit'.

3 Danto himself expresses his gratitude to both Richard Sclafani and George Dickie for rescuing his 'artworld' theory from slumber 'in a back number of the sepulchral *Journal of Philosophy*', and for giving it 'modest fame' by erecting thereon 'something called the Institutional Theory of Art' which is, nevertheless, quite alien to anything he believes. But, as he then notes philosophically: 'one's children do not always quite come out as intended' (Danto 1981:viii). One suspects, however, on the evidence of later writings, that Danto himself has been rather a distant father who has chosen not to engage too closely with such unconventional children, but to prefer the philosophical security of such ancestors as Hegel and Heidegger.

4 Alfred Gell's article (1996) has come out while this book is in press. I have been unable, therefore, to incorporate his arguments fully in this Introduction. Needless to add, I am delighted that someone in anthropology is finally taking up the ideas of the art world and artwork and making – what seems to me at least – a lot of sense!

5 It is precisely such art world participants as connoisseurs, patrons, and those in the art market whom anthropologists and sociologists prefer to leave out of their discussions of art (while proffering the usual lame excuses that such participants impinge on, but do not entirely dictate, the final form of artworks [e.g. Manfredi 1982:176–7]). Just how they do impinge on artworks, just how they do (or do not) influence them, is what needs discussion.

6 This was precisely the problem faced by Yanagi Sōetsu when he outlined his philosophy of *mingei vis-à-vis* conventional Japanese art history.

7 For a more recent example of classificatory problems besetting contemporary Aboriginal art, see Morphy (1995).

8 We might note, too, that the smaller such an art world is, 'the more immediately and personally intimate and intense the appreciation of art which it develops can be' (Hauser 1982:450).

9 It is, of course, *participation* that is crucial to the operation of this anthropology of art world (as of anthropology and art worlds in general). It is those who attend conferences, edit books, contribute to journals, help mount the occasional exhibition, attend opening parties, and generally 'network', who form the core personnel and influence the way in which this world will develop. Somebody someday should do an ethnography of ethnographers!

10 Witness Dickie, for example, who writes: 'if something cannot be appreciated, it cannot be a work of art' (1974:41).

11 And this argument of mine is, of course, in itself interpretive.

12 See Moeran (1996:276–97) for a theoretical elaboration and fuller discussion of this argument in the context of advertising.

13 This section of the chapter relies heavily on Suzuki (1978), and on discussions during 1980–82 fieldwork on the ceramic art market with Fujita Shinichirō, Inui Yoshiaki, Hasebe Mitsuhiko, Maeda Taeji, Sugihara Nobuhiko, Suzuki Kenji, and Yoshida Kōzō. To all of these, but particularly to Professor Suzuki, I owe a great debt of thanks for their patience, time and trouble.

14 The first Ministry of Culture Art Exhibition (Monbushō Bijutsu Tenrankai, abbreviated to Bunten) was held in October 1907. It was superseded by the Imperial Art Exhibition (Teiten), with the establishment of the Imperial Academy of Arts (Teikoku Bijutsu-in) in September 1919. An 'art craft' (*bijutsu kōgei*) section, to which potters were allowed to contribute, was eventually included as the fourth category in the Imperial Art Exhibition in 1927. Both these exhibitions were the forerunners of the present-day Japan Art Exhibition (Nihon Bijutsu Tenrankai, or Nitten) discussed in the Afterword to this book (see Suzuki 1978:216–8).

15 It has also characterized the writings of anthropologists who, over the years, have conducted fieldwork in remote parts of the world. For a more detailed discussion of nostalgic praxis in a Tokyo suburb, see Robertson (1991).

16 Hauser (1982:563) points out that the communal nature of folk art affects its use as well as production, so that it becomes difficult to 'distinguish, in principle, producer from consumer'.

1 The Japanese *Mingei* Movement

1 Some of the material presented in this chapter has been adapted from Moeran (1994).

2 Muneyoshi was Yanagi's given name. Later in life, however, Yanagi sometimes made use of the Chinese pronunciation of the characters with which Muneyoshi was formed to call himself Sōetsu. This is the name by which he is generally known in the west and which I have, therefore, adopted for convenience here.

3 For biographies of Yanagi, see Tsurumi (1976) and Mizuo (1978). Bernard Leach has given a somewhat more subjective account of his friendship with Yanagi in the Introduction to *The Unknown Craftsman* (Leach 1972). Further facts may be gathered from a reading of Leach's conversations with the Japanese potter, Hamada Shōji (Leach 1976). I am grateful to Yanagi's son, Munemichi, for giving me further information about his father's activities during the early part of his life. I have decided not to include here references to Yanagi's works where words or short phrases only are

quoted. Those readers interested in tracing the exact sources are referred to my Ph.D. dissertation, *Social Aspects of Folk Craft Production, Marketing and Aesthetics in a Japanese Pottery Community*, Department of Anthropology and Sociology, School of Oriental and African Studies, University of London, 1980.

4 An enthusiasm which, as we shall see in the Conclusion to this book, was inspired by the two potters Tomimoto Kenkichi and Bernard Leach.

5 We should note here, perhaps, the paradox created by the construction of the Folk Craft Museum: artworks are always transformed when placed in museums and so come to be re-evaluated, often as qualitatively valuable or historically important, in a manner not accorded them in their original form (Hauser 1982:498).

6 For a discussion of Tamba's household development, see Kleinberg (1983). In Koishiwara, the original nine pottery households sharing two cooperative kilns increased over a twenty year period to more than three dozen potteries with their own kilns. This expansion took place mainly through the establishment of branch houses for second and third sons by the original potter households, as well as through the independent setting up of potteries by potters (often outsiders) who had been apprenticed to these households.

7 In this respect, I should add that the use of the word 'craftsman' in this book is intended to refer to both men and women.

8 As Bourdieu (1984:567) points out, just because certain connoisseurs return to a 'popular' style, it does not mean that they necessarily return to the 'people' (whether working or rural class).

9 By following Ruskin and Morris in putting forward the principle that good art could only be produced in a 'healthy' society, Yanagi, Hamada and other adherents of *mingei* philosophy fell into a trap pointed out by Hauser (1982:213–4): they all 'failed to recognize that the so-called health of a society is an uncommonly complex concept and that in the machine age it is subject to different assumptions from what it was in the period of medieval craft, which they regarded as exemplary'.

10 In calling for a surrender to 'natural' feelings, Yanagi might also be accused of 'aesthetic slumming', since the basis of the aesthetic disposition among dominant groups is usually a measure of self-control and a refusal to surrender oneself to nature (Bourdieu 1984:40).

11 The word used here by Yanagi was *bijutsu*, 'art'. It is interesting to note that in the early days of the *mingei* movement, neither Yanagi nor any of his friends had fixed on the idea that *mingei* was a 'craft' rather than an 'art' form. In a letter to Bernard Leach in 1927, Hamada calls the planned museum in Tokyo the *Nihon Mingei Bijutsukan*, or Japan People's Art Museum (Leach 1976:91). Leach himself always referred to *mingei* as 'folk art', and Yanagi has often been criticized (by Miyake Chūichi, for example) for setting *mingei* on a pedestal and making it into an art form, despite his theoretical emphasis on the notion of craft.

12 Yanagi's decision to establish a folk art museum and Morris's decision to devote himself to architecture were also both made on trips with close friends: Yanagi with Hamada and Kawai to Mt. Kōyō in December 1925; Morris on a walking tour in France with Burne-Jones and Fulford in August 1855 (Mizuo 1978:697; Lindsay 1979:65–6).

There are other parallels in the lives of the two men. The astrologist may be glad to hear that both Morris and Yanagi were born under the star of Pisces – on March 24th and 21st respectively. S/he will no doubt draw further evidence of compatibility from the fact that the two men's fathers were obviously very capable mathematicians, and that they died before their sons had reached maturity.

13 Yanagi, too, frequently referred to the various distinctions between 'art' and 'craft' (see, for example, Yanagi 1954:11–36, 227–232), and admitted that Morris's notion of

'lesser art' was more or less equivalent to his own '*getemono*', the word that he used prior to the neologism *mingei* (Yanagi 1955a:112).

14 Readers might like to compare this and the following extract with Bernard Leach's translation (Yanagi 1972:208) from Yanagi's first full length work on crafts, since Leach had a tendency to abbreviate and rewrite certain passages for the benefit of the western reader.

15 But see Morris (1962c:133–134) especially. It is clear from the 'principles of art' that he applied to pottery that Morris preferred hand work to 'mechanical finish' (Morris 1882:188–194).

16 Yanagi pursued this somewhat spiritual approach to *mingei* even further in his revelationary essay, *Bi no Hōmon* (*The Visit of Beauty*) (Yanagi 1973).

17 See, for example, Jugaku (1935); Tonomura (1973); and Mizuo (1978:20–23).

18 In this respect, we should note that both German and Italian fascism were stressing spirituality from around this period (personal communication, Grant Evans).

19 See, for example, how Jacques Maquet relates his own experiences in front of particular art works, like Mondrian's *Broadway* in the Museum of Modern Art, New York (1986:80). Although aware of the fact that he is verbalizing and analysing these experiences retrospectively, Maquet – like Yanagi – tries to argue that the 'meaning' of art works can be 'directly' perceived – and so, without admitting it, tries to counter Gombrich's demonstration that this particular work by Mondrian only takes on its 'full meaning' in terms of previous knowledge of the artist's work and of the expectations conjured thereby (Gombrich 1960:313).

20 Itself borrowed from Aldous Huxley (Firth 1992:16) and more recently supported by a keeper of non-western art and anthropology in England (Shelton 1992:241).

21 I do not intend here to go into all the arguments concerning such concepts as 'individual', 'group', 'harmony', 'class', 'conflict', 'self interest', 'inter-dependence' and so on, since to do so would require at best one extra chapter for this book and, at worst, the final deforestation of south east Asia. Still, those interested in the subject can start by reading Peter Dale's withering – and often hilarious – criticism of *nihonjin* writings (Dale 1986), followed by Chie Nakane (1970) who started a whole sub-disciplinary sect of navel-gazing anthropology by mistaking a *category* of persons for a *group* (Moeran 1996:267).

2 A Pottery Community

1 It is said that a number of (foreign) tourists in search of *ontayaki* end up in Onta and are surprised and disappointed to find that no pottery is made there. They then leave empty-handed, without ever discovering that they should have gone to Sarayama. I myself would have made this mistake when I first went to the community had not the people who kindly gave me a lift from Ōtsuru (during a 'spring offensive' train strike when I had had to hitchhike to Kyushu) taken me directly to Sarayama. It was only three days later, after a pleasant walk over the Otomai Pass and down a wooded valley to the next hamlet, that I was informed that I had been to Onta and that I was conducting fieldwork in Sarayama!

2 To avoid confusion, I will, from now on, refer to the fieldwork community as Sarayama when the community is being discussed independently, and as Onta when it is being compared with another pottery community, such as that of Koishiwara, or when the pottery – rather than the community as such – is being discussed.

3 Miyake Chūichi, leader of the Japan Folk Craft Society, has argued in his magazine, *Nihon no Mingei* (114:3–11), that Sarayama was founded in 1665 (Kanbun 5). At the same time, however, he accepts that Yanase Sanuemon and Kurogi Jūbē (see main text below) were founders of the community. But the Kurogi household mortuary

tablets (*ihai*) show that Jūbē died in 1756, so that it is unlikely that he was old enough to walk, let alone found a community, in 1665, ninety-one years prior to his death. That Miyake's argument is more than suspect may be seen from the fact that the same edition of the magazine advertised in 1965 Onta's 300th anniversary festival – a festival devised and arranged entirely by the Folk Craft Society (despite assertion to the contrary by Miyake [cf. *Nihon no Mingei* 114:34–35]). Yanagi himself says that the old people in Sarayama told him in 1931 that their ancestors had come from Koishiwara some 186 years earlier (Yanagi 1931:6). This would mean that Sarayama was founded in 1745.

4 Umeki (1973:27) supposes that the two men were in some way related. While proof is lacking to substantiate this view, fieldwork investigations revealed that Jūbē's mother (d. 1707) was the daughter of one Yanase Mataemon. Whether Mataemon was related to Sanuemon, however, remains unclear. Unfortunately, all genealogical records of the Koishiwara and Onta Yanase households were lost when the temple in which they were kept was destroyed by fire.

5 Nelson Graburn has pointed out that it is intriguing that the Japanese should think it so important that Leach visited and described Sarayama, and that in effect they are using him as an ultimate reference to judge the quality of Onta pottery. My own feeling is that Leach was used by Yanagi, and Hamada in particular, as a reference point for the *Mingei* movement as a whole. Bernard Leach's influence on Yanagi and others in the early days before the coining of the word '*mingei*' will be discussed at the end of this book.

3 Social Organization

1 Kitano (1963) calls the *ie* the 'traditional Japanese family' and emphasizes its genealogical aspect. Befu, who takes the same approach, argues that 'patrilineal descent in Japan performs what may be called the corporate function, that is, the function of perpetuating the kinship unit called the family' (Befu 1963:1330). There is thus some controversy concerning the exact interpretation of what an *ie* is – probably because of the variety of its forms. The interpretation presented here is based on the views of Yoneyama (1965), and of Nakane (1967), who herself follows the Japanese scholar Ariga Kizaemon.

2 Suenari (1972:123) suggests that 'a patrilineal rule of inheritance, succession and descent are not so dominant in Japanese society as was once thought'. He argues that an eldest daughter can have rights of succession transmitted to her either temporarily or permanently, and cites figures from the Tōhoku area which suggest that first-child, and not first-son, inheritance did exist before the Meiji period (1868–1912). For further discussion of inheritance and succession, see Bachnik (1983).

3 Various terms have been used for this distinction between two types of hamlet. Fukutake (1956) has referred to the two types as the *tōhoku-gata* (northeast) and *seinan-gata* (southwest); Ariga (1956) uses the term *dōzoku-gata* (extended household) and *kōgumi-gata* (association), and Gamō (1962) *jūzokuteki* (dependent) and *dokuritsuteki* (independent), respectively. Johnson (1967) talks of 'hierarchical' and 'egalitarian' types, while Dore (1959) has translated Isoda's terms as 'family status' and 'non-family status'. We should note that both types of hamlet were formed during the Edo period prior to Japan's modernization and that only residual elements of each type are found in rural society today.

4 'The *dōzoku* . . . is a set of households which recognize their relationship in terms of *honke* and *bunke* and which, on the basis of this relation, have developed a corporate function as a group' (Nakane 1967:190–191). In spite of the attention paid to it, and the size of household groups discussed in anthropological literature, the *dōzoku* is

rarely expected to exceed half a dozen households; nor does it usually last for more than about three generations (Nakane 1967:119).

5 It should be made clear that 'household ranking' and 'non-household ranking' hamlets are ideal, rather than actual, types. The distinction is certainly useful, but not absolute. For example, it is possible for an age-grade system to operate alongside a *dōzoku*-type of authoritarian organization of households in the same hamlet (Takahashi 1958:138). It is also probable that a hamlet consisting entirely of a single *dōzoku* will have some kind of honzontally structured alliance between its constituent households (Ariga 1956:25–26). Ariga has therefore suggested that we distinguish 'ranking' from 'non-ranking' relations between *households* in a hamlet, rather than between hamlets as such.

6 Readers interested in a more informal account of life in country valley (which includes some – but not all – of Sarayama's inhabitants), are referred to my book, *Okubo Diary* (Moeran 1985).

7 Those who are celebrated as ancestors include only those who die as members of the household, back to the founder of the *ie* (Nakane 1967:106).

8 Compare this with the urban salary-man's household in which the wife often has control over everyday financial affairs (Fukutake 1967:57). It is said that Kyushu men are particularly authoritarian in their dealings with household money matters.

9 Generally, the eldest son succeeded to the headship of the main household, though there are exceptions. For example, in Yamaichi, the eldest son formed a branch household (Kaneichi), the second son succeeded to the headship of the main household (Yamaichi), and the third son was taken into the retirement household (Iriichi) by his father.

10 Further recognized marriage ties exist between households, one of which has since left the community – e.g., Yamaichi and the Sakamoto *sō-honke*, and Yamasai and Yamau.

11 In fact, the post of cooperative leader has continued to be held according to the criterion of seniority.

4 Ecology and Social Structure

1 I have come across foot-powered crushers being used for pounding clay in a pottery village in northern Thailand, and for pounding paint materials in an umbrella village nearby. A photograph in the June 1977 edition of the magazine *Aruku Miru Kiku* shows that clay in Shigaraki, Japan, was also prepared by a foot-powered crusher of the *battari* type during the Meiji period (Cort 1977:18). The clay in Shigaraki and in the pottery village referred to in northern Thailand is in fact softer than that used in Onta (and in nearby Koishiwara), where anything other than a heavy water-powered crusher would not be effective.

2 Sarayama clay is a form of propylite which is found in an area north of Hita City, stretching from Oku-Yabakei to Iwaya. A further pocket of similar clay may be found around the pottery community of Sarayama (Koishiwara). The mountains were formed geologically in the early Pleistocene era; propylite itself derives from hornblende and andesite (*anzangan*) (see Matsumoto 1961:82–86).

3 Fields owned by Kaneyo in the Gōshiki valley and by Yamamasu at the bottom of Sarayama were still being farmed in the late 80s. Yamaichi also grew rice in his fields immediately above the community, but gave up farming in 1979. This has made it possible for the community to expand up the mountainside toward Ikenzuru, although so far no such developments have taken place.

4 There is some difficulty in establishing the origins of Yamako and Kaneyo. It is possible that Yamako branched from Yamasai and Kaneyo from Yamako. The marriage of the daughter of the founding ancestor of Kaneyo to the head of Yamako

would appear to support this view. However, memorial tablets (*ihai*) include only three Kurogi names in the Yamako household, and these suggest that Yamako and Kaneyo branched at about the same time. Therefore, I have applied the principle of downstream branching to the determination of when and from where Yamako and Kaneyo were formed.

5 Kaneichi, which decided to take up potting again in the late 60s, was able to do so because the Sakamoto *sō-honke* had left Sarayama, making one *ize* dam available for use, and the increased demand for pottery had made it possible for potters to give up agriculture. Both land and water at the top of the hamlet had become available for community expansion.

5 Labour Cooperation

1 As in such other folk craft potteries as Tamba (Rhodes 1970:120), potters measure the temperature of the kiln chamber by eye, rather than by Seger or Orton pyrometric cones, or by colour-check test pieces.

For a detailed description of Tamba-ware pottery production at Tachikui in the 1960s, see Rhodes (1970:101–30).

2 There is one exception: Irisai fires the main mouth of its kiln with oil for five hours. In 1977–79, the potter there claimed that this was a temporary measure only, but he was still using oil in the 1990s.

3 Estimates regarding breakages during firing vary wildly, since potters have been intent on defeating the intentions of the local tax authorities. The number of broken and faulty pots, however, would appear to average about 20–30 per cent.

4 Ten households shared the cooperative kiln when Kaneyo was still potting and Irisai had not as yet built its private kiln (prior to 1927), thereafter nine households till Irisai's breakaway in about 1935. Since Irisai was established as a branch household in 1895, and Kaneichi continued potting until 1910, it is possible that at one period between these dates eleven households were sharing the *kyōdōgama* (provided that Irisai did take up pottery immediately upon branching).

5 Many of the terms used by residents of Sarayama are not standard throughout Japan. Nakane (1967:144), for example, refers to *temagēshi* as *yui*, and Smith (1956:16), as *tema-gae*. Embree (1939:134–136) talks of *kattari* for his village in nearby Kumamoto Prefecture. Much of Embree's valuable description of rural life in pre-war Japan (see also Smith and Wiswell 1982) was still valid for Sarayama in the 1970s. Since some anthropologists of Japan already regarded Suye Mura as 'retarded beyond the average for Japan' (Norbeck 1977:196, fn. 2) in 1935–1936, one wonders what they may think of this description of Sarayama.

6 More frequently, however, the *kō* acted as 'cooperative credit clubs' (cf. Embree 1939:138–153; Fukutake 1967:106–107; Yoneyama 1967b:316–317), and Sarayama households banded together to purchase such items as *futon* bedding, watches, and so on when they did not have the financial means to do so independently.

7 When labour was performed for mutual benefit, as in *moyai*, participating households took it in turns to act as hosts.

8 At that time, before shelving was introduced, all households shared the bottom chamber of the cooperative kiln, because the risk of breakage there was extremely high.

9 Some potters are said to have taken advantage of codes of etiquette that forbade a man, out of politeness, from waking a sleeping comrade, and to have purposely feigned drowsiness in order to get others to fire their chambers for them.

6 Environmental and Social Change

1 Unlike other communities, household labour organization in Sarayama was not affected by mechanization and technological innovation in agricultural methods (cf. Shimpo 1976:46ff).

2 Another reason cited by potters for their giving up farming is that their rice paddy was often ravaged by wild boar. People from non-potting households point out, however, that the wild boar started coming out into the fields from the thickly wooded mountains only when the potters had stopped farming (i.e. from the mid-1970s). For a description of some of the economic problems arising from the curtailment policy, see Robert Smith (1978:96–130).

3 It is generally agreed that the quality of the Kitanamizu clay is far superior to that of any other slip, as was painfully brought home to potters when they had to obtain supplies of slip clay from Arita in the 1970s and encountered all kinds of glazing and firing difficulties. There was talk – but no action at the time of my fieldwork – of going back to the Kitanamizu deposit.

4 It is one of the many ironies of the *Mingei* movement and Onta potters that decisions about forestry made by one group of local government officials should go right against the concept of 'tradition' so dearly held by those in another department of the town hall who were more concerned with promoting Hita's tourism.

5 Cf. Shimpo (1976:103) for the breakdown of the roof-thatching association in Shiwa with the adoption of tiles. In Sarayama, improved economic conditions made it unnecessary for households to participate in *kō* to buy bedding, watches, and so on. Expensive items were now purchased outright or through credit or on hire-purchase terms. For further instances of *kō* which, in most parts of Japan came to an end before the Pacific War, see Cornell (1956:149) and Smith (1956:16).

6 This apparent anomaly in figures stems from the fact that Kaneichi stopped potting in 1910, and then started its own kiln in 1970 after the demand for Onta ware had boomed.

7 The *Mingei* Boom and Economic Development

1 In 1962, the exchange rate was £1 = ¥1,008 and $1 = ¥360. By the mid-70s, the value of the yen had just about doubled *vis-à-vis* these (and other) currencies.

2 Compare this sum with figures quoted by Robert Smith (1978:118) for the village of Kurusu, where the average household savings are quoted as ¥328,812 (ranging from ¥5,792 to ¥1,235,471) for July 1975.

3 Since the time of my fieldwork, potters previously working on their own in Irisai, Yamaichi, and Iriichi have now been joined by their sons working full-time at the wheel, thereby enabling them to fire that much more frequently. Older potters in Yamani and Yamako, on the other hand, have moved into semi-retirement and so affected these households' firing schedules.

4 I made my estimates of kiln capacity when I helped unload, and thereby could count, the total contents of firings by Kaneichi, Yamasai, and Yamani. Before seconds had been discarded, these firings came to ¥833,840, ¥1,667,830, and ¥2,161,010 respectively (calculated at wholesale prices). The head of Yamako admitted to me while under the influence of *sake* that he earned at least ¥2 million per firing, a figure admitted by his brother at Yamani in an unguarded moment when sober. The head of Iriichi also became more forthright as my fieldwork progressed, and one day he confided that each chamber of the cooperative kiln yielded an average of ¥350,000. I have taken this figure for my calculations in Table 4. Both Iriichi and Yamaichi agreed, independently, with my suggestion that Irisai earned about ¥1,600,000 per firing.

5 Other hamlet households contributed ¥100,000 each. To allay the suspicions of the Hita tax authorities, potters agreed to pay only ¥350,000 in cash and to borrow the remainder from local banks, thereby making it appear as if they had no ready cash.

6 Cf. Rhodes (1970:112) who makes a similar, though less strident, argument about the quality of Tamba wares deteriorating as a result of increased demand.

8 The Decline of Community Solidarity

1 The former head of Yamani made no pots at all, and the present head of Yamako's adopting father made very few. Both potters had been working more or less on their own until about 1965. Although Irisai had had its own kiln for several decades by the time of the *mingei* boom, the present head had also been working entirely on his own, since his father (an adopted husband) had left the community just before he was born.

2 My inquiries among retailers, however, revealed that in the late 70s Yamani and Yamasan still tended to price their pots higher than other households.

3 Either this part of the story is sour grapes on the part of the loser, or the tax office did not notice, or decided to ignore, the fact that under-reporting failed to meet the overall income agreed between the tax office and the potters' cooperative.

4 This event emphasizes the strongly-held belief in an art world that differences in quality between artists and their works *must* be accounted for at all times (Becker 1982:231), and so lends support to the argument that *mingei* was in the process of becoming an art, rather than mere craft, form.

5 Nelson Graburn has pointed out that the Folk Craft Museum's decision to distribute an album of what it considered to be 'authentic' Onta pots is extraordinary and almost unparalleled in the ethnographic literature on folk art (*personal communication*). He has documented one other case, for the Canadian Eskimos in the early 1950s (see Graburn 1976:55).

6 For example, in Suye Mura, contributions made by parents for musical instruments to be used in a primary school and for a piano in a middle school were worked out according to income levels. Those who earned more made larger contributions (Tsuchiya 1965:45, 50).

7 Onta's self-imposed restriction is remarkable, and nothing similar exists in potteries such as Koishiwara, for example, where 'anything goes'.

8 The system of 'intangible cultural properties' was instituted in 1952 by the Agency for Cultural Affairs, Ministry of Education, primarily to protect Japan's traditional arts (see Moeran 1987, and Afterword). Two years later, a Committee for the Protection of Cultural Properties made the following revisions. First, a very few craftsmen (including the *mingei* potters Tomimoto Kenkichi and Hamada Shōji) were selected as being the holders of 'important intangible cultural properties' (*jūyō mukei bunkazai*) and received an annual stipend from the Agency. It is these men who are popularly referred to as 'national treasures' (*ningen kokuhō*). Second, the committee simultaneously designated certain individuals and groups of craftsmen as the holders of 'intangible cultural properties'. Although the general public tends to confuse the two groups, it should be made clear that the latter designation is far inferior to that of the 'national treasures'. Holders of the title of 'intangible cultural properties', among whom Onta potters are included, receive no stipend from the Agency for Cultural Affairs.

9 For more recent discussions of tradition in Japanese (urban) communities, see Bestor (1989) and Robertson (1991).

10 In Sarayama (Onta) deities that are specifically connected with the production or marketing of pottery – Akiyasama, the fire goddess (cf. Dore 1978:211), and Ebisu, the god of trade – are celebrated by the whole community. In Koishiwara such deities are celebrated by potting households only.

11 In his discussion of *sake* drinking in Suye Mura, Embree remarks that a quarrel rarely breaks out (1939:104). In Sarayama, *sake* drinking is used as an opportunity to air one's views quite openly; what is said is forgiven, but not forgotten, and community problems tend to be 'discussed' with as much heat as exists in a kiln chamber in midfiring (see Moeran 1984a).

12 At the other end of the extreme, of course, an art work's value is gauged by its rarity and the price that it fetches on the market – a price which is then seen to reflect its 'spiritual' (or, in my terminology, symbolic exchange) value and to surround the art work with what John Berger (1972:21) has referred to as 'bogus religiosity'.

9 Theory and Practice in Japanese *Mingei*

1 Compare Osborne (1955:39) on literary criticism for a similar 'relative' view: 'you may in fact choose any writer you like, any dozen critics you like, and you will find ten different assessments, while the three who rank him more or less level will do so for different reasons'.

2 One can argue that the potters' and dealers' attitude that every individual has her personal taste is defensive, in that it licenses them to make and try to sell all kinds of pottery in spite of aesthetic criticism.

3 According to Yanagi (1955b:371), 'the potter's heart is revealed for what it is in the foot-rim, for it is this that determines a pot's final value'.

4 The same sort of thing has occurred in other potteries throughout Japan. In Aizu Hongō, for example, the old herring pickler has been whittled down and adapted into a rectangular ashtray. Gill (1976:109) also reports on Laguna ceramic adaptations of bowls to 'ash bowls'.

5 Buyers were, incidentally, convinced that their female customers were almost totally influenced by colour and pattern in their choice of pots, and that it was only men who 'understood' form. My investigations revealed that women are more concerned with form than buyers believe, while men take function into serious account when choosing pottery.

6 Potters in Koishiwara, where retailing directly to the general public accounts for a large percentage of sales, also admit to naming prices according to the appearance of a potential customer.

7 There is a paradox here that may well have affected the average person's view of the *Mingei* movement, for Yanagi himself was particularly fond of the tea ceremony. Indeed, it might be argued that his whole philosophy is to some extent a continuation of that put forward by the first great tea master, Sen no Rikyū, at the end of the sixteenth century. Certainly Yanagi's concepts are part of the mainstream of Japanese aesthetic theory. His idea that 'selflessness' gives rise to the appreciation of true 'beauty' is in many ways a revival of the concept of *yūgen* as put forward by Zeami Motokiyo (1363–1443), founder of the classic Nō theatre (cf. Tsunoda *et al.* 1964:288–291). 'The concept of *yūgen* teaches us that in aesthetic experience it is not that "I see the work of art", but that by "seeing" the "I" is transformed. It is not that "I enter into the work", but that by "entering" the "I" is altered in the intensity of a pristine immediacy' (Deutsch 1975:32).

8 All this is also true of critics and art historians where similar patterns of 'relatedness' are cultivated. The same might be said, of course, of the academic world where the system of job references, regular conference participation, and the general ability to get on with and be liked by one's colleagues are all as important as – if not more important than – the actual scholarship produced.

9 Cf. Maquet (1986:186) who notes how sections of tree trunks and branches orient some African wood carvers towards the making of cylindrical shapes and 'a certain principle of geometric composition'.

10 If Pierre Bourdieu (1984:32–4) is right in his alignment in aesthetics of form with the upper, and function or content with the lower, classes, then Yanagi's own theory uniting function with form can be said to have initiated *mingei*'s shift from craft to art. Moreover, in *social* terms, the uniting of form and function serves to *deny* the existence of class in contemporary Japanese society and thus reinforces the Orientalist stereotype of the Japanese as a 'group oriented' people.

11 Sociologists are less ideological on the role of the critic. Hauser (1982:484–8) has suggested that the critic as such emerged because of the commercialization of the press, while Schucking (1974:60–1) has pointed out how the critic's position has – since the end of the nineteenth century – shifted radically from siding with the public against the author, to explaining the artist's work to the public.

10 Folk Art, Industrialization and Orientalism

1 For a full-blown discussion of the relation between the aesthetic disposition, taste and social class, see Bourdieu (1984).

2 This observation is supported by further fieldwork that I have conducted on Japanese art pottery, where all serious collectors encountered were men (Moeran 1987, 1990).

3 This 'feminine' aesthetic of *mingei* (and of arts and crafts in general) can also be linked to the discourse of Orientalism which consistently 'feminizes' the Asian objects of its male cultural gaze.

4 Such differences are accompanied, of course, by a different aesthetic vocabulary (cf. Parker and Pollock 1981:160) – witness, for example, the 'well-rounded', 'full-bodied' 'nature' of functional craft pottery, that is often 'pregnant with beauty', *vis-à-vis* the 'sharp', 'lean' aesthetic of ceramic 'sculpture' with its 'upward thrust of the vertical form' (as described in contemporary English-language pottery magazines and auction house catalogues).

5 Note, however, that in fact those buying and selling in an art world are almost always *known* to one another (Moeran 1990:134), and that it is the relationships between artists, collectors, critics, curators, buyers, dealers, auctioneers and so on which make social values so important to the appreciation of artworks (e.g. Manfredi 1982:92–3). In this respect, the art market tends to be by no means as 'anonymous' as the overall commodity market of which it forms a part.

6 The theoretical background to this brief discussion of the 'political economy of values' has been more fully amplified in the Conclusion to my monograph on a Japanese advertising agency (Moeran 1996:281–97).

7 For a more detailed description of why Leach decided to go back to Japan, as well as of the intricate network of relationships that Leach formed there, see Moeran (1994).

8 At more or less the same time, a third famous member of the *mingei* art world, Hamada Shōji, who was then enrolled at the Tokyo Industrial College (Tōkyō Kōtō Kōgyō Gakkō), used to visit a ceramic workshop on the other side of the capital where he would make and decorate pots every Sunday. This led to his meeting Kawai Kanjirō, the fourth potter involved with Yanagi in the development of the idea of *mingei*, who attended the same college and who also visited the same workshop regularly.

Kawai was actually inspired to take up pottery as a living when he first came across Leach's pots at the Mikaidō Gallery in Akasaka in 1913. Much struck by what he saw as the fresh vitality of Leach's work, he proceeded to visit Leach at his home in Sakuragichō (Mizuo 1982:692) and, after graduation, went to work at the Kyoto Ceramic Testing Institute, where Hamada himself found employment a year or two later (1915–16). The two men then used to visit Tomimoto who had by then left Tokyo to set up his pottery near Nara (Leach 1976:21–2). Hamada eventually

253

completed the quartet of relationships by visiting Leach at Yanagi's Abiko home in 1919, and then accompanied him back to England to set up his pottery at St. Ives, Cornwall, in July of the following year.

Pottery and potters had an enormous influence on the development of the Japanese *Mingei* movement. Korean Yi Dynasty pots affected not only Tomimoto and Leach, but Kawai and Hamada, who used to copy them from the catalogue of an exhibition held at the Metropolitan Art Museum in New York round about 1916 (Leach 1976:23). It was an exhibition of such pottery put on by Yanagi in 1924 that stunned Kawai and finally brought the two men together after Hamada returned to Japan from St. Ives (Leach 1976:79). It was in December of the following year that these three men coined the term *mingei*.

9   In the light of my earlier comments about the difference in emphasis between Morris and Yanagi in their discussions of popular art, it is interesting to note that, in this article, Tomimoto makes no mention at all of Morris's political activities and socialist thought. Instead, he focusses totally on biographical details of Morris's life and on his artistic activities. The same criticism can be made of Tonomura (1973) and, to a lesser degree, Jugaku (1935) in their comparisons of the ideas of Morris and Yanagi.

10 Azuma (1981:140) suggests that Leach's real legacy to the Shirakaba group was his passion for things Chinese. As a westerner, he made Shiga, Arishima, Yanagi and Kishida aware for the first time of oriental traditions and oriental culture.

11 There is evidence to suggest that in his discussion of Korean pottery, Yanagi (1982b:19–20) was further influenced by Leach (1920:45) who had praised Chinese form, Korean line, and Japanese colour. As was mentioned earlier, Yanagi was later roundly criticised by a Korean scholar, Kim Yang-gi, for suggesting that line should be linked with 'sadness' (Tsurumi 1976:22–3; Kumakura 1979:445–8), but we might note that Leach himself (1920:45–6) intimates this link between Korea (Corea) and sadness in a description of a visit to that country in May 1920.

12 In his fascinating discussion of orientalism in design, John MacKenzie (1995:132) makes an unfortunate slip of the pen by referring to Bernard as 'Edmund' Leach. This merely reinforces, perhaps, my earlier point that there is an extremely murky area in which it is difficult to separate the artist from the anthropologist!

13 Cf. W. Burges who, in the July 1862 edition of *The Gentleman's Magazine*, claimed that 'truly the Japanese Court is the real medieval court at the Exhibition' (quoted in Miner 1958:29, and in Sato and Watanabe 1991:27).

14 For further general discussion of these international expositions, see Benedict *et al.* (1983). One of the many ironies concerning western visions of the Japanese and Japanese visions of the west is that, while the international expositions may have permitted non-European art to be subsumed under the single category of 'arts and crafts', they also led to the Japanese themselves making a clear-cut distinction between 'art' and 'craft'.

15 It may be that Yanagi initially adopted *chokkan* to translate into Japanese Leach's frequent use of 'intuition' and that, by one of those curious quirks of inter-cultural communication, Leach himself then decided that *chokkan* signified more than mere 'intuition' when he began translating Yanagi into English (Yanagi 1972) (but see below).

16 For a more detailed discussion of Orientalist writings about Japan in the context of advertising images, see Moeran (1993).

17 For a detailed discussion of the 'aesthetic dialogue' between Japan and Britain, see Sato and Watanabe (1991)

18 In this respect, it is interesting to note that Yanagi's and Muromachi Period (1392–1568) tea masters', distinction between *jōte* (aristocratic) and *gete* (common) objects closely paralleled the western distinction between 'greater' and 'lesser' arts (cf. Jugaku 1935:20).

Afterword: The Art World of Japanese Ceramics

1 This paper is an abbreviation of my article first published in the *Journal of Japanese Studies* (Moeran 1987), whose editors I would like to thank for permission to reprint here.

2 It is unlikely that a potter will be able to hold this kind of exhibition at a national museum of art during his own lifetime. Even the works of Hamada Shōji, holder of a 'national treasureship' and the Award of Cultural Merit, were not so exhibited until his death in 1977. Then 68,750 people filed into the Tokyo National Museum of Modern Art to see the show put on there by the Nihon Keizai Newspaper. It is possible, however, for potters to hold one-man shows at prefectural museums of art.

3 In order to be able to exhibit at the Green Gallery in Tokyo's exclusive Aoyama district during the early 80s, for example, potters used to say that it was vital to establish personal connections (*tsukiai*) with the critic, Yoshida Kōzō.

4 These figures do not apply to oil painting, since galleries have considerable power in this sphere of art. A regular gallery averages 800 names on its customer list (see Havens 1982:124).

5 See Seidensticker (1983:11–15). Kawai Kanjirō was the first potter, and probably the first artist craftsman in general, to hold his one man show in a department store – at Tokyo's Takashimaya, in May 1921 (personal communication, Kujō Yoshihide, Art Department, Takashimaya Department Store; cf. Suzuki 1978:216).

The way in which ceramics is exhibited in Japan may be unusual, but the notion that business should in some form or another sponsor the arts is not unusual. Which art worlds business should decide to sponsor, and how it will do so, may differ from one society to the next. In England, it would seem that the world of classical music is perhaps closest to that of contemporary Japanese ceramics – in particular, its emphasis on teacher/pupil relations, musicians' multiple membership in performing groups, and concert sponsorship by such corporations as the National Westminster Bank, Shell Oil, and McDonald's. Discussion of the relation between business and art should encourage us to look further at the relation between art and all those other activities (such as sporting events, academic research, and publications) currently sponsored by business.

6 For an overall view of the role of newspaper companies and department stores in the promotion of art and culture, see Havens (1982:129–43).

7 Both newspaper and department store employees involved in art marketing use catalogue sales as a ready reckoner of an exhibition's success. In Tokyo, approximately one out of six or seven, and in the rest of the country one out of ten to twelve, visitors buy a catalogue at an average show. This figure can increase to one out of four visitors at a popular exhibition, and compares favourably with one out of twenty quoted me by a museum curator in England.

8 It was this underlying trend which prompted one Asahi employee to write a full-scale account of his newspaper's involvement in the sponsorship of art exhibitions (see Asano 1981:4–5).

9 A good discussion of Nitten can be found in Havens (1982:112–18).

10 The Bunka Kunshō was first instituted in February 1937. In 1981, it was said that the sum required to acquire the Bunka Kunshō was ¥30 million; by the summer of 1985, this figure had increased to ¥100 million – although nobody was prepared to say whether payment was made in cash or in kind. Although this may seem an extremely large sum of money, potters should be able to recoup their outlay within a year or two, thanks to the greatly increased prices that the award allows them to charge for their work. The distribution of 'thank you' money in advance to those involved in the awarding of the Bunka Kunshō, therefore, may be a bribe, but should also be recognized as no more than a sound financial investment.

11 The appointment of two Saga potters – Imaizumi Imaemon and Eguchi Katsumi – to the panel of jurors in the early 1980s, for example, led to a great increase in the number of works by Kyushu potters selected to the Dentō Kōgeiten. This may partly have had something to do with an overall style or 'feeling', in that jurors are likely to appreciate pots which make use of similar types of clay and glazes to their own. At the same time, however, it cannot be denied (and potters themselves do not attempt to deny) that jurors are more likely to recognize the works of potters who live in their own region, and so feel bound by personal obligation to vote for them, regardless of their quality.

12 See, for example, Thompson (1973). For a discussion of some socio-linguistic aspects of pottery criticism, see Moeran (1984b).

13 In the ceramics art world, as in the American art establishment, a number of people fulfill multiple functions of this nature. Collectors act as dealers when there is an opportunity for them to make a profit; museum curators as critics when asked to write catalogue introductions or magazine articles (see Rosenberg 1970:394). 'Great' potters (such as Hamada Shōji, Kitaoji Rosanjin or, in Britain, Bernard Leach) are often those who themselves acted as critics and propagated their own aesthetic philosophy during their lifetimes.

14 It is ironical that, in the West, prizes (e.g. Pulitzer [1917], Goncourt [1902], and Nobel [1901]) were instituted with the aim of overcoming personal connections among those involved in the literary world (see Schucking 1974:53). In general, it would seem that Japanese critics have more power than their counterparts on the American art scene (see Rosenberg and Fliegel 1970).

15 I have described events leading up to and during the holding of my own one-man exhibition in Moeran (1990).

16 Here, perhaps, we should heed Hauser's (1982:512) warning that 'the assumption of an analogy between value and price in the area of art would be the worst example of that objectivization which robs a state of affairs of its meaning'. No wonder scholars such as Katō (1971:34) end up vainly protesting that 'quality cannot be measured', and that 'artistic culture is a culture of quality, not quantity'.

17 On gossip, I should add an explanatory note with regard to my own fieldwork among those connected with contemporary Japanese ceramics. In an art world which takes on its organizational form primarily as a result of networks and personal connections, gossip becomes an important focus of group identity. Some of this gossip is a means of communicating in private what cannot be said in public and would seem to be a close approximation to the 'truth', but some gossip is undoubtedly malicious. As a general rule, when I heard the same story three times from three totally different sources (a potter in Agano, a dealer in Tokyo, and a museum curator in Kurashiki, for example). I used to regard it as being more than a coincidence. It is this oft-repeated and widely known gossip that has on occasion been included in this Afterword (as in, for example, the comment on Bunka Kunshō payments).

BIBLIOGRAPHY

Abramson, J. J. 1976 'Style Change in an Upper Sepik Contact Situation', in N. Graburn (ed.), *Ethnic and Tourist Arts: cultural expressions from the fourth world*, Berkeley and Los Angeles: University of California Press.

Albrecht, Milton 1970 'Art as an institution', in M. Albrecht *et al.* (eds.), *The Sociology of Art and Literature: a reader*, New York: Praeger.

Anderson, J. N. 1973 'Ecological anthropology and anthropological ecology', in J. Honigman (ed.), *Handbook of Social and Cultural Anthropology*, Chicago: Rand McNally.

Appadurai, Arjun (ed.) 1986 *The social life of things*, Cambridge: Cambridge University Press.

Ariga Kizaemon 1956 'Sonraku kyōdōtai to ie' (Village community and household), p.21–49 in *Sonraku Kyōdōtai no Kōzō Bunseki*, Sonraku Shakai Kenkyūkai Nenpō 3.

Asano Shōichirō 1981 *Asahi no Tenrankai – sono kako to mirai (Asahi's Exhibitions: their past and future)*. Tōkyō: Asahijin.

Azuma Tamaki, 1980 *Shirakaba to Kindai Bijutsu (Shirakaba and Early Modern Art)*, Tōkyō.

Bachnik, Jane 1983 'Recruitment strategies for household succession: rethinking Japanese household organization', p.160–82 in *Man* (NS) 18.

Barnett, James 1970 (1959) 'The sociology of art', in M. Albrecht *et al.* (eds.), *The Sociology of Art and Literature*, New York: Praeger.

Bateson, Gregory 1973 'Style, grace and information in primitive art', in A. Forge (ed.), *Primitive Art and Society*, Oxford: Oxford University Press.

Beardsley, Richard K. n.d. 'Stability and adaptation in folk art production in Japan', unpublished manuscript.

—— *et al.* 1959 *Village Japan*, Chicago: University of Chicago Press.

Becker, Howard 1978 'Arts and crafts', p.862–89 in *American Journal of Sociology* 83.

—— 1982 *Art Worlds*, Berkeley and Los Angeles: University of California Press.

Befu, Harumi 1963 'Patrilineal descent and personal kindred in Japan', p.1328–41 in *American Anthropologist* 65.

—— 1980 'The group model of Japanese society and an alternative', p.169–87 in *Rice University Studies* 66 (1).

Bell, Clive 1913 *Art*, New York: Frederick Stokes.

Benedict, Burton *et al.* 1983 *The Anthropology of World Fairs*, Berkeley and London: Scolar Press.

Benjamin, Walter 1969 'Art in the age of mechanical reproduction', in his *Illuminations*, edited and with an Introduction by Hannah Arendt, New York: Schocken Books.

Berger, John 1972 *Ways of Seeing*, Harmondsworth: Penguin/BBC Books.

Bernstein, Gail 1985 *Haruko's World: a Japanese farm woman and her community*, Stanford: Stanford University Press.

Bestor, Theodor 1989 *Neighborhood Tokyo*, Stanford: Stanford University Press.

Blizet, William 1974 'An institutional theory of art', *The British Journal of Aesthetics* 14. (Reprinted in J. Bender and H. G. Blocker [eds.], *Contemporary Philosophy of Art: readings in analytical aesthetics*, Englewood Cliff, NJ: Prentice Hall.)

Boas, Franz 1955 (1927) *Primitive Art*, New York: Dover.

Bohannan, Paul 1961 'Artist and critic in an African society', in M. Smith (ed.), *The Artist in Tribal Society*, London: Routledge & Kegan Paul.

Bourdieu, Pierre 1968 'Outline of a sociological theory of art perception', p.589–612 in *International Social Science Journal* 20.

—— 1984 *Distinction: a social critique of the judgment of taste*, translated by R. Nice, London: Routledge & Kegan Paul.

Brody, J. 1976 'The creative consumer: survival, revival, and invention in southwest indian arts', in N. Graburn (ed.), *Ethnic and Tourist Arts*, Berkeley and Los Angeles: University of California Press.

Bukharin, Nicholas 1972 (1925) 'Art and social evolution', in B. Lang and F. Williams (eds.), *Marxism and Art: writings in aesthetics and criticism*, New York and London: Longman.

Bunzel, R. 1972 (1929) *The Pueblo Potter: a study of creative imagination in primitive art*, New York: Dover.

Cardew, Michael 1971 *Pioneer Pottery*, London: Longmans.

Carrier, James (ed.) 1995 *Occidentalism: images of the west*, Oxford: Clarendon Press.

Charlton, T. H. 1976 'Modern ceramics in the Teotihuacan valley', in N. Graburn (ed.), *Ethnic and Tourist Arts*, Berkeley and Los Angeles: University of California Press.

Chisholm, Lawrence 1963 *Fenellosa: the far east and American culture*, New Haven: Yale University Press.

Clark, Rodney 1979 *The Japanese Company*, New Haven: Yale University Press.

Clifford, James 1988 *The Predicament of Culture: twentieth-century ethnography, literature, and art*, Cambridge, Mass.: Harvard University Press.

Conant, Ellen 1991 'Refractions of the rising sun: Japan's participation in international exhibitions 1862–1910', in T. Sato and T. Watanabe (eds.), *Japan and Britain: an aesthetic dialogue 1850–1930*, London: Lund Humphries.

Coomaraswamy, Ananda 1943 *Why Exhibit Works of Art?* London: Luzac & Co.

Coote, J. 1989 'The anthropology of aesthetics and the dangers of "Maquetcentricism"', p.229–43 in *Journal of the Anthropological Society of Oxford* 20 (3).

—— 1992 '"Marvels of everyday vision": the anthropology of aesthetics and the cattle-keeping Nilotes', in J. Coote and A. Shelton (eds.), *Anthropology, Art, and Aesthetics*, Oxford: Clarendon Press.

—— and Anthony Shelton (eds.) 1992 *Anthropology, Art and Aesthetics*, Oxford: Clarendon Press.

Cornell, John 1956 'Matsunagi: a Japanese mountain community', p.113–232 in *Two Japanese Villages*, Occasional Papers, Center for Japanese Studies 5, Ann Arbor: University of Michigan Press.

—— 1963 'Local group stability in the Japanese community', p.113–25 in *Human Organization* 22.

Cort, Louise 1977 'Shigaraki-gayoi' (Shigaraki trips), p.3–35 in *Aruku Miru Kiku* 124.

Dale, Peter 1986 *The Myth of Japanese Uniqueness*, London: Croom Helm.

Danto, Arthur 1964 'The Artworld', p.571–84 in *Journal of Philosophy* 61.

—— 1973 'Artworks and real things', p.1–17 in *Theoria* 34.

—— 1981 *The Transfiguration of the Commonplace*, Cambridge, Mass.: University of Harvard Press.

—— 1992 *Beyond the Brillo Box: the visual arts in post-historical perspective*, New York: Farrar, Straus & Giroux.

D'Azevedo, Warren (ed.), 1973 *The Traditional Artist in African Societies*, Bloomington: Indiana University Press.

Deutsch, E. 1975 *Studies in Comparative Aesthetics*, Monograph 2, Society for Asian and Comparative Philosophy, Honolulu: University Press of Hawaii.

Dewey, J. 1934 *Art as Experience*, New York: Minton, Balch & Co.

Dickie, George 1974 *Art and the Aesthetic: an institutional analysis*, Ithaca and London: Cornell University Press.

—— 1993 'A tale of two artworlds', in M. Rollins (ed.), *Danto and His Critics*, Oxford: Basil Blackwell.

Dockstader, F. J. 1973 'The role of the individual indian artist', in A. Forge (ed.), *Primitive Art and Society*, Oxford: Oxford University Press.

Dore, Ronald P. 1959 *Land Reform in Japan*, London: Oxford University Press.

—— 1978 *Shinohata: a portrait of a Japanese village*, London: Allen Lane.

—— 1983 'Goodwill and the spirit of market capitalism', in *British Journal of Sociology* 34 (4).

—— (ed.) 1967 *Aspects of Social Change in Modern Japan*, Princeton, NJ: Princeton University Press.

Duvignaud, Jean 1972 *The Sociology of Art*, London: Paladin.

Ellen, Roy 1978 'Problems and progress in the ethnographic analysis of small-scale human ecosystems', p.290–300 in *Man* (NS) 13.

—— 1979 'Introduction: anthropology, the environment and ecological systems', in P. Burnham and R. Ellen (eds.), *Social and Ecological Systems*, London: Academic Press.

Embree John 1939 *Suye Mura – a Japanese village*, Chicago: University of Chicago Press.

Evett, Elisa 1982 *The Critical Reception of Japanese Art in Late Nineteenth-Century Europe*, Ann Arbor: UMI Research Press.

Firth, Raymond 1992 'Art and anthropology', in J. Coote and A. Shelton (eds.), *Anthropology, Art, and Aesthetics*, Oxford: Clarendon Press.

Forge, Anthony (ed.) 1973 *Primitive Art and Society*, Oxford: Oxford University Press.

Foster, Hal (Ed.) 1983 *The Anti-Aesthetic: essays on postmodern culture*, Port Townsend: Bay Press.

Frake, Charles 1962 'Cultural ecology and ethnography', p.53–9 in *Ecology and Anthropology: a symposium, American Anthropologist* 64.

Freilich, M. 1963 'The natural experiment, ecology and culture', p.21–39 in *Southwest Journal of Anthropology* 19.

Friedman, Jonathan 1974 'Marxism, structuralism, and vulgar materialism', p.44–69 in *Man* (NS) 9.

—— 1994 *Cultural Identity and Global Process*, London: Sage.

Fukutake, T. 1949 *Nihon Nōson no Shakaiteki Seikaku (Social Characteristics of Japanese Villages)*, Tōkyō: Tōkyō Daigaku Shuppankyoku.

—— 1956 'Gendai nihon ni okeru sonraku kyōdōtai sonzai keitai' (Village community existence in modern Japan), p.1–20 in *Sonraku Kyōdōtai no Kōzō Bunseki*, Sonraku Kenkyūkai Nenpō 3.

—— 1967 *Asian Rural Society: China, India, Japan*, Tokyo: Tokyo University Press.

Gamō, M. 1962 'Shinzoku' (Relatives), p.233–58 in *Nihon Minzokugaku Taikei* 3, Tōkyō: Heibonsha.

Gell, Alfred 1992 'The technology of enchantment and the enchantment of technology', in J. Coote and A. Shelton (eds.), *Anthropology, Art, and Aesthetics*, Oxford: Clarendon Press.

—— 1996 'Vogel's net: traps as artworks and artworks as traps', p.15–38 in *Journal of Material Culture* 1.

Gerbrands, A. 1957 *Art as an Element of Culture, Especially in Negro Africa*, Medellelingen van het Rijksmuseum voor Volkenkunde, Leiden 12, Leiden: E. J. Brill.

Gill, R. 1976 'Ceramic arts and acculturation at Laguna', in N. Graburn (ed.), *Ethnic and Tourist Arts*, Berkeley and Los Angeles: University of California Press.

Gluck, Carol 1985 *Japan's Modern Myths: ideology in the late Meiji period*, Princeton, NJ.: Princeton University Press.

Goldwater, Robert 1967 *Primitivism in Modern Art* (revised edition), New York: Random House.

Gombrich, E.H. 1960 *Art and Illusion*, London: Phaidon.

Graburn, Nelson 1969 'Art and acculturative processes', p.457–68 in *International Social Science Journal* 21.

—— 1970 'The Eskimos and commercial art', in M. Albrecht *et al.* (eds.), *The Sociology of Art and Literature*, New York: Duckworth.

—— (ed.) 1976 *Ethnic and Tourist Arts: cultural expressions from the fourth world*, Berkeley and Los Angeles: University of California Press.

Hamada, Shōji 1965 'Onta no karausu hoka' (Onta's clay crushers and other things), p.8–9 in *Mingei* 147.

Hannerz, Ulf 1992 *Cultural Complexity: studies in the social organization of meaning*, New York: Columbia University Press.

—— 1996 *Transnational Connections: culture, people, places*, London and New York: Routledge.

Harmon, M. 1974 'Folk visual arts', p.470–81 in *Encyclopaedia Britannica, Macropaedia* Volume 7, Chicago: W. Benton.

Harris, Marvin 1968 *The Rise of Anthropological Theory*, London: Routledge & Kegan Paul.

Harris, Neil 1990 'All the world a melting pot? Japan at American fairs', in his *Cultural Excursions: marketing appetites and cultural tastes in America*, Chicago and London: University of Chicago Press.

Haselberger, H. 1961 'Methods of studying ethnological art', p.351–84 in *Current Anthropology* 2.

Hatae, K. 1970 'Mukei bunkazai to wa donna mono ka?' (What is this thing called 'intangible cultural property'?), p.4–9 in *Nihon no Mingei* 180.

Hauser, Arnold 1982 *The Sociology of Art*, London: Routledge & Kegan Paul.

Havens, Thomas 1982 *Artist and Patron in Post-War Japan*, Princeton: Princeton University Press.

Hess, Thomas and Elizabeth Baker (eds.) 1973 *Art and Sexual Politics*, New York: Collier Macmillan.

Hiller, Susan (ed.) 1991 *The Myth of Primitivism: perspectives on art*, London and New York: Routledge.

Hobsbawm, Eric and Terence Ranger (eds.) 1983 *The Invention of Tradition*, Cambridge: Cambridge University Press.

Inden, Ronald 1990 *Imagining India*, Oxford: Basil Blackwell.

Isoda, S. 1951 'Sonraku kōzō no futatsu no katachi' (Two types of village structure), p.50–64 in *Hōshakaigaku* 1.

Ivy, Marilyn 1988 'Tradition and difference in the Japanese mass media', p.21–9 in *Public Culture* 1 (1).

Jarves, Jackson 1876 *A Glimpse of the Art of Japan*, New York.

Johnson, Erwin 1967 'Status changes in hamlet structure accompanying modernization', in R. P. Dore (ed.), *Aspects of Social Change in Modern Japan*, Princeton NJ: Princeton University Press.

Jugaku Bunsho 1935 'Iriamu Morisu to Yanagi Sōetsu' (William Morris and Yanagi Sōetsu), p.1–30 in *Kōgei* 50.

Kalland, Arne 1981 *Shingū: a study of a Japanese fishing community*, Scandinavian Institute of Asian Studies Monograph Series 44, London and Malmo: Curzon.

—— 1995 *Fishing Villages of Tokugawa Japan*, Scandinavian Institute of Asian Studies Monograph Series 69, London: Curzon.

—— and Brian Moeran 1992 *Japanese Whaling: end of an era?*, London: Curzon.

Katō, Shūichi 1971 *Form, Style, Tradition: reflections on Japanese art and society*, Berkeley and Los Angeles: University of California Press.

Keene, Donald 1971 *Landscapes and Portraits*, London: Secker & Warburg.

Keesing, F. 1958 'The aesthetic aspect of culture', in his *Cultural Anthropology: the science of custom*. New York: Holt, Rinehart & Winston.

Kishida, Ryūsei 1920 'On Leach's departure', in S. Yanagi (ed.), *An English Artist in Japan*, Tokyo: private publication.

Kitano, S. 1963 '*Dōzoku* and *ie* in Japan: the meaning of family genealogical relationships', in R. Smith and R. K. Beardsley (eds.), *Japanese Culture*, Chicago: Aldine.

Kleinberg, Jill 1983 'Where work and family are almost one: the lives of folkcraft potters', in D. Plath (ed.), *Work and Lifecourse in Japan*, New York: SUNY.

Kojima Kikuo 1933 'Nyūmon no omoide' (Initiation memories), p.42–8 in *Kōgei* 29.

Koyama Fujio 1967 *Nihon no Kōgei* (*Japanese Crafts*), Volume 9: *Tōjiki* (*Ceramics*), Tōkyō: Tankō Shinsha.

Krauss, Ellis *et al.* (eds.) 1985 *Conflict in Japan*, Honolulu: University of Hawaii Press.

Kumakura, Isao 1979 'A tocsin for our times: the *mingei undō*', p.445–8 in *Japan Interpreter* 12.

La Farge, John 1986 *An Artist's Letters from Japan*, London: Waterstone.

Lathrap, D. W. 1976 'Shipibo tourist art', in N. Graburn (ed.), *Ethnic and Tourist Arts*, Berkeley and Los Angeles: University of California Press.

Layton, Robert 1991 *The Anthropology of Art*, Cambridge: Cambridge University Press.

Leach, Bernard 1914 *A Review: 1909–1914* Tokyo: private publication.

—— 1920 *An English Artist in Japan*, S. Yanagi (ed.), Tokyo: private publication.

—— 1960 *A Potter in Japan*. London: Faber & Faber.

—— 1972 'Introduction', *The Unknown Craftsman* by Soetsu Yanagi, Tokyo: Kodansha International.

—— 1976 *Hamada, Potter*, Tokyo: Kodansha International.

—— 1978 *Beyond East and West: memoirs, portraits, and essays*, London: Faber & Faber.

Lindsay, J. 1979 *William Morris: his life and work*, New York.

McLuhan, Marshall 1964 *Understanding Media: the extensions of man*, New York: McGraw-Hill.

MacKenzie, John 1995 *Orientalism: history, theory and the arts*, Manchester: Manchester University Press.

Malraux, André 1967 *Museum Without Walls*, New York: Doubleday.

Manfredi, John 1982 *The Social Limits of Art*, Amherst: The University of Massachusetts Press.

Maquet, Jacques 1979 (1971) *Introduction to Aesthetic Anthropology*, 2nd edition, Malibu: Undena Publications.

—— 1986 *The Aesthetic Experience: an anthropologist looks at the visual arts*, New Haven and London: Yale University Press.

Mason, J. 1935 *The Meaning of Shinto*, New York: Dutton.

Matsukata, S. 1955 'Hita kikō' (A call in at Hita), p.15–17 in *Mingei* 27.

Matsumoto, T. 1961 *Nihon Chihō Chishitsu-shi: Kyūshū chihō* (*A Geological History of the Regions of Japan*). Fukuoka: Asakura Shoten.

Mead, Sidney 1976 'The production of native art and craft objects in contemporary New Zealand society', in N. Graburn (ed.), *Ethnic and Tourist Arts*, Berkeley and Los Angeles: University of Californin Press.

Mendieta y Nunez, L. 1957 'Sociologia del arte', p.67–84 in *Revista Mexicana de Sociologia* 19.

Miller Daniel 1987 *Material Culture and Mass Consumption*, Oxford: Basil Blackwell.

—— 1991 'Primitive art and the necessity of primitivism to art', in S. Hiller (ed.), *The Myth of Primitivism: perspectives on art*, London and New York: Routledge.

Miner, Earl 1958 *The Japanese Tradition in British and American Literature*, Princeton: Princeton University Press.

Mizuo Hiroshi 1966 'Gendai to mingei' (Folk crafts and modern times), *Geijutsu Shinchō* 17 (5).

—— 1968 *Gendai Mingeiron* (*Modern Folk Craft Theory*), Tōkyō: Shinchōsha.

—— 1971 'Yakimono no bi – 17: Onta' (The beauty of pottery: Onta), *Nihon Bijutsu Kōgei* 392.

—— 1972 *Minyō no Tabi* (*Travelling by Folk Craft Kilns*), Tōkyō: Geisōsha.

—— 1974 'Teshigoto ni tsuite' (About handicraft work), p.6–10 in *Mingei* 252.

—— 1978 *Yanagi Sōetsu, Nihon Minzoku Bunka Taikei* Volume 6, Tōkyō: Kōdansha.

—— 1982 'Kōgei to kokoro no tomo' (Crafts and a friend of the heart), in S. Yanagi, *Yanagi Sōetsu: Zenshū* Volume 14, Tōkyō: Nihon Mingeikan.

Moeran, Brian 1984a 'One over the seven: *sake* drinking in a Japanese pottery community', in *Journal of the Anthropology Society of Oxford* XV (2).

—— 1984b 'Individual, group and *seishin*: Japan's internal cultural debate', p.252–66 in *Man* 19 (2).

—— 1985 *Okubo Diary: portrait of a Japanese valley*, Stanford: Stanford University Press.

—— 1987 'The art world of Japanese ceramics', p.27–50 in *The Journal of Japanese Studies* 13 (1).

—— 1990 'One man show: anthropologist as potter in Japan', in E. Ben-Ari *et al.* (eds.), *Unwrapping Japan*, Manchester: Manchester University Press.

—— 1993 'The Orient strikes back: advertising and imagining Japan', p.77–110 in *University of Hong Kong Supplement to the Gazette* 40 (1). (Reprinted p.77–112 in *Theory, Culture and Society* 13 (3), August 1996).

—— 1994 'Orientalism and the debris of western civilization: popular art movements in Britain and Japan', in D. Gerstle and A. Milner (eds.), *Europe & The Orient*, Humanities Research Centre Monograph Series 8, Canberra: Australian National University.

—— 1996 *A Japanese Advertising Agency: an anthropology of media and markets*, London: Curzon.

Morawski, Stefan 1974 *Inquiries into the Fundamentals of Aesthetics*, Cambridge, Mass.: MIT Press.

Morphy, Howard 1994 'The anthropology of art', in T. Ingold (ed.), *Companion Encyclopedia of Anthropology*, London and New York: Routledge.

—— 1995 'Aboriginal art in a global context', in D. Miller (ed.), *Worlds Apart: modernity through the prism of the local*, ASA Decennial Series, London and New York: Routledge.

Morris, William 1882 'The lesser arts of life', in his *Lectures on Art*, London.

—— 1893 *Gothic Architecture: a lecture for the Arts and Crafts Exhibition Society*, Hammersmith.

—— 1902 *Hopes and Fears for Art*, five lectures delivered in Birmingham, London, and Nottingham, London: Longmans, Green & Company.

—— 1947 *On Art and Socialism: essays and lectures*, London: J. Lehmann.

—— 1962a 'Art and society', in A. Briggs (ed.), *William Morris: selected writings and designs*, Harmondsworth: Pelican.

—— 1962b 'The decorative arts', in A. Briggs (ed.), *William Morris*, Harmondsworth: Pelican.

—— 1962c 'Useful work versus useless toil', in A. Briggs (ed.), *William Morris*, Harmondsworth: Pelican.

—— 1962d 'The worker's share of art', in A. Briggs (ed.), *William Morris*, Harmondsworth: Pelican.

—— 1962e 'how we live and how we might live', in A. Briggs (ed.), *William Morris*, Harmondsworth: Pelican.

—— 1964 'Art and the people', in R. Peters (ed.), *Victorians on Literature and Art*, London.

Moulin, Raymonde 1967 *Marché de la Peinture en France*, Paris: Editions Minuit.

Mukerjee, R. 1948 *The Social Function of Art*, Bombay: Hind Kitabs.

Nakamura, K. 1956 'Sonraku kyōdōtai' (Village communities), in *Sonraku Kyōdōtai to Kōzō Bunseki*, Sonraku Shakai Kenkyūkai Nenpō 3.

—— 1977 *Nihon no Sonraku Kyōdōtai (Japanese Village Communities)*, Tōkyō: Nihon Shuppansha.

Nakane, Chie 1967 *Kinship and Economic Organization in Rural Japan*, London: Athlone Press.

—— 1970 *Japanese Society*, London: Weidenfeld & Nicolson.

Nakano, T., and Keith Brown 1970 'Changing rural Japan', p.195–206 in E. Norbeck and S. Parman (eds.), *The Study of Japan in the Behavioral Sciences*, Rice University Studies 56 (4).

Netting, R. McC. 1965 'A trial model of cultural ecology', p.81–96 in *Anthropology Quarterly* 38.

Nisbet, R. 1970 *The Sociological Tradition*, London: Heinemann.

—— 1976 *Sociology as an Art Form*, New York: Oxford University Press.

Nochlin, Linda 1973 'Why have there been no great women artists?', in T. Hess and E. Barker (eds.), *Art and Sexual Politics*, New York: Collier Macmillan.

Noma, Y. 1955 'Onta no Sarayama' (Sarayama Onta), p.6–9 in *Mingei* 27.

—— 1965 'Ontagama shinken' (The gravity of Onta), p.13–16 in *Mingei* 147.

Norbeck, Edward 1954 *Takashima: a Japanese fishing community*, Salt Lake City: University of Utah Press.

—— 1961 'Postwar cultural change and continuity in northeastern Japan', p.297–321 in *American Anthropologist* 63.

—— 1977 'Changing associations in a recently industrialized Japanese community', p.45–64 in *Urban Anthropology* 6.

Okada, J. 1976 'Applied arts and handicrafts in Japan', in C. Yamada (ed.), *Dialogue in Art: Japan and the west*, London: Zwemmer.

O'Neill, Patrick 1984, 'Organization and authority in the traditional arts', *Journal of Modern Asian Studies* 18 (4).

Osborne, Harold 1955 *Aesthetics and Criticism*, London: Routledge & Kegan Paul.

Parker, Roszika and Griselda Pollock 1981 *Old Mistresses: women, art and ideology*, London: Routledge and Kegan Paul.

Plath, David 1967 '*Japanese Rural Society* and *Asian Rural Society*', p.518–20 in *Japan Quarterly* 14.

Price, Sally 1989 *Primitive Art in Civilized Places*, Chicago: Chicago University Press.

Rappaport, Roy 1971 'Nature, culture, and ecological anthropology', in H. Shapiro (ed.), *Man, Culture, and Society*, London: Oxford University Press.

Read, Herbert 1936 *Art and Society*, London: Faber & Faber.

—— 1961 'Comments' and 'A personal point of view: summary of proceedings', in M. Smith (ed.), *The Artist in Tribal Society*, London: Routledge & Kegan Paul.

Rhodes, Daniel 1970 *Tamba Pottery: the timeless art of a Japanese village*, Tokyo: Kodansha International.

Robertson, Jennifer 1991 *Native and newcomer: making and remaking a Japanese city*, Berkeley and Los Angeles: University of California Press.

Rogers, Maria 1970 'The Batignolles group: creators of Impressionism', in M. Albrecht *et al.* (eds.), *The Sociology of Art and Literature*, New York: Praeger.

Rosenberg, Bernard and Norris Fliegel 1970 'The artist and his publics: the ambiguity of success', in M. Albrecht *et al.* (eds.), *The Sociology of Art and Literature*, New York: Praeger.

Rosenberg, Harold 1970 'The art establishment', in M. Albrecht *et al.* (eds.), *The Sociology of Art and Literature*, New York: Praeger.

Ruskin, John 1963 *The Genius of John Ruskin: selections from his writings*, edited by I. Rosenberg, London: Allen & Unwin.

—— 1985 'The nature of gothic', *The Stones of Venice* Volume 2, in C. Wilson (ed.), *Unto This Last and Other Writings*, Harmondsworth: Pelican.

Said, Edward 1978 *Orientalism*, New York: Vintage.

Sakamoto, K. 1953 'Suiden shakai no seikaku' (The character of irrigation societies), p.143–64 in *Jinbun Gakuhō* 3.

Sato, Tomoko and Toshio Watanabe (eds.) 1991 *Japan and Britain: an aesthetic dialogue 1850–1930*, London: Lund Humphries.

Sclafani, Richard 1973 'Artworks, art theory and the artworld', p.18–34 in *Theoria* 39.

Schucking, Levin 1974 (1944) *The Sociology of Literary Taste*, Chicago: University of Chicago Press.

Seidensticker, Edward 1983 *Low City, High City*, New York: Knopf.

Seki, K. 1962 'Nenrei shūdan' (Age groups), p.127–74 in *Nihon Minzokugaku Taikei* Volume 3, Tōkyō: Heibonsha.

Shelton, Anthony 1992 'Predicates of aesthetic judgement: ontology and value in Huichol material representations', in J. Coote and A. Shelton (eds.), *Anthropology, Art, and Aesthetics*, Oxford: Clarendon Press.

Shiga Naoya 1933 'Rīchi no koto' (About Leach), p.26–31 in *Kōgei* 29.

Shimpo, Mitsuru 1976 *Three Decades in Shiwa: economic development and social change in a Japanese farming community*, Vancouver: University of British Columbia Press.

Silbermann, A. 1968 'A definition of the sociology of art', p.567–88 in *Arts in Society: International Social Science Journal* 20.

Smith, Marion (ed.) 1961 *The Artist in Tribal Society*, London: Routledge & Kegan Paul.

Smith, Robert J. 1956 'Kurusu', p.1–112 in *Two Japanese Villages*, Occasional Papers, Center for Japanese Studies 5, Ann Arbor: University of Michigan Press.

—— 1961 'The Japanese rural community: norms, sanction, and ostracism', p.522–33 in *American Anthropologist* 63.

—— 1978 *Kurusu: the price of progress in a Japanese village, 1951–1975*, Stanford: Stanford University Press.

Smith, Robert and Ella Wiswell 1982 *The Women of Suye Mura*, Chicago and London: The University of Chicago Press.

Smith, Thomas C. 1959 *The Agrarian Origins of Modern Japan*, Stanford: Stanford University Press.

Smith, W. W. 1973 *Confucianism in Modern Japan*, Tokyo: Hokuseido.

Steiner, Kurt 1956 'The Japanese village and its government', p.185–99 in *Far Eastern Quarterly* 15.

Steward, J. 1955 *Theory of Culture Change: the methodology of multilinear evolution*, Urbana: University of Illinois Press.

Suenari, Michio 1972 'First child inheritance in Japan', p.122–26 in *Ethnology* 11.

Sumiya, K. 1953 'Sonraku kyōdōtai to yōsui kyōsei' (Village communities and water usage coercion), p.39–60 in *Shakaigaku Hyōron* 3.

Suzuki Kenji 1978 *Tōgei* (*Ceramic Art*), Volume 15 in T. Aiga (ed.), *Genshoku Gendai Nihon no Bijutsu* (*Modern Japanese Art*), Tōkyō: Shōgakkan.

Takahashi, T. 1958 'Nihon ni okeru nenrei shūdan soshiki no shoruikei' (Some types of

264

age group organization in Japan), *Tōyō Daigaku Kiyō* 12.

Takamura Kōtarō, 1933 'Nijū-roku nen mae' (26 years ago), p.13–7 in *Kōgei* 29.

Tanaka Takashi 1969 'Onta e no osasoi' (Invitation to Onta), p.44–48 in *Mingei* 195.

—— 1971 'Arita to Onta ni miru dentō' (Traditions seen in Arita and Onta), p.16–25 in *Mingei* 225.

Tanaka Toyotarō 1961 'Kyūshū no minyō' (Kyushu folk kilns), p.6–10 in *Mingei* 101.

—— 1966 'Nihon mingeiten nyūsen sakuhin kōhyō: tōki' (An appraisal of selected contributions to the folk art exhibition: ceramics), p.10–13 in *Mingei* 160.

Tanaka Yōko 1965 'Onta no tōgyō' (Onta pottery production), p.17–25 in *Mingei* 147.

Terakawa, Y. 1975 'Ontagama no rekishi' (The history of Onta) and 'Ontagama nenpyō' (An Onta chronology), in *Onta no Dentō to Tōki* (*Traditions and Pottery of Onta*), Ōita-ken Bunkazai Chōsa Hōkoku-sho.

Thompson, Robert 1973 'Yoruba art criticism', in W. d'Azevedo (ed.), *The Traditional Artist in African Societies*, Bloomington: Indiana University Press.

Thompson, Michael 1979 *Rubbish Theory: the creation and destruction of value*, Oxford: Oxford University Press.

Tomars, Adolf 1940 *Introduction to the Sociology of Art*, Mexico City.

Tomimoto Kenkichi 1920 'On Mr Bernard Leach', M. Toyoda and E. Speight (trans.), in S. Yanagi (ed.), *An English Artist in Japan*, Tokyo: private publication.

—— 1981a 'Takushoku Hakurankai no ichi nichi' (A day at the Colonial Exposition), in his *Tomimoto Kenkichi Chosakushū* (*Selected Writings of Tomimoto Kenkichi*), Tōkyō.

—— 1981b 'Kōgeihin ni kansuru shiki yori' (From thoughts about crafts), in his *Tomimoto Kenkichi Chosakushū* (*Selected Writings of Tomimoto Kenkichi*), Tōkyō.

—— 1981c 'Uiriamu Morisu no hanashi' (About William Morris), in his *Tomimoto Kenkichi Chosakushū* (*Selected Writings of Tomimoto Kenkichi*), Tōkyō.

Tonomura Kichinosuke 1965 'Kawaranai Onta-gama' (Unchanging Onta), p.10–12 in *Mingei* 147.

—— 1973 'Yanagi Muneyoshi to Uiriamu Morisu' (Yanagi Muneyoshi and William Morris), p.6–12 in *Mingei* 247 and p.8–11 in *Mingei* 248.

Tsuchiya, Y. 1965 'Sonraku shakai no hendō – seisan to shōhi o chūshin to shite' (Changes in village society – a focus on production and consumption), in *Shiga Daigaku Gakugei Gakubun Kiyō* 15.

Tsunoda, R. *et al.* (eds.) 1964 *Sources of Japanese Tradition* Volume 1, New York: Columbia University Press.

Tsurumi Shunsuke 1976 *Yanagi Muneyoshi*, Tōkyō: Heibonsha.

Umeki, H. 1973 *Ontayaki – yakimono no mura* (*Onta Pottery: a pottery village*), Ōita: San'ichi Shobō.

Vasquez, Adolfo S. 1973 *Art and Society: essays in Marxist aesthetics*, London: Merlin Press.

Veblen, Thorstein 1925 *The Theory of the Leisure Class*, London: Allen & Unwin.

Warner, Langdon 1958 *The Enduring Art of Japan*, New York: Grove Press.

Watkinson, R. 1983 *William Morris As Designer*, New York.

Wichmann, Siegfried 1981 *Japonisme: the Japanese influence on western art in the 19th and 20th centuries*, New York: Harmony.

Williams, Nancy 1976 'Australian aboriginal art at Yirkala: introduction and development of marketing', in N. Graburn (ed.), *Ethnic and Tourist Arts*, Berkeley and Los Angeles: University of California Press.

Williams, Raymond 1958 *Culture and Society 1780–1950*, London: Chatto & Windus.

—— 1976 *Keywords*, London: Fontana.

Wittfogel, Karl 1955 'Developmental aspects of hydraulic societies', in J. Steward (ed.), *Irrigation Civilizations: a comparative study*, Washington: Pan-American Union.

Wolff, Janet 1983 *Aesthetics and the Sociology of Art*, London: Allen & Unwin.

Yanagi Sōetsu 1931 'Hita no Sarayama' (Sarayama, Hita), p.1–11 in *Kōgei* 9.

—— 1932 'Sakubutsu no kōhansei' (The after-life of crafts), p.52–71 in *Kōgei* 15.

—— 1946 'Mingei undō wa nani o kikō shita ka?' (What has the folk craft movement contributed?), p.1–22 in *Kōgei* 115.

—— 1947 *Teshigoto no Nihon* (*Handcrafts in Japan*), Tōkyō: Seibunsha.

—— 1949 *Folk Crafts in Japan*, Tōkyō: Kokusai Bunka Shinkōkai.

—— 1954 *Kōgei Bunka* (*Craft Culture*), *Selected Works* Volume 3, Tōkyō: Nihon Mingeikan.

—— 1955a *Kōgei no Michi* (*The Way of Crafts*), *Selected Works* Volume 1, Tōkyō: Nihon Mingeikan.

—— 1955b *Cha to Bi* (*Tea and Beauty*), *Selected Works* Volume 6, Tōkyō: Nihon Mingeikan.

—— 1961 'Ontagama e no kenen' (Apprehension for Onta), p.4–5 in *Mingei* 101.

—— 1972 *The Unknown Craftsman: a Japanese insight into beauty*, adapted and translated by B. Leach, Tokyo: Kodansha International.

—— 1978 'Getemono no bi' (The beauty of vulgar things), in H. Mizuo (ed.), *Yanagi Sōetsu, Nihon Minzoku Bunka Taikei* Volume 6, Tōkyō: Kōdansha.

—— 1982a 'Leach-Riichi', in *Yanagi Sōetsu Zenshū* (*Collected Works of Yanagi Sōetsu*) Volume 14, Tōkyō: Nihon Mingeikan.

—— 1982b 'Tōjiki no bi' (The beauty of ceramics), in *Yanagi Sōetsu Zenshū* (*Collected Works of Yanagi Sōetsu*) Volume 12, Tōkyō: Nihon Mingeikan.

Yoneyama, T. 1965 'Kazoku to ie no shakai jinruigakuteki kenkyū yosetsu' (A social anthropological study of family and household), p.129–52 in *Jinbun Gakuhō* 21.

—— 1967a 'Kaminosho: a farm village suburban to Osaka in south central Japan', in J. Seward (ed.), *Contemporary Change in Traditional Societies* Volume 2, Urbana: University of Illinois Press.

—— 1967b 'Kurikoma: a farm village in the mountains of the Tohoku district of north central Japan', in J. Seward (ed.), *Contemporary Change in Traditional Societies* Volume 2, Urbana: University of Illinois Press.

Yoshino, Kosaku 1992 *Cultural Nationalism in Contemporary Japan*, London and New York: Routledge.

Yoshino, Michael 1971 *The Japanese Marketing System: Adaptations and Innovations*, Cambridge, Mass.: MIT Press.

Zola, Emile 1968 *The Masterpiece*, translated by T. Walton, Ann Arbor: University of Michigan Press.

INDEX

Aboriginal art 154, 196, 244
adoption 63–4, 69–70
aesthetic, agnosticism 5, 8, 210;
   appreciation/appraisal 30, 188–97, 208,
   241; disposition 182, 215, 245, 253;
   experience 10, 138; ideals 4, 141,
   207–9, 225; specificity 10, 182, 200; *see
   also* aesthetics *and mingei*, theory and
   practice of
aesthetics 9–12, 13, 32, 216–7, 253; and
   society 19, 21–4, 33, 35, 44, 62–180,
   202–3, 208–9, 241–2; definition of 9;
   language of ix, 253; moral aspects of
   30–3, 35–6; *see also* aesthetic *and*
   anthropology *and* art *and* beauty *and*
   values
age, associations 65, 79–82, 83; grade
   seniority 84, 169–71, 177, 208
agricultural cooperative 82, 145
agriculture 88, 100, 111–2, 131, 144, 145,
   157, 250; and irrigation 65, 84, 88, 97;
   see also environment
ancestors 68–9, 80, 248; return of 68, 109
anthropology 44, 189, 193, 200; ecological
   anthropology 3, 87; of aesthetics 1,
   9–11, 84, 216; of art xi, 4, 5–9, 10, 216,
   218, 244; of Japan 3–4, 34, 42, 44, 123;
   of values x, 11, 85, 211, 216, 217; *see
   also* art *and* material culture
Arakawa Toyozō 15, 199, 234
Arita 45, 50, 125, 138
art 5, 12, 17, 20, 26, 162, 193; and
   anthropology 7–8, 44, 154, 223; and
   capitalist society 21–4, 154; and
   commerce 24, 37, 139, 153–4, 225,
   228–242; and industrialization 21–2, 23;
   as commodity 154, 253; by destination
   5; by metamorphosis 5; folk crafts as
   199, 200, 208; institutional theory of
   6–7, 10, 243; market 154, 193–7, 205,

243; philosophy of 6, 8, 9; primitive 5,
   6, 217, 224; *see also* aethetics *and*
   artworld *and* beauty *and* ceramics
   exhibitions *and mingei and* nature *and*
   values *and* women
artist 11, 34, 138, 139, 178–9, 207; *vis-à-
   vis* craftsman 155, 164–8, 177, 187–8,
   199, 206, 216, 220
Arts and Crafts Movement 4, 12, 19, 20–4,
   40, 214, 220, 223, 225
artwork 6, 7, 8, 9, 11, 138, 141, 216, 245,
   252, 253
artworld (art world) ix, x, 9, 10, 11, 155,
   210, 244, 251, 253, 255; and philosophy
   6–7, 243; and sociology 7–9; definitions
   of 5, 7; Japanese ceramics 13–4, 15,
   228–42, 256; *mingei* 1, 85, 139, 202; *see
   also* art
Award of Cultural Merit (*bunka kunshō*)
   211, 228, 233, 255

beauty 17, 18, 36–7, 141, 155, 193, 215, 217;
   absolute and relative concepts of 210; and
   cooperation 9, 18, 32, 185–6, 207; and
   individual 33, 187; and intellectualism 32,
   33; and nature 18, 32, 186; and truth 22,
   29; functional aspects of 33–4, 141,
   189–90; standard of 30, 184–5, 202, 207,
   209; Yanagi's concept of 2, 18, 25, 31–2,
   188; *see also* art *and* environment *and*
   mingei and tradition *and* Yanagi Sōetsu
bisque firing 67, 103, 197
bon see ancestors
Buddhism 32, 42, 226; Zen 212
buraku see hamlet
buyer *see* pottery, dealer

Carlyle, Thomas 21–2
ceramics 13, 187, 228–242; art of 13; *see
   also* ceramics exhibitions *and* pottery

267